ARCHANA R SINGH

BEYOND THE HASHTAG

A Decade of Twitter Activism in India

Published by
Renu Kaul Verma
Vitasta Publishing Pvt Ltd
4348/4C, Ansari Road, Daryaganj
New Delhi - 110 002
info@vitastapublishing.com

ISBN: 978-81-19670-68-0
First Edition 2024
MRP ₹ 695

All Rights Reserved.
No part of this publication may be reproduced, stored in a retrieval system, or transmitted in any form, or by any means–electronic, mechanical, photocopying, recording or otherwise–without the prior permission of the publisher. Opinions expressed in this book are the author's own. The publisher is in no way responsible for these.

Edited by Soumitro Das
Cover Design & Typeset by Rohit Gautam
Printed at Chaman Enterprises, New Delhi

Table of Contents

Preface ix

Acknowledgement xi

Viral Vanguard: Social Media Surge in Social Movements 1

Theoretical Tapestry: Communication's Role in Activism 22

Paving the Path: A Journey through Literature 44

Unearthing Digital Footprints in Social Activism: Methodological Insights 113

Medium, Message, and Masses: Decoding the Data 124

Synthesis and Insights: Unpacking Findings, Unveiling Perspectives 217

The Ripple Effect: Implications and Recommendations 248

Pathways Forward: Lessons from the Activism Landscape 256

Endnote 267

References 269

List of Figures

Figure 1:	Digital News Report	8
Figure 2:	Timeline of Twitter	17
Figure 3:	Medium - Message, Channel, Source, Receiver and Content	37
Figure 4:	Representational Metafunction	122
Figure 5:	Interpersonal Metafunction	123
Figure 6:	Compositional Metafunction	123
Figure 7:	Chronology of the Nirbhaya Case	131
Figure 8:	Total Activity of Three Hashtags - 16 Dec 2012 to 16 Jan 2013	133
Figure 9:	Overall Activity of Three Hashtags	134
Figure 10:	All-time Influencers	135
Figure 11:	All time Influencers	136
Figure 12:	Discovery as per Acceleration	147
Figure 13:	Discovery as per Momentum	147
Figure 14:	Discovery as per Peak	148
Figure 15:	Overall Exposure	149
Figure 16:	Top Photographs	151

Figure 17: Original Photo	152
Figure 18: Timeline of Farmer's Protest	165
Figure 19: Total Tweets in Three Hashtags,#Farmersprotest, #tractortotwitter, #Iamwithfarmer	166
Figure 20: Top Trending Hashtags	168
Figure 21: Farmers' Agitation - Total Tweets of Three Hashtags	171
Figure 22: Peaks in Twitter Activity	174
Figure 23: Economic Value of the Report	176
Figure 24: Economic Value of Tweets and Users	177
Figure 25: Most Expensive Tweet	179
Figure 26: Second Most Expensive Tweet	180
Figure 27: Third Most Expensive Tweet	181
Figure 28: Top Accounts	182
Figure 29: Most Expensive Users	184
Figure 30: Sentiment Timeline	187
Figure 31: Overall Sentiment Score	189
Figure 32: Sentiment Data	190
Figure 33: Most Active Handles	191
Figure 34: Most Original Tweets	194
Figure 35: Most Popular Handles	194
Figure 36: Highest Impact	195
Figure 37: Original Tweets with Hashtag - Top Average RTS	196
Figure 38: Most Favourite, Most Mentioned	201
Figure 39: Tweets Per Contributor	202
Figure 40: Age of Account & Length of Tweet	203

Figure 41: As Per Followers	204
Figure 42: Most Retweeted Tweet	205
Figure 43: Most Liked Tweet	206
Figure 44: Top Photo Contributors	207
Figure 45: Most Liked Image - @almeidaJugnu	208
Figure 46: Most Retweeted Photo - @indijaswaloye	213
Figure 47: Sanjoy Mujumdar's Tweet - Police Action on Protestors	258
Figure 48: Tweet Inviting People to Memorial Meet	259
Figure 49: Tweets - TV Programmes on Nirbhaya	259
Figure 50: New Trending Hashtags - #nirbhayaneedjustice, #nirbhayarapistout	260
Figure 51: Hashtags for Unrelated Topics	263

Preface

It is almost as if you were frantically constructing another world while the world that you live in dissolves beneath your feet, and that your survival depends on completing this construction at least one second before the old habitation collapses.
-Tennessee Williams, Camino Real

My principal motivation for writing this book is our situation today: We stand on the precipice of a new era, where the convergence of artificial and human intelligence has altered the landscape of communication in profound ways. This interaction between human and machine learning models has far-reaching implications that are destined to reshape the dynamics of human expression forever. It is crucial to preserve the record of the last two decades of social media activity as a significant cultural stage, because the advent of the multiverse has the potential to irrevocably redefine public engagement. The timeline studied in this book is the period spanning 2012 to 2022. Two prominent case studies on the Twitter platform, the Nirbhaya rape case and the Farmers' agitation serve as testimonies to the initial levels of public participation. The concerns that weigh upon me today shall undoubtedly resonate with future generations; a resonance magnified manifold. The onset of a new era is often marked by technological innovation, but it is important to recognise that this represents a continuous journey, wherein the pursuit of progress is never truly halted.

Acknowledgement

Silent gratitude isn't much use to anyone.

-G.B. Stern

The inception of an idea, the impetus of motivation, and the culmination through perseverance all necessitate substantial external support. The nascent idea, fragile and ephemeral, undergoes a transformative journey from the recesses of the mind to tangible form on paper. The process of discovery brings with it daily revelations, surprising data, and remarkable methodologies; yet it can also be a solitary expedition through uncharted territories, fraught with uncertainty and doubt. My own journey follows this trajectory, and I am indebted to numerous individuals whose contributions warrant recognition.

Foremost, I express my gratitude to Zizi Papacharissi, from the Department of Communication, University of Illinois, Chicago, whose pioneering work on 'Affective News' and its implications within the realm of Twitter has greatly influenced this undertaking. Enthralled by her research, I reached out and she responded with utmost enthusiasm, generously providing me with invaluable resources and methodological guidance.

In my quest for methodological insights, I intensively studied the works of Arthur Asa Berger, whose writings on semiotics have proven enriching and accessible. Additionally, I extend my gratitude to the brilliant minds of the big data scientific community, whose pioneering efforts have yielded remarkable tools and techniques that have developed the landscape of contemporary research.

Among the luminaries who have indelibly influenced this work is Marshall McLuhan, whose succinct aphorisms have consistently captivated me. Delving deep into the concept of 'the medium is the message' I found a profound intellectual engagement, which served as the springboard for my arguments. I pay homage to the genius of Prof McLuhan.

I am indebted to the numerous scholars, researchers, and experts in the field whose published works and academic contributions have been instrumental in informing and enriching this study. This collective body of knowledge has served as a beacon of inspiration and provided the intellectual foundation to my own work.

I am indebted to Panjab University for affording me the privilege of a sabbatical period dedicated to this endeavour. My sincere gratitude to Prof Arun K Grover, the esteemed former Vice Chancellor, whose unwavering support for sabbaticals among the faculty enabled me to immerse myself in this work. I would also like to extend my sincere appreciation to Prof Renu Vig, the present Vice Chancellor of our institution, for giving me the invaluable opportunity to delve into my research interests. Under her leadership, I have been able to explore and pursue my academic passions, contributing to the advancement of knowledge within my field. also express my heartfelt gratitude to the Registrar and the administrative team for efficiently handling the official intricacies.

Closer to home, I sought guidance and found the answer to countless queries through the invaluable support of esteemed colleagues, professors, administrative staff, research scholars within my home department of the School of Communication Studies. Engaging in spirited discussions with my colleagues constituted crucial brainstorming sessions, while the attentive listening and valuable input from my research scholars proved indispensable.

Undoubtedly, conducting independent research can be arduous when undertaken single-handedly. Daunting deadlines, monotonous and time-consuming work, and the occasional confusion present formidable challenges. In these circumstances, solace is found within the family, which serves as a steady source of motivation, urging one to exert their utmost efforts. Thus, I extend my gratitude to my husband, Rakesh Singh, and my daughters, Sowmya and Pallavi, my sons-in-law Aditya and Ronak, my sister Shilpa and brother-in-law Dhiraj Singh for their unwavering support, which allowed me to devote myself wholeheartedly to my studies. Moreover, I am grateful to my mother, Sudha Shukla, whose confidence in my abilities exceeds even my own. She propelled me continuously to surpass my self-imposed limitations. My family stands as my support system, providing a nurturing environment where I can candidly acknowledge my shortcomings. I am grateful to my friends Prof Navneet Agnihotri, Prof Shubhini Awasthi, Dr Ruhi Tabassum Khan, Ms Meena Iyer and Dr Anu Dua Sehgal for their unflagging encouragement, support and understanding. Their presence has served as an abiding source of strength enabling me to strive for excellence.

I extend my profound gratitude to Renu Kaul Verma and the esteemed publishers, Vitasta Publications, for generous allocation of time, and provision of a contemplative space. Their steadfast commitment has been invaluable, enabling me to refine and elevate the scholarly calibre of this work. Through their dedication, they have provided an environment conducive to academic rigor, enhancing the overall quality of this research endeavour.

I wish to express my heartfelt gratitude to all those individuals who, despite not being mentioned explicitly, have made significant contributions to this work.

Lastly, I extend my gratitude to Twitter itself, as well as platforms such as www.topsy.com and www.twitterbinder.com, for their indispensable contributions in terms of tweet analytics and the vast array of tweets that I was able to access. I am indebted to all the Tweeters whose active participation has enriched this research. To one and all, my profound thanks.

ARCHANA R SINGH

Viral Vanguard
Social Media Surge In Social Movements

> *A social movement that only moves people is merely a revolt. A movement that changes both people and institutions is a revolution.*
> –Martin Luther King Jr.

SOCIAL MOVEMENTS HAVE been an integral part of human history, serving as catalysts for change and agents of social transformation. These movements often gain momentum and eventually reach a tipping point when they become a force capable of bringing about significant societal shifts. They can be defined as organised efforts by a group of individuals who come together to achieve common goals and address specific grievances within a society. These movements are often driven by a shared vision of social justice and seek to challenge existing power structures and institutions. Through collective action, social movements strive to bring about meaningful changes by raising awareness, mobilising supporters, and influencing public opinion. 'A social movement is a collectivity acting with some degree of organisation and continuity outside of institutional channels for the purpose of promoting or resisting change in the group, society, or world order of which it is a part' (Smelser, 1962).

Smelser's definition of a social movement is one of the most widely used in the field of sociology. It emphasises the

following key elements of social movements:
- A social movement is set in motion by a group of people who share a common goal or interest.
- Social movements are organised to some degree, even if they are not formally structured.
- Social movements are not short-lived phenomena. They persist over time, even in the face of opposition.
- Social movements operate outside of formal institutions such as the government or the media.
- Social movements can either promote or resist change. They can seek to change the status quo, or they can defend the status quo against change.

The rich history of India is punctuated by significant social movements that have played a transformative role in shaping the country's socio-political landscape. Prior to the advent of internet, these movements harnessed traditional communication channels such as newspapers, pamphlets, and public gatherings to disseminate their message and generate participation. The most long lasting and effective socio-political movement in India was the struggle for Indian independence, led by iconic figures such as Mahatma Gandhi, Jawaharlal Nehru, and Subhas Chandra Bose. It represents an example of collective mobilisation against British colonial rule. Employing nonviolent resistance, civil disobedience, boycotts, and mass protests, this movement received immense support from the masses. Newspapers and pamphlets played a pivotal role in galvanising public sentiments and disseminating nationalist ideals. For instance, Mahatma Gandhi's newspaper, *'Young India',* effectively propagated the principles of nonviolence and self-reliance, resonating with readership and inspiring collective action. Similarly, the Non-Cooperation Movement launched in 1920, aimed to unite Indians in nonviolent resistance against British rule. By advocating for the boycott of British institutions, including educational institutions and law courts, the movement effectively challenged the legitimacy of colonial authority. The movement's success can be attributed to its adept utilisation of newspapers like *Navjivan*, which Gandhi established to articulate the movement's objectives. Through its extensive coverage, *'Navjivan'* disseminated information, promoted public awareness, and mobilised widespread participation. Mahatma Gandhi also organised the Salt Satyagraha in 1930, as a powerful protest against the British salt tax that burdened the common people. Gandhi's march to Dandi, where he symbolically violated the salt laws by producing salt from seawater, attracted significant attention. Newspapers played a crucial role in raising public awareness and fomenting dissent against British rule. The *'Harijan'* newspaper, founded by Gandhi, served as an influential medium for advocating social justice and equality, amplifying the impact of the Salt Satyagraha. In free India, the Chipko Movement of the 1970s based in Uttarakhand, assumed a prominent role in advocating the protection of forests for sustainable development. Distinguished by the active participation of women, the movement involved tree-hugging as a nonviolent method to prevent the felling of trees by commercial loggers. The Chipko Movement too effectively utilised newspapers, such as *Sarvodaya*, to draw attention to the ecological consequences of deforestation and recognise the local communities' rights over forest resources. When India faced the imposition of Emergency during 1975-77, the Anti-Emergency Movement emerged as a robust social response, encompassing various political parties, activists, and citizens.

Through protests, strikes, and acts of civil disobedience, the movement tried to restore democracy and protect fundamental rights. Newspapers like *'The Indian Express'* and *'The Statesman'* played a pivotal role in galvanising public opinion. There have been other movements such as the Assam Movement between 1979-1985 which was against the integration of undocumented immigrants to Assam, and Anti-reservation protests in 1990 and 2006. The earliest of social movements used the idea of 'passive resistance' (Govindu, 2019), and each was led by a prominent socio-political leader(s) accompanied by their followers. Post Independence protests took a more democratic stance but were still classified under readymade categories such as students, women, LGBTQ+, elderly, disabled and a host of other identities (Edelman, 2001).

The Social Network

In recent years, social movements have discovered a novel instrument for amplifying their momentum, namely, social media. Prominent platforms such as Facebook, Twitter (Now known as X), and Instagram have been harnessed as powerful tools to enhance awareness regarding pertinent issues, to facilitate the organisation of protests, and to motivate supporters. Moreover, social media serves as a medium through which narratives and firsthand accounts from the forefront of social movements can be documented and disseminated, effectively garnering public support and exerting pressure for transformative change. Besides, the social media platforms reach a large audience, often in ways that are more personal and engaging than traditional media. This can help to raise awareness of issues that might otherwise have been ignored, and it can also help to build support for social movements.

One can imagine social media as a form of plaza protest. Plaza protests, also known as Public Square protests, have been potent arenas for social movements. These protests often take place in central gathering spaces within cities, symbolising the intersection of power and the public sphere. By occupying public squares, protesters aim to disrupt the everyday functioning of society, attracting attention, and generating discourse around their cause. A social media platform fulfils these criteria and presents itself as an effective medium for collectivity. Social media can be seen as a plaza in many ways. It is a place where people come together to share ideas, connect with others, and learn about the world around them. It is also a place where people can express themselves freely and build communities.

Like a plaza, social media is a public space. Anyone can access it, and anyone can participate. This makes it a powerful tool for social change. However, like a plaza, social media can also be a place of conflict. People with different ideas and opinions come together on social media, and this can sometimes lead to heated debates, wars of words, trolling, and threats.

While plaza protests possess the unique power of capturing public attention through their physical presence, visual impact, and symbolic significance, the social media does it by their online presence throughout the day. In a plaza protest, the occupation of a central plaza or square becomes a visible reminder of the movement's existence and demands, ensuring that their message reaches a wide audience. The iconic images and footage of crowded squares filled with passionate protesters can have a profound impact in shaping public opinion and sparking conversations about the issues at hand. On social media the images reach far and wide and communities of interest come together regardless of geographical boundaries. They act as catalysts for community mobilisation and formation of networks of solidarity. The gathering of like-minded individuals fosters a sense of belonging, unity, and collective identity while the online gatherings empower participants by the presence of others who share their concerns, strengthening their resolve and commitment to the cause. These collectives often become hubs for exchange of ideas, knowledge, and strategies, further enhancing the movement's efficacy.

The combination of plaza protests and social media activism has the potential to shape public opinion, influence societal discourse and, ultimately, policy outcomes. When a movement reaches the tipping point, it garners substantial media coverage, forcing public and political figures to take notice. The ensuing discussions and debates help to mainstream the movement's concerns, generating support and placing pressure on policymakers to address the grievances. In some cases, plaza protests combined with social media involvement have led to significant policy changes and reforms. Social media should have a significant presence for this to happen. Changes in technology have led to changes in media systems.

Each medium creates a new space for itself and transforms society in apparent and invisible ways while forever affecting the pattern and direction of growth. Technology has also affected news and changed the latter's identity every time, by evolving new forms of writing styles; for example, the popular inverted pyramid pattern was a fallout of the Associated Press Lead which was necessitated by the invention of the telegraph. A similar change is currently visible, and it seems to be affecting the very ideals of present-day journalism. As the old order changes, the traditional media give way to the more unorthodox means of information flow. As of now, in the spirit of convergence, the old media co-exists with the new and thereby creates multiple platforms for news flow.

Four crucial dimensions brought about by the new fluidity of information flow—depth, breadth, diversity, and speed—differentiate one medium from the other (Zhang Shixin, Ivy, E. D., 2013). The Information Age expanded the media tremendously through the advent of cable television, growing numbers of niche print publications, internet websites, mobile telephones and so on. Meanwhile, the Knowledge Age has made media lose their independent identities and converge on one platform making them nearly ubiquitous. When a medium is invented or introduced to a society, it is always a novelty, a miracle, and an unbelievable reality which in due course of time becomes an inescapable part of life. One can follow the links in the chain of technological advancements and find oneself at the centre of a modern media scenario. One can visualise a world that survived on speech alone, where communication was face to face. This immediately morphed into one which relied on delayed communication in the form of printed word. Next was the amalgamation of the oral with the visual created by cinema and television, and finally, over a period of time, all these strands were brought together and there was convergence.

The social network as an invention was never created for news gathering and dissemination. Nevertheless, the media, which relies on such a network, has turned into a meeting point of likeminded people who share and disseminate news and information. The network comprises of societies within societies, all brought together by communities of interest.

Amongst the social networking sites—LinkedIn, Facebook, Instagram, and Twitter—it is Twitter (now known as X) which strikes one as being the most useful for the purpose of journalistic news storytelling and for disseminating messages to a large mass of people for offline action. Twitter has developed into a platform for news storytelling, enabling collaborative story writing, but more typically, collaborative filtering and curating of news (Schonfeld, 2010). It has gained importance due to its unique features of being always-on, its emphasis on informal scripting, maintaining an open and ever expanding base of users, and a portable back-end interface (T. O'Reilly, 2004). Collaboratively produced news feeds by citizens committing independent or coordinated acts of journalism present an important alternative to the dominant news economy (A. Bruns, & J. Burgess, 2012).

As per digital news consumption-based survey of over 93,000 online news consumers in 46 markets covering half of the world's population, carried out by Reuters Institute and published by Oxford University (Reuters Institute Digital News Report 2022), news consumption on social media is increasing. The table below reflects the usage on various platforms (Krishnan, 2023).

Brand	For News	For All
YouTube	53%	76%
WhatsApp	51%	76%
Facebook	43%	62%
Instagram	32%	55%
Twitter	22%	35%
Telegram	21%	41%

Figure 1: Digital News Report

Although Twitter appears to lag behind other social media platforms, it is this medium which is most used by newsmakers and plaza protestors for announcements and mobilisation.

Media theorists such as Nicholas Negroponte predicted that in the future, online news would give readers the ability to choose only the topics and sources that interested them (Negroponte, 1995). The phenomenon is visible now. Individuals have now turned into content creators for a seamless cyberspace experience filled with continuously updated messages hurled back and forth. The internet has provided a forum for discussion along with the tools for discussion in the form of various websites ranging from the most general to the most specialised. Since the coming of smart phones, these sites are available in the pockets of most people around the world.

Convergence, Social Media, and News

Convergence has redefined the practice of journalism in ways that were unimaginable a decade ago. With the internet making lateral, horizontal and vertical inroads into the realm of journalism, path breaking changes and challenges can be discerned. The formal structures of news organisations and traditional systems of news gathering, production, and dissemination are now as old fashioned as snail mail. We are in a phase of transition, where new and old media co-exist.

New information technologies have created a virtual community that is faster and more competitive. Initially, the intention perhaps was not to compete with the traditional media, but the floodgates were soon opened leading to an unstoppable barrage of information which goes on creating waves of news, views, opinions, and debates.

The new community of news producers, disseminators and

consumers with its virtual existence can influence real concerns. A. J. Liebling once said, 'Freedom of the press is guaranteed only to those who own one' (A. J. Leibling, 1960). Millions of people armed with laptops and smart phones now own the entire paraphernalia to send and receive news and information. It is a world where news meets views in a confused blur, a world where opinions are formed from fact and falsehood alike, where sentiments are expressed without hesitation, where everybody has a point of view and is free to enunciate it.

Search engines have played a pivotal role in granting individuals instantaneous access to information, thereby empowering seekers with an unprecedented ability to attain success in their inquiries. This transformative invention has brought about a profound shift in the dynamics of communication, effectively converging face-to-face, interpersonal, and group interactions within the realm of cyberspace. Consequently, the landscape of communication systems has undergone an irrevocable transformation, forever altering the way we engage with one another. As you read this, the influence of Artificial Intelligence tools on the creation of media content is already discernible, introducing a paradigm shift in the very fabric of media production dynamics. The rapidity of these changes is such that a complex amalgamation of truth and falsehood, authenticity and deception, coexists in a manner that often eludes immediate recognition.

Content prosumers can interact on collaborative websites in many ways such as to create, to inform, to entertain, to gain status and build a reputation in the community, to create connections with others who have similar interests, online and offline, for sense making and understanding.

The intersection of consumers and producers within the

realm of online platforms yields a discernible outcome: the generation of opinions. Regardless of the motives behind individuals' engagement with a particular website and its community, the consequence is an emergence of perspectives. As a result, the traditional media systems find their exclusive rights to delivering 'breaking news' increasingly undermined. In today's landscape, a growing amount of news not only finds its way into discussions and debates but also breaks first on social networks such as Facebook and Twitter.

Online media exhibits various classifications based on different criteria, including the pursued objectives or aims, the targeted audience, the application of professional, structural, editorial, and ethical journalistic standards, and the utilisation of possibilities offered by the digital realm. Additionally, the constant updating of content plays a pivotal role in defining the diverse nature of online media platforms.

In India, internet penetration increased by 4 per cent to 866 million subscriptions in December 2022. Thirty-two million Indian households have a wired broadband connection. The smartphone user base increased to 538 million in 2022 from 448 million in 2020 – this indicates penetration into around 38 per cent of India's population. Though this appears to be lower in percentage terms as compared to many other countries, in absolute terms, India is the second largest market in terms of the number of users (Report, 2023). Sam Pitroda, former advisor to the Prime Minister on public infrastructures and innovations said a decade ago in 2013: 'As traditional media becomes increasingly dictated by monetary decisions and establishment structures, social media will emerge as the more untainted voice of the citizens' (Sam, 2013). Presently, India has the second biggest social media user base with 755.47 million users (Ruby, 2023).

Twitter

Twitter, a micro-blogging service was launched in 2006 and as of December 2022, Twitter's audience accounted for over 368 million monthly active users worldwide, (Dixon, 2022) and 27.25 million users in India as of early 2023 (Kemp, S, 2023).

This mechanism of news selection and gathering is visible since the time the Social Networking Sites (SNS) became prominent in urban lifestyle. Ever since control over the content of the media space, once held by traditional news outlets, began to be shared by bloggers and other social media participants one can observe the involvement of opinions expressed in SNS featuring in the news broadcasts of traditional media. Questions are asked, answers are sought, and debates are carried out on the social networking sites alongside the traditional media. Twitter news feeds of journalists and news organisations are typically modelled after the news values and practices of parent organisations. Most trending topics on Twitter tend to be headlines of breaking or persistent news on sports, cities, or brands (Kwak, 2010). News organisations forward print and broadcast stories to their news feeds, delivering the same news over a different platform. Such uses may undermine the potential of Twitter, which works best in pre-mediated situations where the story changes so quickly that TV or print media do not have the time to develop a fully sourced story.

Twitter was not conceived as a predominantly news-oriented platform. It was primarily info-mediation or recreational. However, the tendency of the forum to give voice to opinions has made it a favourite with journalists who share space with the common man to create content. Although there is a clear distinction between what is created for the conventional media on the internet (such as newspapers' websites) and that which is created exclusively for the online media. Twitter feeds are incorporated in the more traditional news websites. The data, when it moves from one medium to the other, changes in shape and form, but the spirit remains the same. This is so, because the messages that are picked up by the mainstream media are the ones that are already approved and accepted by the philosophy of the new medium. The message therefore transforms in shape, size, format, and looks but does not change in terms of the nuances that it carries because those nuances helped it to be transported from one media to another in the first place. One can safely say that even in the absence of Twitter and despite its presence, the news that leapfrogs from one medium to the other is a veritable blend of humor, opinion expression, and emotion. This concoction is being dished out to unsuspecting network users and from there it is being picked up by the mainstream media. This blend broadcasted and listened to via Twitter has been called 'Affective news' by Papacharissi and de Fatima Oliveira in their study about the Egyptian uprising and the collaboration between networked publics around #Egypt (Z. Papacharissi & M. de Fatima Oliveira, 2012). Twitter has been used most effectively during the Arab Spring for the first time, and later during the Hong Kong protests, and the Black Lives Matter protests, all of which prove that it has been effective across the world.

Twitter exerts tremendous impact on information creation and circulation. It speeds up the process of news collection and usage by other media. It is a medium on its own and a source of information for other media. It is the content of other media as McLuhan said. The entire mechanism of news collection and dissemination has gone through a drastic change. In the legacy media the viewers are exposed to news much later than the producers of news. The writer, reporter, news agency, news desk used to go through the news before it was released to the masses through publishing, radio broadcast, TV broadcast, etc. In the digital age, information trickles down to the masses even as the same news is accessed by professional news workers. Therefore, journalists are no longer the sole occupants of the first row in the drama of life.

Of all the media, Twitter seems to have a full-time monopoly over the reach and access of news. Even while the news workers seem to be struggling to put together the news for the formal media networks, the viewer exposition through social media is complete with Twitter taking the lead.

The role of the editor was to check that stories are factually correct before they release them to the public at large (Herman, 2014). On Twitter, it can break with a single Tweet, and the editor has no role in it. The reporter has the wherewithal to share the information on his personal handle and also operate the official handle. Many a times, the reporter presents the information through 'going live' on social media. The era of pre-publishing verification has given way to an era of post-publishing correction. The receiver has the power to verify and also to vilify. Every message is open for discussion and debate.

Besides it's apparent influence on the news flow, Twitter has shown itself to be remarkably useful in collective action and collaboration. Twitter has developed into a platform for news storytelling, enabling collaborative story writing, but more typically, collaborative filtering and curating of news. Although only about 5 per cent of Twitter content is devoted to news, mainstream news networks frequently poll the

Twitterverse for public opinion; independent bloggers use it to promote each other's or their own content, and journalists use it to supplement their own reporting (K. Ryan, 2009).

The roles played by news workers, be it that of editors, reporters, critics, or independent observers are also in a flux and are being played interchangeably. Journalists use Twitter in a way that supplements their traditional role as information disseminators and prompts news agencies to issue guidelines regarding the use of social media. Citizens, on the other hand, are likely to use a particular medium as a mechanism for public accountability. The conversations on Twitter are carried out with organically produced hashtag feeds. This may include news, opinion, emotion, promotion, or a blend of all the above.

Growth and Development of Twitter

Twitter has been used for this research in order to collect primary data through data scraping. Twitter has opened up vast possibilities for research in various fields such as media and communication studies, linguistics, sociology, psychology, political science, information and computer science, education, and economics. The immense amount of content generated and shared on Twitter by individuals and institutions offers a rich source of data for analysis. To fully harness this potential, it is crucial to develop innovative methods and approaches that can effectively handle these new sources of research data. Furthermore, it is essential to train a new generation of scholars who are well-versed in these methodological frameworks. Accessing large datasets from Twitter is made possible through the Twitter Application Programming Interface (API). Researchers can retrieve these datasets and employ specialised tools, such as programming languages, statistic packages, network analysis frameworks, and text and data mining tools, to analyse the data. The availability of API-based access has also given rise to a variety of tools and services that aim to measure and compare impact, influence, and audience reach on Twitter (Katrin Weller, Axel Bruns, Jean Burgess, Merja Mahrt, Cornelius Puschmann, Steve Jones, 2014).

Date	Event	Participant
2004	Odeo founded by Evan Williams, Biz Stone, and Noah Glass	Evan Williams, Biz Stone, Noah Glass
21 March 2006	Jack Dorsey sends the first tweet ('just setting up my twttr')	Jack Dorsey
July 2006	Twitter debuts as a completed version	Evan Williams, Biz Stone, Jack Dorsey
October 2006	Williams, Stone, and Dorsey buy out Odeo, start Obvious Corp.	Evan Williams, Biz Stone, Jack Dorsey
November 2006	Twitter Inc. created as a corporate entity	Evan Williams, Biz Stone, Jack Dorsey
April 2010	Twitter unveils 'Promoted Tweets' as intended primary revenue source	Twitter
15 January 2009	Tweet by Janis Krums breaks news of US Airways flight 1549 water-landing	Janis Krums
June 2009	Twitter becomes a prominent outlet for news during the Iranian presidential election	Twitter
September 2013	Twitter files to become a public company	Twitter
November 2013	Twitter's IPO raises $1.8 billion, giving it a market value of $31 billion	Twitter
October 2015	Jack Dorsey returns as CEO, Moments feature added	Jack Dorsey
March 2016	Twitter replaces chronological timeline with algorithmic timeline	Twitter

January 2017	Moments replaced with Explore feature	Twitter
2017	Character limit of a tweet increased to 280 characters	Twitter
Early 2019	Twitter switches to 'monetizable daily active users' metric	Twitter
November 2020	Fleets feature introduced, designed to vanish within 24 hours	Twitter
May 2021	Spaces feature introduced for hosting live audio conversations	Twitter
November 2021	Jack Dorsey steps down as CEO, Parag Agrawal becomes CEO	Jack Dorsey, Parag Agrawal
2022	Elon Musk announces bid to purchase Twitter for $44 billion	Elon Musk
July 2022	Twitter sues Elon Musk to force him to buy the company	Twitter
September 2022	Twitter shareholders vote to accept Musk's offer	Twitter

Figure 2: Timeline of Twitter (Zeidan, 2023)

Tweet and Tweeter

The news feed on Twitter is called Tweet. A tweet is a short text comprising of only 280 characters that include letters and punctuation marks. When Twitter was introduced, the length was restricted to 140 characters but later doubled to 280. Tweets, like other texts, are a sign system. The emphasis is on its structure, which must be precise and tightly packed. Tweets are a virtual medium for discussions created by the users of Twitter. While Tweets offer a commentary on the events around us, they also construct a virtual reality at the same time which is juxtaposed with the real world.

Twitter, therefore, in addition to immediacy, sensationalism, quotes, prominence, action, drama, also has biases, viewpoints, and opinions. It also caters to the privileged class and creates a divide amongst the haves and have-nots in terms of not just infrastructure to produce tweets but also in viewpoints. India ranks third in the world when it comes to the use of Twitter (Oberlo, 2023) and has in place a remarkable process of 'trickle down' of messages across various media.

The real impact of Twitter was felt in the 2014 elections when most politicians used the medium to make political pronouncements and to gain political mileage. It was believed to be an election contested primarily on social media. A new form of journalism emerged. This journalism is called 'hashtag journalism' because it used the Twitter symbol of hashtag (#) to identify persons, events, groups or organisations. Presently, Twitter is being cited on television and a symbiotic relationship has been forged by the two media.

The people who are on social media are people who have access to all modern gadgets of information reach. One may argue that the digital divide has broadened to totally marginalise the non-internet savvy population from this world of inter-media give and take. On the other hand, though only a minuscule population uses Twitter it is also the population that reads the mainstream English language newspapers, sits in decision making positions, get retweeted by the common man, and falls under the influential category.

Twitter is blurring boundaries between information, news, and entertainment by creating 'subtle, but important shifts in the balance of power in shaping news production' and creating 'an awareness system [with] diverse means to collect, communicate, share and display news and information, serving diverse purposes on different levels of engagement' (Chadwick, 2011). Analysing tweets could potentially open a whole new area of knowledge as it floats through cyberspace. Blogs and microblogs rise to prominence as news disseminators on occasions when access to mainstream news and/or other communication media is restricted or blocked (Papacharissi, 2009). Social media is being used for several purposes including social action and activism.

The term 'Tweeters' is introduced here to identify the individuals who tweet. The other terms 'Twitterers' or 'Tweeples' are used commonly for people who use Twitter. In this book, merely being on Twitter as a Twitterer or being a part of the mass that constitutes all those people who tweet as 'Tweeple' was not enough to form the population to draw the sample. Individuals who had accounts and who actively participated in the discussion using the selected hashtags had to be 'persons who tweet,' hence the term being introduced here is 'Tweeter' which is distinct from Twitterer and Tweeple.

The theoretical strength is derived from Habermas's public space and communicative action theories, agenda setting theory by McCombs and Shaw, the concept of choreography of assembly by Paulo Gerbaudo and the Diffusion of Innovation theory by Rogers. The conceptual framework is provided by the Social Network theory of Charles Kadushin. Underlining all theories that bear impact, is the simple notion formulated by Marshall McLuhan, 'Medium is the message'. Marshall McLuhan's aphorism meant the key impact of media lay in its structure rather than its content (W. T. Gordon, 2003). McLuhan's philosophy predicted that the medium was powerful enough to impose a mindset such as linear and sequential for print and for radio, which he believed to have returned to the oral and musical tradition of the tribal societies, with the only difference being their global reach. He predicted that the trend of pervading information would also imply the emergence of a hyperconnected global village.

Just as the Twitterer who gives importance to the medium, the Tweeter holds the message as paramount, yet whatever the Tweeter has to say, he or she will have to follow the rules set by the medium. In the Indian context, increasing visibility of Twitter in news dissemination has created an alternative force of 'collectives' who may sometimes be pro-sumers, at other times regular media persons and sometimes may be anonymous users hiding behind a fake profile.

This book aims to explore the role of Twitter in mobilisation and coordination of social movements and protests. The background of the book is rooted in the use of social media in collective action and the increasing importance of Twitter in this regard. Twitter has been used in various protest movements such as the Arab Spring, the Black Lives Matter and the Hong Kong pro-democracy protests. This has led to a growing interest in understanding how Twitter is used in the choreography of assemblies and the impact it has on the success of these movements.

The significance of the book lies in its contribution to the literature on the intersection of social media and collective action. By analysing case studies and conducting a thorough analysis of Twitter data, related to two prominent cases, the book aims to provide insights into how Twitter is used to mobilise and coordinate social movements in India. Much has been written about the movements across the world, but the users of Twitter in India have effectively used the medium many times but more so in the case of two important events nearly a decade apart, the Nirbhaya Rape Case of 2012 and the Farmers' agitation of 2021. As we follow the asynchronic communication of the news feeds on Twitter by concerned individuals, journalists, and news organisations these two cases occupy a unique position in the din of social media and stand out among the complex haze of the networked system of social awareness.

This book provides insights into how social media can be leveraged for effective collective action. It has practical implications for activists and policymakers alike and can inform the development of policies and strategies for social movements and activism.

This book is an essential read for students of Mass Communication who are ready to participate in the world of media of which social media is a huge part, for students interested in activism, in policy building, and for students who are interested in this form of research. The book makes a significant contribution to the academic literature on social media and collective action.

Theoretical Tapestry
Communication's Role in Activism

> *A new medium is never an addition to an old one, nor does it leave the old one in peace. It never ceases to oppress the older media until it finds new shapes and positions for them'.*
>
> -Marshall McLuhan

WE LIVE IN an amazing era. It is during our time when the grassroots media is exploring the possibilities of international readership through the internet, where small and medium newspapers are rubbing shoulders with the trans-national media corporations, where media products are integrating into each other by sometimes providing content and sometimes providing environment to each other, where all media is a mix with the coming together of technologies and businesses. We live in a time when horizontal and vertical integration creates media giants who treat all media as vehicles for carrying messages suitable to each other, where audiences are fragmented into targeted groups and the masses are de-massified for the benefit of the message.

The emergence of the internet and subsequently social media follows the path described by the Diffusion of Innovations Theory. Pioneered in 1943 by Bryce Ryan and Neil Gross of Iowa State University, Diffusion of Innovations Theory was substantiated by Thomas W Valente and Everett M Rogers (Valente, T. W., Rogers, E. M., 1995). This theory traces the process whereby a new idea or practice is communicated through certain channels over time among members of a social system. The model describes the factors that influence people's thoughts and actions and the process of adopting a new technology or idea. Control over the contents of the media space, once held by traditional news outlets, is today shared by bloggers and other social media participants. Some are faster than others in adapting to new technologies. This virtual race makes some media universally accepted while others are accessed by only an exclusive set of people with the necessary resources needed to access them.

Twitter remains a medium that is yet to make inroads into the hands of the common man and is still being used by the intellectual, political, or social elite of the society. Although the medium itself has not diffused amongst the masses, the message percolates through inter-media sharing. There are many reasons for this inter-media sharing amongst different platforms. The horizontal and vertical integration of media in the presence of conglomerates, makes it sensible to have one set of news gatherers operate across platforms. No wonder, the reporters on their beats are seen as reporting for the online edition from the site. With the coming of social media, we have witnessed that news is being broken by the common man as soon as the events occur because of the availability of the instruments of data collection and dissemination. Every individual who has gadgets for recording and transmitting messages across platforms can behave as a citizen journalist. This emerging unorganised sector creates pressure on the organised sector of media organisations to perform with equal alacrity.

The journalists seek out and share videos and audios

prepared by 'citizen journalists' because of their presence on the scene. In the era of 24x7 news it is impossible for media organisations to provide 'breaking news'. Young people are more in tune with the news as it is being shared on social media platforms rather than the traditional media avenues because they easily get news snippets in the Twitter or Facebook news feeds. This news is short, crisp, and unconfirmed. It makes sense for traditional media to use these platforms to provide authentic information so that rumour does not make its permanent home on these platforms.

In such a scenario, media must work doubly hard to use the variety of platforms for functioning optimally. Media can create viewpoints and thus, influence the decisions of their users. McCombs and Shaw in their Agenda Setting Theory (McCombs, 1972) highlight the ability of the media to influence the significance of events in the public's mind. It says that the media is not always successful at telling the masses what to think, but they are quite successful at telling us what to think about. The media set the agenda for the audience's discussion and intellectually order and organise their world. The agenda-setting function of the media fosters a correlation between the media and public ordering of priorities. Since different stakeholders of information are present on different media, they create a world according to their perception and reveal the same through their messages. Across platforms the messages reverberate, then settle down to exert maximum influence through the richest medium.

Agenda Setting Theory becomes even more significant in the context of Twitter. The reason being that it is already a significant platform for news dissemination and allows individuals and organisations to share news and information in real time. Specific topics can be followed, and news can be curated. Besides, Twitter's algorithm plays a role by prioritising content based on engagement metrics such as likes, retweets, and replies. As a result, popular topics tend to get amplified while less popular ones are suppressed. The site allows for the creation and spread of viral hashtags which can focus attention on specific issues and topics.

Similarly, consider the Media Richness Theory which was formulated by Daft & Lengel in 1984, also known as the Information Richness Theory. This theory is related to communication effectiveness. Each communication medium is classified according to the complexity of the message that it can handle effectively. One may believe that the 280-character restriction on Twitter may be too narrow to convey rich relational messages, considering that media richness construct is defined theoretically by four sub-dimensions such as number of cue systems supported by a medium, immediacy of feedback, potential for the usage of natural language and message personalisation. Anticipating the inclusion of all the dimensions in social media interaction would be too ambitious.

In the original formulation, face to face was considered as the richest medium. However, social media does offer all the above traits and may be considered rich. Yet, theoretically, its bandwidth has been considered narrow because of the other keyword, 'equivocality' present in the theory. Equivocality is defined as the degree to which a decision-making situation and information related to it are subject to multiple interpretations. The theory argues that greater richness is required in the media for greater equivocality. A deeper study is required to examine the degree of equivocality in social media (Daft, R. L. & Lengel, R. H., 1984). However, it is still felt that social media such as Twitter has brought back the oral tradition of group conversations. It resembles a gathering of like-minded friends, discussing and arguing over issues in voices loud enough to be heard across the platform.

Considering the theory in the context of Twitter, one can discern that Twitter's character limit and emphasis on brevity may make it more difficult to convey complex information. Yet, the presence of emojis, videos, and other nonverbal cues enrich the communication. One should also underline the fact that Twitter allows the user to attach documents which can be opened and read by the users who want detailed information. The restriction on size is there—documents cannot exceed 5 MB in size—but the attachment can still be present in the Tweet adding to the depth of information. The real time nature of the medium allows for immediate feedback and interaction which can enhance the richness. Users can respond to tweets, engage in conversations, and share additional information, leading to a more interactive and dynamic communication process. Most importantly, the use of hashtags on Twitter allows users to organise and categorise information, making it easier to find and share information on specific topics.

The information in the Twitter system is beyond the reach of the great digital divide. However, those who are inside the elite circle of users, bear resemblance to what Habermas calls the public sphere (Jürgen Habermas; Sara Lennox; Frank Lennox, Autumn, 1974). The public sphere is defined as a segment of social life which allows citizens to exchange views on matters of importance to the common good, so that public opinion can be formed. This public sphere comes into being when people gather to discuss issues of political concern. Habermas's work refers to a historical moment during the seventeenth and eighteenth centuries when coffee houses, societies, and salons became the centres of debate, and sets this up as an ideal of participation in the public sphere for today. He talks about media and democracy, emphasising the critical role of the media in revitalising the public sphere.

Cyberspace is the new public sphere and Twitter may be called Twittersphere. Public participation is visible in the virtual world which flows into the real world as new communities of interest where virtual relationships are being forged over the internet. Habermas also propounded the Theory of Communicative Action, which he later called 'strong communicative action' in *Some Further Clarifications of the Concept of Communicative Rationality* (Habermas, 1989) where speakers coordinate their action and pursue individual (or joint) goals based on a shared understanding that the goals are inherently reasonable or merit worthy. While strategic action succeeds insofar as the actors achieve their individual goals, communicative action succeeds insofar as the actors freely agree that their goal (or goals) is reasonable, and that it merits cooperative behaviour. Communicative action is thus an inherently consensual form of social coordination in which actors 'mobilise the potential for rationality' given with ordinary language of rationally motivated agreement (Habermas J., 2014). The information floats over each medium which is structured as per its potential. Society tends to favour the media for its ease of operation and in creating a rich medium with its usage. The social influence approach to media richness was elaborated by Fulk, Schmitz and Steinfeld in 1990. It focuses on the factors that change users' perceptions about the capacity of social media and its consequent use (Fulk, 1990).

The democratic platform offered by the medium allows anyone on the right side of the digital divide to have an opinion and to disseminate it through this rich media throughout the network.

Twitter is an open network (Kadushin, 2012). Social Network Theory talks about three kinds of networks: ego-centric, socio-centric, and open-system networks. Ego-centric networks relate to a single node or individual. A person with many good friends whom he or she can count on is said to have a large 'network'. Socio-centric networks are in a box. Connections between children in a classroom, between executives or workers in an organisation are closed system networks and the ones most often studied in terms of the fine points of network structure. In open system networks the boundaries are not necessarily clear. The elite of a country, or connections between corporations, or the chain of influencers of a particular decision, or the adoption of new practices constitute closed networks. The open networks created by social media comprise of users of a particular site having their own viewpoints and airing them as and when they deem fit. In some ways these are the most interesting networks, but they are also the most difficult to study.

The connections forged amongst the users of social networking sites can be viewed in the context of the 'weak ties' theory of sociologist Mark Granovetter. In his seminal 1973 study entitled *The Strength of Weak Ties*, Granovetter analysed the link between micro-level interactions and macro-level patterns in social networks. He concludes by saying that the strength of weak ties lies in their potential for 'diffusion, social mobility, political organisation, and social cohesion in general', across different networks. The advantages of weak ties over strong ties lie in their ability to diffuse information and ideas across social groups. He illustrated his theory by taking 'rumour' or 'the grapevine' as examples. It is only through the sharing of the rumour that information is spread. In the online world the weak ties of connectivity are utilised for political or social mobilisation (Granovetter, 1973). On the face of it, the weak ties of social media have the potential of turning into ties stronger than others because they are capable of motivating users into offline action which would not have happened in the absence of such social networks.

Considering Twitter, one can easily see that it has all the qualities of what Granovetter describes as 'weak ties'. It enables users to connect with a large and diverse group of people, including individuals they have never met. It can facilitate the formation of weak ties which can provide access to new perspectives and information that may not be available through one's strong ties. Since Twitter emphasises the sharing of information, serendipitous connections and opportunities may arise which would not have a chance in the offline world. Use of hashtags facilitates the formation of communities around shared interests and topics. Thereby likeminded individuals connect and expand the weak ties network.

Medium is the Message: McLuhan Revisited in Twittersphere

In the present scenario, McLuhan's famous pithy aphorism, 'Medium is the message', is reinforced. If there is any phrase that encapsulates the relationship between media and its products, it is this aphorism proposed by McLuhan in 1962, and its relevance has been further re-established. He enunciated catchy, precise phrases and small witty sentences as if he had a premonition that there will be a day when everyone on social networks will vie with each other to do the same. The Facebook status, the LinkedIn updates, and, most importantly the 280-character tweets are examples of small being beautiful on social network.

Marshall McLuhan called new media the 'electric' media in the 1960s. We now call it the 'electronic' or 'digital'. While the hardware and software have evolved since he first wrote about it, the impact of new media hasn't changed much at all. Additionally, 'All media are extensions of some human faculty—psychic or physical' (Marshall McLuhan, 2001).

Marshall McLuhan was way ahead of his time. The world was slow to recognise his genius and it took almost 50 years to really understand the meaning of simple arguments thrown at us in easy conversational language from the first version of *Understanding Media* that was published in 1962.

One of McLuhan's famous sentences that prophesied the state of media has been dissected into 10 different phrases by Kerckhove & McLuhan who gave us a 10-point mantra to understand McLuhan.

'The next medium, whatever it is may be the extension of consciousness, will include television as its content, not as its environment, and will transform television into an art form. A computer as a research and communication instrument could enhance retrieval, obsolesce mass library organisation, retrieve the individual's encyclopedic function and flip into a private line to speedily tailored data of a saleable kind.' *McLuhan Decalogue* (Derrick de Kerckhove, Eric McLuhan, 2011). This decalogue explains all we need to know; let me elaborate:
The next medium, whatever it is…
1. It may be the extension of consciousness.
2. Will include television as its content, not as its environment.

3. Will transform television into an art form.
4. Have computer as a research and communication instrument
5. Enhance retrieval,
6. Obsolesce mass library organisation,
7. Retrieve the individual's encyclopedic function and,
8. Flip into a private line to
9. Speedily tailored data of
10. A saleable kind.'

Each phrase in the paragraph above is the definition of a phenomenon as we witness it, a phenomenon that includes the technological as well as the business aspects of the media environment today.

Here's a look at the Decalogue in the context of Twitter and how each of its tenets is applicable to the new medium.

The Medium, Twitter

1. Is an extension of consciousness. Many ideological battles and opinionated arguments ensue over Twitter. Whether it is a celebrity such as Shashi Tharoor with his cattle class comments or Salman Khan with his Yakub Memon faux pas, or a commoner such as one Justin Stacco who got into trouble because of her tweet posted in jest.
2. Uses television as its content and not its environment. Not only television, but also personal videos, audios, and links are used as content and the facility is used remarkably to tide over the 280-character limit.
3. Transforms all media into an art form and not just television (video). The connection between the media strung together by simple @ or # brings together people, places, audios, videos, and links on one platform each substantiating the other.
4. The computer is THE research instrument like none other.

5. Retrieval is enhanced manifold as all libraries are virtual. This answers point number 6 also.
7. Everyone can create his own encyclopedia. On Twitter, one can follow and pursue persons and topics of interest and customise one's feed to his or her liking; transforming the Twitter feed into a private space with only topics of interest and people who one follows and who are followed by an individual appear on the feed. This answers points 8 and 9.
10. Twitter is being used to promote events, personalities, and agendas. It is a method by which to measure the popularity of businesses and the assessment of Twitter feeds has turned into an occupation of its own.

It is amazing how effortlessly the prophecy fits into our present-day reality. No wonder it is believed that McLuhan had the insight and perspicacity to see just how electronics will be changing us. Today as we are a part of the convergence culture, we find that the old and new media come together as parts of one another. We are witness to the presence of pro-sumers who are both consumers and producers at the same time. We are part of the group that carries all the media paraphernalia with them, thereby being ready to transmit a message in an instant. Medium therefore, is not only the message but also the messenger, because the producers and the consumers combine their energies for the production of the message.

The ability of media to work us over as proclaimed by McLuhan becomes more and more evident every day. McLuhan also observed that media shapes societies in its own image with the help of the content and the men who manage the content, in terms of new technology; messages as they are constructed for various media, intrapersonal to mass; the role of the medium in understanding the message, the grammar of the message and the characteristics of the medium. He also said messages are metaphors and medium is context that is, the content is the reader. When consumers and producers of messages come together as one, the medium and the message emerge as one entity. Medium is the message and messages invariably are the medium too.

McLuhan (1995) attached another meaning to the medium with his assertion that the user ultimately is the creator of content and therefore controls the content itself through the process of customisation (E. McLuhan, & F. Zingrone, eds., 1995). This is so because the internet is customised to such an extent that each user can create, produce, disseminate, and access content as per his personal choice. The user therefore is defined by the content that he accesses over the medium and all data would hence be guided by the choices he makes. This is precisely how the Search Engine Optimisation and customised advertising work on the new media.

Regarding media effects McLuhan had a critical stance. He used the term 'narcissus narcosis' to refer to the numbing that is brought about by the adoption of new inventions, and the fact that we do not have an awareness of our intimate connection to the media which is an extension of our senses. To quote McLuhan, 'It is numbing of our very consciousness, transforming us into sleepwalkers' (Strate, 2012).

McLuhan did not think that content was the most important part of communication as we are prone to think. Content, he believed, changes its form and each new medium provides the environment and the content to the old medium. The medium is the message would then imply that to get the message, we need to study the medium and not just the content alone. The message, in this sense, refers to significance rather than information, but the term is also synonymous with content, suggesting that this phrase also means that the medium is the content. Taking the argument further, one can see the convergence of media as the amalgam of medium and content. As the world gets digitised, this convergence emerges as the future of journalism. Citizen journalism is a phenomenon which turns everyone into a sender of information for public dissemination. When BBC turned to citizens to bring the news to the nation after the London terrorist attacks, within six hours the BBC received more than 1,000 photographs, 20 pieces of amateur video, 4,000 text messages, and 20,000 e-mails (Sambrook, 2009). The messenger was the content which was the medium and finally when the broadcast was aired it was also the message.

To follow the dynamic nature of the statement 'Medium is the message' we find that each aspect of communication models is changing its characteristics. The model that has been chosen for the purpose of studying in the modern context is the Shannon and Weaver's model. This model was specially designed to portray the possibility of effective communication between sender and receiver. At first the model was developed to improve technical communication. Later it was widely applied in the field of communication. It is one of the earliest attempts at providing a structure to the process of communication.

Shannon and Weaver's model, as shown in Figure 3, breaks the process of communication into eight discrete components:
1. An information source, presumably person who creates a message.

2. The message, which is both sent by the information source and received by the destination although interspersed by noise, is encoded and decoded through stereotypes on either sides.
3. A transmitter, for Shannon's immediate purpose a telephone instrument that captures an audio signal, converts it into an electronic signal, and amplifies it for transmission through the telephone network. Transmission is generalised within Shannon's information theory to encompass a wide range of transmitters. The simplest transmission system, associated with face-to-face communication, has at least two layers of transmission. The first, the mouth (sound) and body (gesture) create and modulate a signal. The second layer, which might also be described as a channel, is built of the air (sound) and light (gesture) that enable the transmission of those signals from one person to another. A television broadcast would obviously include many more layers, with the addition of cameras and microphones, editing and filtering systems, a national signal distribution network (often satellite), and a local radio wave broadcast antenna. Then there are the layers of interpretation and biases which have to be considered as well.
4. The signal, which flows through a channel. There may be multiple parallel signals, as is the case in face-to-face interaction where sound and gesture involve different signal systems that depend on different channels and modes of transmission. There may be multiple serial signals with sound and/or gestures turned into electronic signals, radio waves, or words and pictures in a book.
5. A carrier or channel, which is represented by the small unlabelled box in the middle of the model. The most

used channels include air, light, electricity, radio waves, paper, and postal systems. Note that there may be multiple channels associated with the multiple layers of transmission as described above.
6. Noise, in the form of secondary signals that obscure or confuse the signal carried. Given Shannon's focus on telephone transmission, carriers, and reception, it should not be surprising that noise is restricted to noise that obscures or obliterates some portion of the signal within the channel. This is a restrictive notion of noise by current standards, and a somewhat misleading one. Today we have at least some media which are so noise free that compressed signals are constructed with a minimal amount of information and little likelihood of signal loss. In the process, Shannon's solution to noise redundancy has been largely replaced by a minimally redundant solution: error detection and correction. Today we use noise more as a metaphor for problems associated with effective listening. Noise could also be the pictures in the head as Walter Lippman described. The pictures act as filters whenever one tries to comprehend a message.
7. A receiver, in Shannon's conception, is the receiving telephone instrument. In face-to-face communication the receiver is a set of ears (sound) and eyes (gesture). In television, there are several layers of receiver, including an antenna and a television set.
8. A destination, presumably a person who consumes and processes the message (Foulger, 2004).

The concept of Entropy refers to messages which convey highly unpredictable information to the receiver and that of redundancy to messages which convey highly predictable information to the receiver. These lead to a variety of noise. For instance, listeners/receivers proceed on the principle of least effort (Sperber, D. and Wilson, D., 1995). This implies that listeners always balance their effort with the relevance of the message. The amount of background knowledge they must retrieve to result in cognitive benefits depends on both entropy and redundancy. If they must make too much effort to understand or if they are exposed to the same information repeatedly, they lose interest in communication. A perfect balance must be struck.

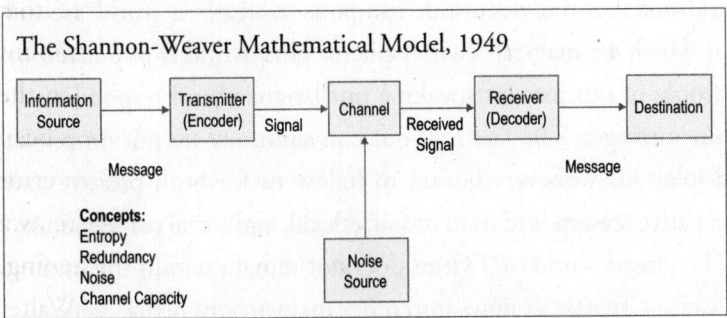

Figure 3: Medium is the message, channel, source, receiver and content.

The Information Source and the Receiver

In the present context of multiway communication, the source, and the receiver change roles almost instantly. McLuhan himself has put them in one category by calling them 'user', which is a very modern term for all pro-sumers (C. Willis, S. Bowman, 2003) of internet who keep creating material to fill up cyberspace with what is called the 'user generated content'. According to McLuhan, the user is the content and hence, the content that is generated by the user in the modern media ecology is the content that signifies what is important to him.

The user and the 'user generated content' are no different from each other because the user being the pro-sumer in the contemporary context participates in content generation. The user brings his or her own experience and understanding to a medium and transforms the content according to his or her own need and ability. The content reflects the pro-sumers' thought process making the World Wide Web a complex network of opinions. On Twitter, each tweet reflects the tweeter. Even when a tweet is retweeted, it is done so only if it matches the ideology of the tweeter.

The 280-character message on Twitter, replete with the additional audio/video/link component creates a world around us which we may call Twittersphere. This world is populated by people of our interest speaking our language and responding to our messages. The fact that our conversations are put on public display for whoever chooses to follow us for both positive and negative reasons lead us to moral, ethical, and social consequences. The closed world of Twitter does not remain within the limited vistas of Twitter. It flows into other mainstream media.

Medium has changed the structure of the content, the look, and the plan. The depth and breadth of the content has been altered too. So have the thought processes of the sender and the receiver. Their methods of information sharing, whether it is disseminating or retrieving, represent media seeking habits and usage of technology for communication.

The brevity of messages used by McLuhan is present in the form of 280-character messages on Twitter that are not only able to tell the whole story but also carry within them information encapsulated into tiny URLs, which, when opened, lead to the whole story in detail. McLuhan's famous probes, that is, short ideas expressed without elaborate explanations are the modern-day equivalent of tweets and SMS messages. Their brevity embodies their economy of words but not their insight. McLuhan rightly described, and to some extent predicted, how messages need not be unidirectional. When he argued that technology is an extension of the senses, he did not argue that a select few had agency over the shaping of the message. He argued, on the contrary, that *any* person had that potential. Specifically, he described how alternate modes of literacy allowed non-literate people to participate in a global discourse. This is McLuhan's legacy and part of why his work should be celebrated today (St-Louis, 2014). Twitter as a platform has democratised information.

Having discussed all the theoretical aspects of the subject under study, it is important to point out the two theories that provide the platform on which the entire phenomenon can be framed and discussed. The theory of Collective Action by American sociologist Mancur Olson and the Choreography of Assembly by social anthropologist David Graeber and activist film maker Amin Husain in their 2018 book titled, *'The dawn of everything: A new history of humanity'* published by Penguin Press in US and Allen in UK.

Theory of Collective Action

This theory was first proposed in a 1965 book titled, *The logic of Collective Action: Public goods and the theory of groups*. Olson was an economist and political scientist who focused on collective action in the context of interest groups and public policy. His work has been influential in social sciences and has widely been cited and applied in the allied fields of sociology and economics too. This theory seeks to explain why and how individuals engage in collective action to achieve a common goal. The theory posits that individuals have limited resources and face collective action problems that can make it difficult to coordinate and achieve their goals. Collective action problems refer to situations in which individuals may be better off if they cooperate and work together, but face obstacles that make it difficult to do so. Examples of collective action problems include the free-rider problem, in which individuals may choose not to participate in collective action because they can benefit from the efforts of others without contributing themselves. It suggests that individuals will engage in collective action if they perceive that the benefits of doing so outweigh the costs. This means that individuals will weigh the potential benefits of achieving their goal against the costs of participating in collective action such as time, effort, and resources. The theory also suggests that individuals will be more likely to engage in collective action if they perceive that their actions will make a difference in achieving the goal. It has been applied to a wide range of social and political phenomena, including social movements, political protests, and labour strikes. It has been used to explain why some collective action efforts are successful while others fail, and to identify the factors that contribute to the success or failure of collective action. Overall, the Theory of Collective Action provides a framework for understanding how individuals can work together to achieve the common goals, despite the obstacles and challenges they may face.

Choreography of Assembly

The relationship between choreography and protest was established by dance historian Susan Leigh Foster in 2003. Foster argues that movement and dance have been used to create powerful images of collective action, and she emphasises the need to understand the role that choreography plays in the dynamics of protest. By examining historical and contemporary protests, Foster demonstrates the crucial role of choreography in shaping the meaning and impact of these movements. However, she also acknowledges the challenges and limitations of choreography as a tool for political mobilisation, including the tension between individual agency and collective action, as well as the potential for choreography to be co-opted or used for purposes that contradict the protest's goals (Foster, 2003).

Social anthropologist David Graeber and activist/filmmaker Amin Husain built upon Foster's ideas and introduced the concept of the 'Choreography of Assembly'. This concept describes the organisation and execution of social movements and protests. It emphasises creative and intentional organising strategies that go beyond traditional notions of leadership and control, aiming to establish decentralised and democratic forms of collective action. The Choreography of Assembly focuses on three key elements: space, time, and bodies. Space refers to the physical locations and environments where protests occur, as well as their utilisation and contestation. Time encompasses the rhythms and patterns of social movements, creating a sense of urgency and momentum. Bodies represent the participants in social movements, that is, those whose movements and actions convey meaning and establish a collective identity. This approach promotes creativity, improvisation, and flexibility in organising protests, encouraging activists to move away from hierarchical structures and engaging a diverse range of participants. The Choreography of Assembly has influenced the study and practice of social movements, inspiring new forms of creative and decentralised activism worldwide. In 2012, Paolo Gerbaudo popularised the term 'Choreography of Assembly' by examining the relationship between social media and emerging forms of protest. He argues that social media, such as Twitter and Facebook, are not detached from physical reality but instead contribute to the re-appropriation of public space. Activists utilise social media platforms to organise protests in specific locations, building a symbolic construction of public space that facilitates the physical gathering of dispersed individuals. Gerbaudo notes that although these movements lack visible leaders, there are indirect leaders or 'choreographers' who set the stage for participants to exercise creativity and improvise. In the case of the Nirbhaya story as well as the farmers' agitation, although the first aspect was visible, the second was not. No leader emerged out of the uprising, no one came forward to claim leadership either. It seemed to be a revolution which was leaderless in one sense but brought out the leadership in many. However, he also acknowledges the risks associated with the use of social media in the Choreography of Assembly (Gerbaudo, 2012).

These risks include the potential evanescence of protest sites as they trend and gradually disappear from social media platforms, as well as the potential for social media to obscure power dynamics within social movements by employing the discourse of 'horizontalism' to avoid addressing questions of leadership and organisation. The risks outlined by Gerbaudo are very much a part of the life cycle of a Tweet. After analysing over 1.2 billion tweets, the Sysomos team found that only 29 per cent of tweets produce a reaction—that is, a reply or a retweet. According to Sysomos, just 6 per cent of all tweets are retweeted and these retweets have a very short lifespan. Virtually all retweets happen within the first hour after the original tweet (Lardinois, 2010). The tweet, although present in cyberspace, will not be picked up again. In such a short life span the tweet must start the process of 'trending'. The emotions associated with the case kept the tweets alive and thriving, keeping the discourse horizontal.

This fleeting nature of tweets underscores the need for them to quickly gain attention and become 'trending'. While the use of social media can keep the discourse horizontal and sustain emotional engagement, it also poses challenges in maintaining lasting impact and may conceal power dynamics within social movements. The following chapters will further explore how tweets were employed by users, examining their role and participation.

Paving the Path
A Journey through Literature

> *I am always doing that which I cannot do, in order that I may learn how to do it.*
> -Pablo Picasso

A BOOK IS a result of many books. An academic book is a result of not just many books, but also research papers, articles, theoretical foundations and thoughts of many theorists, experts, and leaders in the subject. In the following pages I will take you through the variety of literature that exists in the concerned subjects. A remarkable body of work can be discerned, emanating from all parts of the world. This is a tapestry of intellectual threads, intricately woven together to reveal the rich heritage of human understanding, allowing us to contribute our own unique strand to the fabric of knowledge.

For the convenience of my readers, I have divided the review into five distinct themes:

- New Media and User Generated Content
- Role of social media in collective action and social movements
- Impact of Twitter on protest movements
- Overview of Choreography of Assembly theory
- Previous research on the two Indian case studies

New Media and User Generated Content

Media has evolved at such a fast rate over the last couple of decades that it is no longer a two-way interactive forum. It is a multi-way medium due to the presence of the internet. The internet is a platform where ideas, issues, opinions, and discussions bounce back and forth amongst all the stakeholders on every side of the issue at hand. No longer is the legacy media, with its organisational support and technical paraphernalia, seated smugly on the first row in the drama of life. The curtains are never down, and the drama unfolds to a universal gathering of participants breaking the barriers of time and space.

Social Networking Sites started to gaining popularity amongst educated urban individuals who wish to remain connected to the virtual world for many reasons. Barnes is credited with coining the term 'social networks' (Barnes J., 1954). This view of society was first enunciated by Simmel who saw it as a complex skein of partly overlapping relatively loose networks that he called 'social circles' (Simmel, *The Sociology of Georg Simmel,* 1950). Gans (Gans H. , 1979) characterised a communication network as consisting of interconnected individuals who are linked by patterned communication flows and the interpersonal linkages created by the sharing of information in the interpersonal communication structure.

Faust (Faust S. W., 1994) applied the social Network Science theory and found that prominent individuals identified as gatekeepers have a more advantageous position in shaping community-wide framing of an event. Williams connected the aspects of online media that had the potential to diffuse the gatekeeping function of traditional media, thereby altering the latter's agenda-setting function with far reaching and irreversible changes in media practices (Williams B., 2000). Newman, a physicist explained that social network science theory has revealed the ubiquity of power laws or rich-get-richer effects, a scenario where a few users are able to capture an inordinate amount of attention in open, growing web systems as a result of age (entering the network earlier) and of preferential attachment (receiving greater connections from incoming nodes due to their celebrity status). He also points out a practical difficulty with profound theoretical implications, namely, the matter of multiple flows and crosscutting statuses (Newman, *The Structure and Function of Complex Networks,* 2003).

We have since moved on from bloggers to digitally connected citizens as proponents of free speech through online media, especially the social media. To see the Internet as simply a free market is a grave mistake and one born of utopianism that ultimately neutralises the power of capital (Terranova T., 2000). Yet it is found that, today, news media in a multi-channel communication environment, have a high content uniformity (G. Ku, 2002). The reason could be that all media converge when news and views are aired on informal portals called social media.

Bowman and Willis have suggested a number of ways in which content prosumers (producer+consumer) can interact on collaborative websites to create, inform, entertain, gain status and build reputations, create connections, online and offline, be informed and be entertained. Whatever the reason for their engagement with the site and its members, one thing is clear, when the consumer meets the producer of messages, as one entity, there is likely to be a generation of opinions. This opinion leads to taking away from the traditional media systems their right to 'breaking news' (C. Willis, 2003)

In recent years, proponents of the internet have proclaimed that new media technology will lead to a democratisation of the mass media (Rodman G., 2003). Earlier theorists believed the social network to be an elitist phenomenon. Newman found that prominent and influential users are at the head of the power law curve (Newman, 2003). Charles Kadushin explained the theory in the context of social sciences in his book *Introduction to Social Network Theory*. The theory applies to a variety of levels of analysis from small groups to entire global systems (Kadushin C. 1976).

Any set of nodes in real life has multiple flows with one another so there is never one network connecting the nodes but many. This is true at all levels: people, organisations, nations, etc. To construct a network connecting the nodes is a challenge because a theoretical calculus for indexing or adding one type of flow to another does not exist (unless they are all reduced to money in which case social network analysis is severely limited). The social reality, however, is that many network clusters are composed of crosscutting smaller units built up into larger ones which in turn overlap with one another. Perline found that the top 10 per cent to 20 per cent of users command the most attention in web-based networked environments (Perline, Strong, *Weak and Inverse Power Laws*, 2005). There are three main aspects in social networks which are studied by researchers and analysts: 1) How a user joins a community/group, 2) How the group will evolve, and 3) How it will change over a period of time. These three aspects are also termed as membership, growth, and change. That is the reason why an assumption based on the popularity of an issue on social media could be erroneous because of the variety that exists amongst users in terms of their behaviour online

(Backstrom L., 2011). The users of a social network have been categorised as passive members, who do not perform any activity, the inviters who encourage offline friends to join the social network and the linkers who fully participate in the social evolution of the network (Sharma Sanur, 2012).

Paying particular attention to the role that the audience plays in the process of mass communication given that the term 'audience' has over time become embedded within the literature of mass communication studies. This illustrates a contemporary approach to mass communication and can be reiterated as a more robust conceptualisation of the idea of the 'mass' in which the term refers to both the senders and receivers of information. Such a formulation of the concept of mass communication and the role of the audience within it reflects the contemporary dynamics of interactive media and user-generated content. (Napoli P., 2008). This mass is evident in large numbers on social media. Considering the role of social media such as Twitter and Facebook during political events such as election campaigning;, one finds that partisan ideologies use the platform effectively.

Good News for the Future? Young People, Internet Use, and Political Participation by Tom P. Bakker and Claes H. de Vreese focuses on offline and online political participation in the Netherlands. For this study, an online survey of ten thousand people in the age group of sixteen to twenty-four was conducted and it was found that using the internet for news is a positive predictor for all forms of political participation. The study highlights that quality newspaper reading only shows significant positive associations with traditional forms of participation; whereas public television viewing which is often seen as strongly correlated with news viewing, only proves to be a positive predictor of passive forms of participation; while commercial television viewing is not a significant predictor for any type of participatory behaviour. Given the systematic positive association of news use on the internet and the mixed results of newspaper reading and watching television, the study partially confirms that news consumption via newspapers, television, and the Internet is positively related to political participation. Looking at the internet as a medium, a considerable number of variables are positive predictors of participation. Concerning surfing activities, particularly news service and club/organisation are significantly and positively related to most forms of participation. The same tendency is found for online forms of communication. Significant positive relationships were found between online forms of communication (mainly e-mail and forum use) and participation, supporting the expectation that interactive online communication is positively related to participation. The study concludes that internet use is a stronger predictor for newer forms of political participation than traditional forms (Tom P. Bakker and Claes H. de Vreese, 2011). A lot of development in research on political campaigning on the internet provides numerous new options to study political behaviour and online public opinion.

Twitter has been used for political campaigning in a big way. Developments in research on political campaigning on the internet reflect on the 'live' and temporal aspects of social media and on how to deal with public communication from a flow (i.e., 'real time') perspective. Tweets are not just objects to be analysed, distant from the event they originate from. These new online grassroot platforms foster internal debate about parties and their leaders. Yet they are not considered rivals of official party platforms, because they are particularly popular in non-election periods. Internet research in general and political communication in particular are incomplete without the presence of social media platforms (Vergeer M., 2012). It is interesting to note that the globally reachable platforms of social media are being referred to as the 'new grassroots media' because this is the place where local and global meet.

Although the internet had been around during previous elections and politicians and parties had tried to make use of it, it really came to life in 2009 (Hewlette S., 2010). A similar development was noticed in the Indian political scenario in the 2014 general elections and the coming to power of the NDA government. Besides, political campaigning, the new media has been credited with several modern-day revolutions such as the Egyptian 'Arab Spring' protests. However, some researchers have dismissed or downplayed the existence of a causal relationship between the use of social media and subsequent Egyptian protests (Gladwell, *Why the Revolution Will Not Be Tweeted*, 2010). There have been studies that widely acknowledge the fact that social and other forms of new media 'have not caused' social unrest in the Middle East and North Africa, but there is also, strong support for the view that 'they have most certainly aided it'. Media technologies have always influenced man and his behaviour. From the invention and growth of the printing press to the contemporary social media, all have facilitated revolutions in the past (Ingram M., 2001). For instance, the role of telegraph in disseminating Woodrow Wilson's Fourteen Points speech which helped 'spark' the Egyptian upheavals of 1919 (Anderson L., 2011) could be a predecessor of the 'Twitter Revolution' rhetoric of the Egyptian uprising. There is, however, no denying that the new media has provided the common man with the tools of message collection and dissemination. As a result, the erstwhile consumer of media messages has now turned into the producer of messages in this three-way interactivity platform. This has given rise to a new term, 'prosumers', which is a simple amalgam of producer and consumer. The prosumer has emerged as a central figure in both mainstream and radical visions of the future. Through the melding of production with consumption, both mainstream and progressive analysts conceptualise 'pro-sumption' to be a liberating, empowering and, for some, a prospectively revolutionary institution. These fantastic associations situate pro-sumption activities, including contemporary online applications as 'co-creation'. Pro-sumption (particularly its Web 2.0 iterations), constitutes an emerging hegemonic institution, one that effectively frames and contains truly radical imaginations while also tapping into existing predilections for commodity-focused forms of self-realisation (Comor E., 2011). The activity of the prosumer is not limited by time, location, or organisational policies. He is located on the scene of the event and reports live most of the time.

Web 2.0 is now making way for Web 3.0. The developed countries were leading the social web but, in the future India as the most populous economy has the potential to be a leader. Eleven per cent of global Web3 talent is in India, making it the third-biggest talent pool in this sector, after the US and China. This pool is growing at a fast rate worldwide, as there are over 450 Web3 startups in the country that have got $1.3 billion in investments in the last two years (Tripathi, 2023). Web 3.0 is likely to change the dynamics of social activism totally. We are standing at the brink of a great technological breakthrough which will rely on blockchain technology for its business. It will inherit the characteristics of blockchains such as decentralisation, distributed, transparent, immutable, and running on consensus. This system will allow every individual to access, append, collaborate and vote for desirable solutions. If it doesn't get concentrated into a few hands, it will prove to be a game changer (Ghose, 2022).

In order to fully utilise the tools of modern-day media systems a certain amount of media literacy is necessary. It helps prosumers to consume, modify, and even create many media types. In essence, media literacy may assist someone in thinking critically about what they read, see, or hear in the media. Every individual who is armed with the paraphernalia for content creation must be adept at decoding media content and understanding both the medium and the message. Knowledge of media laws is important too. Since the users are ready to take the responsibility to create content and freely distribute it too, they need to be aware of the policies that guide them. Twitter itself has a set of guidelines posted on its help centre at https://help.twitter.com/en/rules-and-policies/twitter-rules. Besides the policy guidelines of the website, every country's government has its own rules and regulations in place. India has Information Technology (Intermediary guidelines and digital media ethics code) Rules, 2021. Intermediaries such as Twitter fall under the provisions of this law (Techcrunch, 2021). It is under these laws that accounts get suspended. The professionals and common men alike fall within the jurisdiction of this law and have to comply with it.

Many times the media workers are not just aware of the laws but also of their own social responsibility in sharing content online. The concept of 'gatekeeping' was introduced by Kurt Lewin. As per this concept, those media persons are 'gatekeepers' who control what goes or does not go into the public domain (www.communicationtheory.org, 2023). The gatekeeping mechanism that holds back the reporter in a formal medium may or may not exist for the prosumer. The prosumer has challenged the regular reporting and editing staff in the news production business. Zvi Reich in his study *Comparing reporter's work across print, radio and online: Converged origination, diverged packaging* compares how eighty reporters from three domains—media-print, online, and radio—obtained a sample of their items, seeking to establish which of two schools of thought is closer to reality: scholars who contend that each news medium embodies a unique 'regime' of content creation or those who argue that different media maintain similar news reporting standards. The findings of this paper suggest that the studied media are not unique factories of news but rather unique packing and distribution houses of similarly obtained raw materials. It is important to note that the selected media were high-profile, competitive national news organisations, a decisive majority of which were employers of substantial reporting staff (Reich Z., 2011). This emphasises the medium is the message concept.

Distinct features of online communication call for a radically processual explanatory framework. Online communication must be explained in terms of its dynamic fluidity; a theory that is able to grasp the communicative process as process is needed. Such a theory explains online communication as that which is determined by the ability to invite collaboration and the willingness to participate in collaboration (Just, 2011). Keeping the Habermas concept of 'communicative action' as the background, this theory can evolve.

The internet has emerged as an alternative medium, a space in which alternative views and voices have the possibility of being made visible and obtaining potency. This 'possibility' provides no guarantee as to what makes certain online cultural products powerful and not others. The answer gives no assurance of high visibility. Thompson's (1995) concept of 'symbolic power' has been applied to an internet phenomenon in China, namely the 'grass-mud horse'. A grass-mud horse is an imaginary animal that resembles an alpaca. It has an impressive number of web pages and is popular because its Mandarin translation is a profanity. In the tightly controlled media environment in China, this depicts defiance. (www.ischool.berkeley.edu) A symbolic product needs to possess certain characteristics before it emerges as a powerful one, able to create events and influence people's actions. It is likely to be representing the shared sentiments, emotions, or experiences of a large number of audiences. What the internet makes easy is to produce follow-up discourse once a powerful symbol has appeared. With the aid of supporters and their follow-up discourses, the symbol creates a symbolic network and quickly and deeply takes root in the society (Tang, 2011).

Concentrating on one particular site, Twitter on the internet, Dhiraj Murthy asks a simple question in the article titled *Twitter: Microphone for the masses?* This article examines citizen journalism and Twitter. The site's role in two prominent cases, being the first to report the Mumbai bomb blasts in 2008 and the downed US Airways flight in 2009, are used as case studies. This article also explores the question of whether Twitter has transformed ordinary individuals into citizen journalists whom the news-reading public follows or whether their voices are merely subsumed by traditional media. In other words, has Twitter really produced a new space in which ordinary people meaningfully interact with ordinary people from around the world who have rich insider accounts pertaining to diverse forms of socioeconomic life? An argument is made that ordinary people on Twitter are producing news and consuming news (especially 'breaking news') produced by other ordinary people. However, counterarguments are presented which make the case that perhaps the individual tweets and Twitter users' breaking news stories experience a short-lived fame as the public follows stories of interest and relies on professional news media outlets for serious news content. Another issue that is pertinent to citizen journalism and Twitter is the digital divide. As has previously been argued, there remain persisting and multiple digital divides in many Western countries which keep marginalised and vulnerable populations away from Twitter. These divides are generally amplified by Web 2.0. Though new social networks and communities of knowledge are supported by Twitter, they are strongly socioeconomically stratified (Murthy D., 2011). Any doubt about the future of journalism confronted with social media should be laid to rest because journalism has changed forever and the good old days of pen pushing journalists breaking news stories are over. The present data as mentioned in Chapter 1, already tells us that YouTube and WhatsApp are the best sources of news for nearly half the news consuming public. The content on these applications is from professionals as well as common people, the veracity of which cannot be substantiated.

In his article *News bytes can satisfy all appetites*, Peter Barron gave clear pointers on how journalism on the web is going to change the nature of journalism the world over.

His nine points about the forthcoming changes are:
- Journalism will be of more open form
- The emergence of the 'read later' tool
- Doing clever things with technology
- Changes in the conventions and structure of storytelling
- Journalism will be more open-minded
- Pooling resources and sharing content
- Transformation in the way story ideas emerge
- Journalism will be increasingly open-sourced
- Local people get to the scene faster (Barron P., 2011)

Adding to this is a tenth point from an interesting paper *I've seen tomorrow and it's female* by Hilly Jane, which says that there will be increasing importance of women news workers in a digitised newsroom (Hilly J., 2011). We can observe all these in the networked environment of today.

Kevin Marsh in his article, *Our only hope is to stand - and Deliver,* talks about the challenges being faced by the traditional journalistic forms in the face of new media. He talks about Sohaib Athar a non-journalist, IT consultant who live-tweeted the catch-or-kill operation in Abbottabad that eliminated Osama bin Laden and Janis Krums another non-journalist who took the iconic photograph of US. Airways flight 1549 floating on the Hudson River. The underlying assumption drawn by Marsh is that paid-for, mainstream, big-audience journalism has to adapt to new forms of journalism, news from and through amateurs, happenstance, random social media. It will be possible in the future only if the press that emerges from the firestorm is genuinely accountable to the public and transparent about its methods. As we all look at the web, at Twitter and YouTube and Facebook, at the remorseless growth in Google's and Apple's profits, and then at the relentless downward graphs on newspaper sales and readership charts, it is easy to think the answer is to go for a slice of the web's free for-all. That's precisely the wrong conclusion. If we fail to use this unsought opportunity to work out what it is about journalism that the public values and deliver it to them, but instead carry on just as unaccountable and opaque as before, we shouldn't be surprised to find the public don't value the journalists at all (Marsh K., 2011).

Blogging and tweeting are becoming indispensable modalities of news dissemination, which further makes internet journalism an inevitable part of the media environment. The smarter ones even acknowledge that the future has, in some respects, already arrived. The future has arrived in the form of Artificial Intelligence (AI). We are observing the potential and scope of AI to transform journalism in many ways, including automated content creation, personalisation of news content, fact-checking, analysis of large data sets, audience engagement, and translation. AI is ready to enhance the speed, accuracy, and relevance of news coverage, while also improving the engagement and satisfaction of audiences.

This presents a massive opportunity rather than a threat to traditional journalism. They can work collaboratively such as the blogosphere can actually teach the mainstream media a thing or two about fact-checking, about expert opinion, about being generous with sourcing and doggedly pursuing a story. For its part, the mainstream can certainly teach bloggers a thing or two about how to write concisely, accessibly, and elegantly. In some areas, their relative merits balance out (Waugh P., 2011). Those who post good content turn into social media celebrities called 'influencers' and are used for all types of promotion. Popular celebrities are also present on social media, revealing their personal life and many a times sharing their opinions about current public issues.

In their article *To See and Be Seen: Celebrity Practice on Twitter* Alice Marwick and Danah Boyd talk about social media technologies and the way they let people connect by creating and sharing content. They examine the use of Twitter by famous people to conceptualise celebrities as a practice. On Twitter, celebrity-hood is practiced through the appearance and performance of 'backstage' access. Celebrity practitioners reveal what appears to be personal information to create a sense of intimacy between participants and followers, publicly acknowledge fans, and use language and cultural references to create affiliations with followers. Interactions with other celebrity practitioners and personalities give the impression of candid, uncensored looks at the people behind the personas. But the indeterminate 'authenticity' of these performances appeals to some audiences who enjoy the game playing intrinsic to gossip consumption. While celebrity practice is theoretically open to all, it is not an equaliser or a democratising discourse. Indeed, in order to successfully gauge celebrity presence on Twitter, fans must recognise the power differentials intrinsic to the relationship (Boyd, 2011).

When a celebrity operates a social media tool, he gains direct access to his fans or followers. The exposure to a politician's Twitter page develops a sense of direct, face-to-face conversation with him among those more prone to get immersed in a mediated experience offered by the medium, leading them to have a more favourable impression of the politician. The engaged group also presents a stronger intention to vote for him. Whereas when the readers read newspaper interviews of the candidates, they better recognise the issues mentioned and have fewer thoughts about the candidate, suggesting that people adopt medium specific processing strategies, focusing more or less on the source (Shin, 2012).

There is a relationship between language and identity in the community and it is heightened during a politically challenging time. As a result of direct interaction with the political candidate or any other celebrity, the public discourse oscillates between stance-taking and identity construction which in turn, is a result of public biases. Language is both a social process as well as a social practice. In considering examples of different forms of Egyptian public discourses related directly to identities that emerged during the 2011 revolution of Egypt—at a time when state TV media stations were casting doubt on the identity of the protestors by utilising linguistic resources—it was found that speakers use public discourse in order to construe language as a classification category and an identity builder (Bassiouney R., 2012). Attention was drawn towards the power of social media active within the Egyptian uprising in 2011. Newspaper coverage of the 2011 protests in Egypt by Nawaf Abdulnabi Al-Maskati analyses the coverage of the 2011 Egyptian protests by Al Ahram, Arab News, China Daily, Guardian International, International Herald Tribune, and Jerusalem Post, according to the following criteria: the type and intensity of the coverage, potential shifts in tunes, and interaction with some types of social media. The study reveals that national policies and diplomatic relations determined the type and intensity of coverage, as much as prevailing news themes. Moreover, a shift in tune, although not significant, was found in the coverage of Al Ahram and Arab News. The study also emphasises that journalists demonstrated a clear preference for conventional sources against social media sources in their stories (Al Maskati, 2012).

Although social media crosses all barriers of space and time, culture plays a role in dictating the usage and content of these media. Gustavo S. Mesch, Ilan Talmud, and Anabel Quan-Haase studied the importance of relational and cultural variables in social media, in their paper *Instant messaging social networks: Individual, relational, and cultural characteristics.* The researchers collected social network data in Israel and Canada to investigate the effect of individual, relational, and cultural variables on the frequency of Instant Messaging (IM) and the multiplicity of communication topics. The researchers conclude that geographic distance continues to matter in interpersonal contact in spite of heavy reliance on digital tools for connectivity. The paper suggests that even though IM is a communication channel well suited for long-distance communication and for the maintenance of weak ties, a large proportion of IM communications also took place among close and local friends. This result is counterintuitive because IM's low-cost is a factor in overcoming the constraints resulting from distance (Gustavo S. Mesch, Ilan Talmud, and Anabel Quan-Haase, 2012). It is due to such facilities that the established distinctions between amateurs and professionals are blurring as the impact of social media, changes in cultural consumption, and crises in the copyright industries' business models, are felt across society and economy. The growing ubiquity of social media platforms help in better understanding the sources of disruption and innovation in audio-visual production and distribution in wealthy western markets that are as significant as those found in informal practices outside the West. On the one hand, there is an exponential increase in creative expression and communication facilitated by the explosion of social media while at the same time there are crises threatening the business models of the established media like music, newspapers, films, and broadcasting. The concepts of co-evolution and social network markets offer a way out of such binaries and explore emergent practices of enterprises and proto-enterprises along the dynamic boundaries between the market and the non-market, between the cultural and the economic, between the commercial and the community, boundaries that are converging around the affordances and constraints of social network markets (Cunningham S., 2012).

The participatory nature of this medium, which has given rise to the concept of citizen journalist leads many non-journalists to participate in story building. *'iReporting' an Uprising: CNN and Citizen Journalism in Network Culture* by Lindsay Palmer studies a series of interviews conducted by iReporters who covered the Iranian elections and protests of 2009, in order to address the complex political imperatives that inspired their unpaid labour for CNN. The paper highlights the numerous obstacles hindering the citizen journalists who increasingly draw on corporate visibility to tell their stories. In turn, it suggests that corporations like CNN are not monolithic structures, allowing for internal complexity, especially as network culture fuels the ever-growing interdependence between corporate news organisations and citizen journalism. The paper ultimately reveals that citizen journalism is less a story of exploitation and more a story of negotiation, as hegemonic journalistic representations of world events ultimately unfold within the increasingly disruptive informational milieu that is the product of network culture (Palmer L., 2012).

The public sphere on the Internet is populated by people and groups of all types. Blogs are sites where detailed views on specific topics are presented by an individual who is called a Blogger. Blogs are also open for interaction to those who are interested in the given topics. This virtual space, just like the real world, offers its own set of problems. It creates a social circle within the precincts of the virtual world which may or may not coincide with the real world. In drawing a connection between the real and the virtual, it was found that with regard to mediation, the higher the bloggers' social anxiety the more motivated they are to make new friends via blogs and the more intimate the information they disclosed on their blogs. Both these factors were, in turn, associated with more new friends and a higher quality of new friendships (Tian Q., 2011). Yet it is evident that a network culture is being created and nurtured by the youth in most countries because the youth take to the new technology more naturally than the older age groups. Hence, most of this media brings forth youth generated content. The youth are able to connect and mobilise revolutions through the use of this medium. However, the lines between the old and the new media are blurring.

In the context of youth-generated media, the blogs offer lenses to explore cultural politics in the why and the how of organised street revolutions especially with regard to the mobilisation of participants, the printing and the conceiving of fliers, the shooting, editing and uploading of videos, the broadcasting of images (on Al Jazeera and other networks) and the sharing of texts and images on social media. If anything, Al Jazeera, Facebook, and Twitter are the trees that should not be mistaken for the forest of youth-generated media (Khalil

J. F., 2012). Social media are either addressed in terms of economic and socio-political value creation, as in the exercise of power, exploitation, and business revenues or in terms of value creation as sense-making, as in creative explorations of the self and the management of social relationships in everyday life. These different interests in value creation have consequences for the conceptualisation of the media user as a participatory agent. Social media can be discussed in terms of processes of value creation (Bechmann A., 2012). The values can be created by information sharing amongst all stakeholders. To imagine that social media lack space would be a mistake. With the use of hyperlinks a great depth can be added to a 280-character tweet. The hyperlinks can add a whole new dimension to the message. Hyperlinks have also been used as research objects in social sciences despite some barriers and limitations to the study of links. There are issues of unobtrusiveness, the importance of interpreting links in context, and the possibilities of large-scale, automatic link studies. However, the variety of fields applying link studies, as well as the multiplicity of possible interpretations, should not lead to the conclusion that these tools and methods are chaotic or sterile. A univocal, unambiguous interpretation of the link does not exist (Maeyer J. D., 2012).

The social networking sites are now mediating the new urban environment through the processes of surveillance, and the surveillant assemblage, and how the self interacts with these technologies to produce an authentic self in mediated urban spaces. Instead of constructing an open public sphere, these technologies operate to build a 'second city' of commodified urban space in which the recording of banal activities recounted from an everyday setting is the authentic lived experience of people using this technology. Emerging from this new form of surveilled corporeality, urban settings have the possibility to move towards a kind of re-medievalisation of what may well become 'village life', that is, the formation of well-knit communities where information is shared quickly and efficiently. This means a move away from the grand schemes of modernity, and into a fully realised postmodern fragmentary life (Owen S., 2013).

The second city created by this mediated reality has different actors who negotiate and ultimately shape the manner in which the internet and related digital technologies are embedded in the newsroom. The newsroom changes. The place which was the front row in the drama of life becomes a place that watches all dramas being enacted by actors who are also story tellers. This places journalism in a state of flux. Professional culture—articulated in skills, ideas, and practices—acts as a network that weakens the potential impact of technology on innovation and audience-oriented models of journalism.

The internet and related tools are seen as empowering journalists to do their (traditional) jobs better. However, instead of moving on to the next stage built around a stronger commitment to capitalise on the growing sociotechnical potential of the amateur, the journalists are reaffirming their faith in traditional and conventional modalities. A study conducted in the news rooms of Greece found that radical changes in the media environment and widespread economic uncertainty have pushed Greek journalists into a defensive posture. Instead of engaging in innovative practices, they now promote the perpetuation of established routines (Lia-Paschalia Spyridou, Maria Matsiola, Andreas Veglis, George Kalliris and Charalambos Dimoulas, 2013). On the other hand, ICT (Information and Communications Technology) helps to change the political attitudes and behaviours of the youth. Motivations and psychological factors that affect patterns of new media use in political participation also differ. Data from 23 interviewees and 69 focus groups amongst Bangladeshi youth participants reveal that they have a passion for shaping their opinions through social networking instead of joining processions, attending party meetings, or indulging in political violence. This study finds that youth engagement through virtual communication has no direct impact on political decision-making but may play a pivotal role in some policy-making processes in Bangladesh (Ullah M. S., 2013).

While journalists participate in social media dialogue along with the youth a consensus develops that leads to the creation of public opinion based on who follows whom on social media. Examining the relationship between youth, digital technology, and civic engagement within the context of the authoritarian democracy of Singapore, Weiyu Zhang explains how activism has been understood in the Singaporean context, and how young activists appropriate or reject this concept.

Through this exercise of (re)defining activism, we are able to see how ICT goes beyond its function as a tool, and for young activists becomes an important component of their political lexicon. The article examines generational shift through the young activists' own accounts of their parents and seniors, including how the prominence of ICT differs between older and younger activists. The Singapore situation suggests how young activists perceive the contribution of ICT to their work is limited by the historical trajectory of political development and by the current arrangement of institutions. If there is a new horizon in youth activism, it is definitely the increasing prominence of ICT (Zhang W., 2013). The time is now for a consolidated media that uses the tools of both online media and traditional media such as the newspapers. The newspapers are slowly progressing towards a model of global networked communication that would enable the masses to communicate while following certain standards or norms issued by web 2.0 technologies. The news outlets recognise the ways in which social media can promote conversation between journalists and readers and thus promote more information exchange in the production of news. At the same time, the lack of norms and standards for communication signifies that newspaper editors are just beginning to realise the potential of these new media (Said-Hung, 2013).

Live research: Twittering an election debate by Greg Elmer draws upon research collaboration with the news division of the Canadian Broadcasting Corporation (CBC) to understand how Canadian political parties increasingly work to strategically intervene, in real time, on Twitter, during a broadcast political debate. This paper questions how vertical tickers on leading social media platforms (blogs, Facebook, and in particular the Twitter micro-blogging platform) pose new challenges to research that focuses on political communications campaigns. The collaboration discussed in this article furnished researchers the ability to showcase the role that new media platforms play in important social and political issues of our day in the context of public debates. Live research, as such, serves not only to question and understand the interface time of social media practices and platforms but also challenges the time-compressed and space-delimited sphere of academic scholarship. Live research, in other words, should not only be concerned with re-presenting the world of things or their imprints but rather work to offer concepts, theories, and methods that might critically help us to understand how users mobilise and sustain texts and other digital objects (by uploading, sharing, remixing, and downloading) across the field of networked communication. Live research serves as an important and contingent step in recognising the ever-shifting social media plane and the tactics deployed to sustain meaningful communication in a socially networked media age (Elmer G., 2013).

Role of Social Media in Collective Action and Social Movements

'Every revolution was first a thought in one man's mind, and when the same thought occurs to another man, it is the key to that era.' Ralph Waldo Emerson

The first recognisable social media site, in the format we know today, was Six Degrees—a platform created in 1997 that enabled users to upload a profile and make friends with other users (OurWorldInData.org., 2019). It was a revolution of sorts because it changed the course of history. All actions by man would henceforth be counted as offline or online creating a clear distinction between real and virtual. Social media became that conversation starter from where many ideas began to originate. Many times, social media behaved as a force multiplier leading the discussion on issues concerning the masses who were also social media users. The number of users grew steadily, and today social media is the most used space for protest movements. For this book, I am concentrating largely on Twitter related reviews to stay focused. Some reviews about the entire social media appear due to their relevance.

A book by Bimber, Flanagin, and Stohl (2012) explores

the ways in which technological change is affecting collective action in organisations. The authors argue that advances in communication technologies such as the internet and social media, have created new opportunities for organisations to engage in collective action and to interact with stakeholders. The book is divided into three parts. The first part provides an overview of collective action and its relationship to technology. This includes a discussion on the theoretical foundations of collective action and the ways in which technology is shaping this field. The second part focuses on the role of technology in organisational communication, including a discussion on how technology is being used to facilitate collaboration and engagement among organisational stakeholders. The third part explores the challenges and opportunities of using technology for collective action, including a discussion on the potential risks and benefits of using technology to mobilise and engage stakeholders. Overall, the book provides a comprehensive and interdisciplinary analysis of the ways in which technology is changing the landscape of collective action in organisations. It argues that technological change has created new opportunities for organisations to engage in collective action, but that these opportunities are accompanied by new challenges and risks (Bimber, B., Flanagin, A. J., & Stohl, C., 2012).

The use of Twitter during protests is not a new phenomenon. The term 'Twitter Revolution' has been around for some time and has both fans and critics. Schectman (Schectman, 2009) in his paper, *Iran's Twitter Revolution? Maybe not yet* felt that it is a preposterous idea. On the other hand, Potts studied the role of Twitter in the London bombings and the Mumbai bombings and found a strong presence (Potts, 2009). Similarly, Jewitt (Jewitt, 2009) studied the use of Twitter during the 2008 terrorist attacks in Mumbai when Twitter was being used to not only break news but also to monitor rumours reported as facts. Yet, it cannot be denied that revolutions were successful even before the advent of social media.

In an essay called *Four stages of social movements*, Jonathan Christiansen (Christiansen, 2009) talks about collective behaviours during social movements. He argues that social movements grow through four stages viz. Emergence, Coalescence, Bureaucratisation, and Decline; decline is when an organisation becomes established within the mainstream. That is, their goals or ideologies are adopted by the mainstream and there is no longer any need for a movement that requires participation. It shifts our energies from organisations that promote strategic decline or 'institutionalisation' and does not necessarily mean failure for social movements. It may mean Repression, Co-optation, Success, and lastly, Failure. He discusses a fifth reason for disciplined activity as that which promotes resilience and adaptability. It makes it easier for activists to express themselves and harder for that expression to have any impact.

The kind of activism associated with social media isn't like the activism in the real world at all. The protests against racism started in a small café in Greensboro, North Carolina and spread across entire South with more students joining in every day. Nearly 70,000 students participated in this protest in July 1960. This fever of protests was fueled without the presence of social media (Wilson, 2020).

The platforms of social media are built around weak ties. Twitter is a way of following (or being followed by) people you may have never met. Social networks are effective at increasing participation—by lessening the level of motivation to physically meet or get involved with the issue at hand. It is easier to appear interested online.

However, several studies have highlighted that Tweets contain factual information of high value. Several instances of the use of Twitter as a mobiliser have come to light. The tweets that were posted during Australia's worst fire disaster—Black Saturday—were studied by Sinnappan et al. Black Saturday is the name given to nearly 400 bushfires that started in Victoria in Australia on 7 February 2009. They caused 173 deaths and many injuries. The authors propose a new coding scheme for further research into how Twitter can be used as an alternative communication tool during crisis to support official communications, in particular, where reporting ground level conditions is concerned. Further, they also found that tweets made during Black Saturday were laden with actionable factual information which contrasts with earlier claims that tweets are of no value (Sinnappan, Farrell, & and Stewart, 2010).

Nunns and Idle studied the concept of Twitter as 'alternative press'. The Arab world witnessed a wave of revolts in December 2010, while commentators struggled to explain these phenomenal movements. No one saw this coming. Searching for a distinctive factor contributing to the revolt, many experts attributed the revolt to a powerful solidarity that emerged on Facebook and Twitter. In an inevitable backlash, others have pointed out that revolutions happened long before computers were invented. However, it is undeniable that in these revolts, Twitter became a means for those on the ground to report what was happening for the benefit of their fellow citizens and the outside world. It became a place for emancipating bursts of self-expression. Of course, the internet was also an organising tool (Idle, Alex Nunns and Nadia, 2011).

The prolific commentary disseminated via Twitter on the riots in London and other British cities in August 2011 led people to ask whether its appearance in social media forums may have added to the unrest. Investigators analysed 600,000 tweets and retweets about the riots for evidence that Twitter was used as a central organisational tool to promote illegal group action. Results indicated that irrelevant tweets died out and that Twitter users retweeted to show support for their beliefs in others' commentaries. Tweets offered by well-known and popular individuals were more likely to be retweeted (Emma Tonkin, Heather D. Pfeiffer, Greg Tourte, 2013).

Public squares are turned into centres of networks of mobilisation in a way which contradicts Manuel Castells' vision of a centre-less network. Castell has carved out a set of common patterns of networked social movements that provide a useful set of analytical categories.

Multimodal networking of emerging social movements. They connect online and offline networks, society with the movements, etc. They can work without a center or hierarchical leadership.

This de-centred structure maximises the chances of participation in the movement and reduces the possibility of repression.

Incidents that trigger online outrage usually happen in the physical environment, not in virtual spaces. Hence the role of internet is mainly instrumental and cyber-activism translates only into an influential movement by occupying urban space.

'A third space' between communication networks and physical action is a space of autonomy.

Inspired by other movements around the world he states that 'movements are local as well as global at the same time'.

Incidents that turn into media events and cause networked social movements are 'spontaneous in their origin, usually triggered by a spark of indignation'.

One of the most striking characteristics is the accelerated pace with which messages, news and images are spread. According to Castells, movements become viral when they generate hope.

Multimodal networks create a feeling of 'togetherness' not in the classic sense of community because there is no shared set of values. Instead there is a common purpose.

On account of integrating multiple demands and generally lacking a unifying ideology, Castells categorises networked social movements as 'programmatic movements'.

For Castells the internet is an autonomous space of communication because it facilitates a new type of 'mass communication of the self' which is directly related to the development of social and political autonomy (Castells M., 2012).

Very closely related to this work is the paper titled *The agenda building function of political tweets* by John H Parmalee which expands the scope of agenda-building research that has traditionally focused on the ability of press releases, press conferences, and political ads to influence media coverage. In-depth interviews with political reporters and editors at US newspapers during the 2012 campaign found that tweets from political leaders are used by journalists in ways that suggest first-and second-level agenda building. Participants gave examples of how political tweets shaped their coverage in the events they cover, the sources they interview, the quotes they use, and the background information they rely on to decide how to cover an issue. In addition, political tweets that contribute the most to coverage tend to have several elements in common (Parmalee, 2013).

Is Twitter just social media or is it a news outlet? Four researchers from the Korea Advanced Institute of Science and Technology's Department of Computer Science have performed a multi-part analysis of Twitter and how it works. The group wanted to find out whether Twitter is just a social network or a news media outlet by itself? Haewoon Kwak and his associates Changhyun Lee, Hosung Park, and Sue Moon built an array of twenty personal computers to trawl the entire contents of Twitter for a period of one month in July 2009 (Moon, Haewoon Kwak Changhyun Lee Hosung Park Sue, 2010).

According to Kwak and his team, the role of traditional news media is played by traditional news accounts in Twitter. Moreover, based on their findings, these news accounts are more powerful than traditional news media and the reasons are two-fold. One is motivation. Some studies report that different motives lead to different levels of attention and show that motivation to gain information for personal or social use leads to greater cognitive involvement. A Twitter user actively follows others and subscribes to their tweets. Also, they can stop subscribing to tweets whenever they want. In other words, Twitter users themselves actively choose and subscribe to their favourite news sources and the motivation to read tweets emerges from the desire to gain information or be entertained. This motivation is stronger than the one of just passing time (Alejndro, 2010).

The other is the form of news. The study argues that for politically inattentive citizens, soft news is more effective than traditional hard news. Both a short message (tweet) and social interaction (retweet) among users puts Twitter ahead of other sources of news. Thus, Twitter can be an effective medium of disseminating political messages. They also argue in favour of the retweet and believe it has a powerful impact.

The use of Twitter for news has been termed the Twitter Effect. which is defined as a rapid spread of information through the micro blogging service Twitter. The tweets can spread out like the branches of a tree and reach a very large number of Twitter users. Pingdom, a company that tracks site availability suggested this formula.

The Twitter Effect = (Original tweet x followers) + (retweets x followers of retweeters) + (retweets of retweets x followers of those) and so on (S. Shankland, 2009).

The Twitter Effect is also visible in information regarding a protest, or an agitation that also spreads through Twitter.

Impact of Twitter on Protest Movements

Twitter has seen a lot of growth since it was launched in October 2006. Some researchers view the impact of social media as pivotal in current events of the recent past. Such network clusters are now visible in the form of social and professional networks in cybersphere, for example, on Facebook, LinkedIn, Twitter etc. Twitter, a popular micro blogging service, has received much attention recently. Twitter enables users to post messages ('tweets') of up to 280 characters. The participants use the facility to converse with individuals, groups, and the public at large and are able to address a large number of people at once. This makes Twitter a medium of interpersonal as well as mass communication all at once. Mainstream news media has for years maintained a gatekeeping function that serves to control the flow of information to audiences. This phenomenon has changed the role of media personnel from being gatekeepers to gate watchers of news, a term coined by Bruns (Bruns, 2005).

Social media is a nebulous term since it can refer to an activity, a software tool, or a platform. Moreover, all media have to some extent, a social element (Donath, 2004). The social media aspect of the internet cannot be highlighted enough. This dissemination of news and views happens in the absence of the kind of gatekeeping system which has been the mainstay of mainstream news media for years. Twitter has been used as a powerful tool for protests over the last decade. It has been used to organise and mobilise people for various causes, from political uprisings to social justice movements.

One of the main advantages of Twitter for protests is its ability to spread information quickly and widely. Protest organisers can use Twitter to share information about the events such as time and location, as well as updates during the protest itself. They can also be informed about sit-ins or marches, livestream protests which include offsite participants and in general, they can spread the word across geographical boundaries.

The use of Twitter for protests has revolutionised the way social movements are now being organised. The real-time information dissemination and the use of hashtags to spread the word in a very focused manner has made Twitter a popular medium with the activists. It has also given voice to the marginalised groups who had hitherto been overlooked. Having said that, one must also point out that there are risks associated with using Twitter for protests. For instance, any authority may monitor social media and identify key players. Many a time, such a powerful tool in the wrong hands has been used to spread propaganda or misinformation which can be harmful to the cause and to society in general.

Several instances of the use of Twitter as a mobiliser have come to light. Ifukor studied the use of Twitter by citizens to influence people to participate in public discussions and serve as watchdogs during the electoral process of the 2007 elections in Nigeria (Ifukor, 2010). Hermida in an extensive study found that Twitter allowed communication and access to the protesters, following the 2009 elections in Iran, despite state censorship of other media (Hermida, 2013). He also suggests that Twitter made public the information about the Iranian conflict when access to other media was blocked. The same applies to the Egyptian uprisings that led to the resignation of Hosni Mubarak, as Twitter enabled the global broadcasting of dissent to an international audience that united in support. Moreover, the continuous stream of tweets with #egypt provided a news-worthy insight on the uprising.

Power play amongst the users and influencers has also been studied. Singh and Jain in 2010 found that content in select hashtags on Twitter follows a power-law distribution in terms of popularity, time, and geolocation. A similar distribution was found by Cha in their findings which showed that mainstream media were prominent in the retweet category while celebrities tended to be more prominent in the mention indicator (Cha, 2010).

Boyd talks about the function of retweet as a form of endorsement; often raising the visibility of content. He pointed out that the retweet syntax involves verbatim reposting of the tweet or editing the tweet syntax to include additional commentary. While global media has brought the communities together in the form of 'communities of interest' they have also magnified the sense of 'localisation' in a globalised world. Once this premise was established researchers started working on the effects of social media (Boyd D. S., 2010). Cha and Boyd have found a great degree of interdependence amongst formal and social media. Using

Twitter for public relations and journalism is common, but citizens use it to further their causes, voice opinions, create a personal image of self and society. Individuals balance social benefits with privacy costs when performing identity and sociality through online media. Re-tweeting news has been found more on mainstream media and it is done as a form of endorsement (Cha, 2010) (Boyd, 2010).

Yardi and Boyd suggested the presence of homophily in the form of replies between like-minded people. He also says that this strengthens group identity and reinforces in-group and out-group affiliations (Yardi, 2010).

Twitter had been assumed to be a medium used by the newly created 'haves' of the new mediated society. This assumption was proved wrong in the preliminary research done by Lotan who suggested influence by non-élites in the framing of the Egyptian movement (Lotan, 2011). Following on the footprints of previous studies, Meraz ascribed a powerful role to ordinary users of Twitter during times of natural disasters such as the Tsunami Indian Ocean Quake (Meraz, 2011). The operation of homophily—the tendency to follow likeminded individuals—is similarly prevalent on Twitter as it is on other social media applications. When present in conversations around controversial topics, Cottle studied the retweeting aspect of Twitter and found that Twitter participants retweet using different styles and for diverse reasons. As a Twitter convention, retweeting is analogous to broadcasting, and helps explain how virality, meme propagation, and opinion formation occur on Twitter (S. Cottle, 2010).

In a widely cited statistic, technology commentator Morozov reports that there were only 19,235 registered Twitter accounts in Iran at the time of the 2009 uprising, representing only 0.027 per cent of the population (Morozov, 2009). Similarly, Rich observes that, 'only some 20 per cent of those masses involved in the Egyptian protests, had internet access (Rich, 2011). In the light of such statistics, 'inflated claims about social networking led to charges of media centrism and technological determinism that detract from the complexities that are in play in these conflicts.'

Lysenko and Desouza have found that terms such as 'Facebook Revolution' have been used for events in Tunisia, Egypt, and Libya, and the term 'Twitter Revolution' was subsequently applied to the revolution in Moldova of the same year. The dynamics at work in the application of a social network is of spreading the information through the trickledown theory and message reinforcement. Restricted access to these technologies by activists and the general populace in the countries involved is a key reason why the people suspect the authorities of wanting to suppress the free circulation of information under the circumstances (Lysenko, 2012).

Use of Twitter always increases after a crisis. Soon after the Boston bombing incident on 15th April, 2013, Stahl Jeremy wrote in his blog, 'Twitter has only made the business of news gathering and sharing in the wake of a disaster more treacherous. If, as a wise journalist once said, journalism is the first rough draft of history, then Twitter is the first rough draft of journalism' (Stahl, 2013).

The Government of India has recognised the power of Twitter and the Planning Commission went live on Twitter in March 2013. The idea behind this move was to make the 12th plan more accessible and easier to read (Dave, 2013). Several early cases of internet-related activism have come to light such as those that encouraged ethnic clashes amongst

Bodo tribals. The arrest of cartoonist Aseem Trivedi can also be cited in this regard (International Federation of Journalists Asia Pacific, 2013).

India, the most populous country in the world, is also a country with a very high proportion of young people. Social media is popular amongst the youth. Initially used for making online friendships, developing relationships, business contacts and interacting with global masses, social media has recently been used for mobilising youth for revolutions and riots (Bute, 2014).

Social media activists like Clay Shirky saw immense potential in supporting civil society and the public sphere and stated that they will facilitate slow change over a longer time. He argued that social media are new tools enabling new forms of group formation. These new tools are making our lives easier; making our communication faster, that is, invariably better: 'as more people adopt simple social tools, and as those tools allow increasingly rapid communication, the speed of group actions also increases' (Shirky C., 2011).

Social network analysis techniques were used to generate and analyse the online networks using tweets during the Australian 2010-2011 floods. The goal of the researcher was to identify the online communities disseminating critical information and the important online resources disseminated by these communities. Important and effective players during the Queensland floods were found to be local authorities (mainly the Queensland Police Services), political personalities (Queensland Premier, Prime Minister, Opposition Leader, and Member of Parliament), social media volunteers, traditional media reporters, and people from not-for-profit, humanitarian, and community associations. Twitter activity varied from region to region. This is a predictable change in the nature of journalism where all stakeholders participate in information sharing (Cheong, 2011).

Talking about the power of Twitter in her paper by the same name, Joy Johnson does not believe that Twitter alone has the ability to change mindsets. Expressing her doubts over the agenda setting capability of Twitter she says that Twitter is not a magic bullet. It is a naive belief that the Arab Spring was a Facebook revolution. She stresses that Twitter, blogs, and online campaigns really get traction only when the mainstream media take up the cause. But modern technology and social media are bringing to public platforms evidence that once would have remained hidden; and giving people a new and powerful voice (Johnson, 2012). Twitter is a space where 'interconnected individuals are linked by patterned communication flows and the interpersonal linkages created by the sharing of information in the interpersonal communication structure' (Papacharissi Z., 2012).

In a larger research project at BBC, asking how social media changed the fundamentals of journalism it was found that the 2008 Mumbai terrorist attack, the 2009 Iranian elections, and the 2011 Arab Spring are amongst international news stories broadcasted by the BBC, highlighting the contribution of social media in journalism and also how important the medium is for the institution, not just at the User Generated Content (UGC) level but also at the social media level which includes UGC (Belair-Gagnon, V. Mishra, S. and Agur, 2014).

In the coming paragraphs I will discuss some studies related to uprisings from different parts of the world, where Twitter has been used effectively.

Arab Spring

The Arab Spring was a series of uprisings and protests that swept across several countries in North Africa and the Middle East in 2010 and 2011. The protests were sparked by a range of grievances, including political repression, corruption, economic hardship, and the lack of basic freedoms and human rights.

Twitter played a significant role, and the platform was used by the protestors to bypass the government-controlled media outlets and communicate directly with the world. They used hashtags such as #Jan25 for the protests in Egypt to coordinate action and share information about police brutality, government corruption and other issues fueling the protests further. In Tunisia, where the protests first began, Twitter was used to organise people and share videos and photos of demonstrations. They also shared information about the government response to them, thereby attracting international attention.

In a paper by Lotan et al., the authors analysed the use of Twitter during the 2011 Tunisian and Egyptian revolutions. The authors collected and analysed millions of tweets related to the protests in order to understand how information was shared and circulated through the platform. The authors used both quantitative and qualitative methods to analyse the data, including social network analysis and content analysis. The authors found that Twitter was used to coordinate and mobilise protesters, with users sharing information about protest locations and strategies. The authors noted that Twitter played a particularly important role in the early stages of the protests before traditional media outlets began to cover the events. However, the authors caution that while Twitter may have played a significant role in spreading information about the protests, it is unclear to what extent it influenced the outcomes of the protests themselves (Lotan, G., Graeff, E., Ananny, M., Gaffney, D., Pearce, I., & Boyd, D., 2011).

A paper by Howard et al. (2011) examines the role of social media in the Arab Spring uprisings, with a particular focus on how social media platforms were used to challenge authoritarian regimes in the Middle East and North Africa. The authors use a comparative approach, analysing the use of social media in several countries, including Egypt, Tunisia, Libya, Bahrain, and Syria. The authors found that social media played a significant role in the Arab Spring uprisings by providing a platform for citizens to mobilise, organise, and share information. They also found that social media enabled citizens to bypass traditional media channels, which were often controlled by authoritarian regimes, and to communicate directly with each other and with the international community. The authors note that social media played a particularly important role in the early stages of the uprisings before traditional media outlets began to cover the events. The paper also examines some of the challenges and limitations of social media as a tool for political change. The authors note that while social media played a significant role in shaping the Arab Spring uprisings, it was not the sole cause of these events, and that the impact of social media on the outcome of the uprisings is still a subject of debate. Additionally, the authors note that social media can also be used by authoritarian regimes to monitor and suppress dissent, and that the use of social media for political change is not without risks (Howard, P. N., Duffy, A., Freelon, D., Husain, M. M., Mari, W., & Mazaid, M., 2011).

In a book titled, *Twitter and Tear Gas: The Power and Fragility of Networked Protest* by Zeynep Tufekci, the author explores the ways in which social media and other digital technologies have transformed the landscape of political activism and protest movements around the world. Tufekci draws on a range of case studies from the Arab Spring to the Occupy Wall Street movement, to examine the role of social media in shaping the dynamics of collective action and social change.

The book argues that social media has empowered activists and protestors in new ways, providing them with new tools for communication, coordination, and mobilisation. At the same time, Tufekci also highlights the challenges and limitations of digital activism, including issues of surveillance, censorship, and the risks of co-optation by powerful interests. Overall, the book offers a nuanced and complex analysis of the relationship between technology, politics, and social change in the twenty-first century (Z.Tufekci, 2017).

The Political Power of social media is a thought provoking article written by Clay Shirky and published in the journal *Foreign Affairs* in 2011. The article explores the role of social media in contemporary political activism and protests, drawing on a range of case studies, including the Arab Spring and the election protests in Iran. Shirky argues that social media has transformed the dynamics of collective action, empowering citizens to communicate and organise in new ways, often outside the control of traditional power structures. He also suggests that social media has created new opportunities for governments to monitor and control dissent, highlighting the challenges and risks of using these technologies for political change (Shirky, 2011).

One can observe the common thread in most discussions related to social media and activism concentrating on the potential and limitations of social media in the context of political activism and protest movements.

Black Lives Matter

The Black Lives Matter movement began as a response to police brutality and systemic racism against Black people in the United States. The movement gained momentum in 2013 after the acquittal of George Zimmerman, the man who fatally shot Trayvon Martin, an unarmed Black teenager, in Florida. The phrase 'Black Lives Matter' first appeared on social media when activist Alicia Garza posted her response to the Zimmerman verdict on Facebook. Garza's friend and fellow activist Patrisse Cullors saw the post and repurposed the phrase as a hashtag, sharing it on Twitter and launching the online campaign (Black Lives Matter Topic Overview, 2014).

In 2014, the shooting of Michael Brown, an unarmed Black teenager, by a white police officer in Ferguson, Missouri, sparked widespread protests and unrest in the city and beyond. The shooting brought attention to the issue of police violence against Black people and the broader issue of systemic racism in law enforcement and criminal justice. In July 2014 a mobile phone footage was released of a white New York City police officer Daniel Pantaleo using excessive force on Eric Garner, an unarmed African American man. Garner died during the encounter. He could be heard repeatedly saying 'I can't breathe' in the footage, and the phrase became a rallying cry for BLM supporters. The movement also gained momentum and the protests were also driven by broader issues related to racial inequality, including disparities in education, housing, employment, and healthcare (Black Lives Matter Topic Overview, 2014).

Overall, the Black Lives Matter movement has been driven by a deep frustration and anger which through Twitter was brought to national and international attention and subsequently, spurred important conversations and actions towards achieving greater racial justice and equity. Twitter once again played a crucial role, as it allowed protesters to share information, coordinate actions, and spread their message to a wider audience. Twitter was used to share videos and images of police brutality against Black people, including the killing of George Floyd, which helped to generate public outrage and support for the movement. Protesters used hashtags such as #BlackLivesMatter and #JusticeForGeorgeFloyd to organise and share information about rallies, marches, and other events.

They also used Twitter to share information about legal resources and support for protesters who were arrested. Twitter provided a platform for Black activists and organisers to share their stories and amplify their voices, which helped to challenge mainstream media narratives about the movement. Let us discuss some scholarly work done on the subject.

A study by Davis, J. L., & Lovejoy, K. (2018), examines how Black Lives Matter (BLM) activists used Twitter to shape discourse and affect change. Through content analysis of 10 prominent BLM activists' Twitter data and in-depth interviews with BLM activists, this research explores the communication tactics that activists employed on Twitter to call for justice and social change. The findings indicate that Twitter is an important site for activists to engage in social movement activities, particularly across communities, spreading awareness, and directly challenging state power. However, activists also faced significant challenges in using Twitter and discovered that the platform had its limitations. It was difficult to reach a diverse audience, and the risk of backlash from both law enforcement and hostile Twitter users was real (Davis, 2018).

An article by Kitchin, A. T., & Lupton, D. (2018) drawing on a case study of three Twitter publics in US, UK and Australia explores how publics are formed through practices of knowing and being known in place. The analysis reveals that place operates as an important factor in shaping the composition and dynamics of Twitter publics. Place is used to position oneself and others within Twitter publics to establish the relevance and legitimacy of messages and to provide a basis for shared understanding and interaction. By focussing on place, the authors show that Twitter publics are more nuanced and complex than is often assumed and are shaped by multiple and intersecting factors including geography, democracy and culture. The article concludes by reflecting on the implications of these findings and understanding the relationship between social media and place (Kitchin, 2018).

A study on news media framing the Black Lives Matter movement in the context of the protest paradigm was conducted by Moody-Ramirez, M., & Smith, A. (2020), about how these frames differed across platforms. Specifically, they conducted a content analysis of 221 news articles and 1,825 social media posts to investigate the themes present in news coverage and how they were represented on social media. The findings suggested that news media coverage of BLM was primarily framed around protest and violence, while social media content was more likely to focus on issues of race, justice, and community. Furthermore, they found that the framing of BLM on social media was more varied and nuanced than in news coverage, with users expressing a wider range of perspectives and positions. These findings highlight the importance of analysing the representation of social movements across different media platforms and suggest that social media can provide a space for alternative narratives and perspectives to emerge (Moody-Ramirez, 2020).

This study compared how Twitter users responded to police brutality incidents in which the victim was either Black or White. Specifically, the authors examined the use of the hashtags 'Black Lives Matter' and 'All Lives Matter' in tweets related to these incidents, as well as the sentiment expressed in those tweets. They conducted a content analysis of 2,000 tweets related to police brutality, which were collected in the aftermath of two incidents: the shooting of Michael Brown in Ferguson, Missouri, and the shooting of Daniel Shaver in Mesa, Arizona.

The findings suggested that the use of the hashtag 'Black Lives Matter' was more common in tweets related to the shooting of Michael Brown, while the hashtag 'All Lives Matter' was more common in tweets related to the shooting of Daniel Shaver. They also found that tweets using the hashtag 'Black Lives Matter' were more likely to express anger and frustration, while tweets using the hashtag 'All Lives Matter' were more likely to express support for law enforcement. These findings suggest that the choice of hashtag is an important factor in shaping public discourse around police brutality, and that Twitter users may respond differently to incidents depending on the race of the victim (Pang, N., & Kim, Y. M., 2018).

The Women's March in 2017

The Women's March in 2017 was a historic moment for women's rights and activism. It was a global protest that took place on 21 January 2017, a day after the inauguration of President Donald Trump, to advocate gender equality, women's rights, and to protest various issues, including reproductive rights, racial and gender equality, LGBTQ+ rights, and immigration reform. The march brought together millions of people from all around the world, including celebrities, politicians, and activists.

The Women's March was not just a one-time event but rather marked the beginning of a movement. It sparked a wave of activism and mobilisation, with many people joining local organisations and taking part in various forms of resistance. The movement helped to inspire and empower women, and its impact was felt across the globe.

The Women's March in 2017 was also significant because it was an intersectional movement, highlighting the importance of addressing multiple issues and recognising the intersection of different identities such as race, class, and gender. This intersectional approach helped to broaden the movement's appeal and support, and it became a symbol of unity and solidarity. It was a powerful moment in the history of women's rights and activism. It brought together people from all walks of life and inspired a new generation of activists. Its impact was felt globally, and it helped to highlight the importance of intersectionality in social movements.

Twitter played a significant role during the Women's March in 2017, with many participants and observers using the platform to share their experiences, photos, and messages of support. According to Twitter, there were more than six million tweets related to the Women's March on 21 January 2017, making it one of the largest global social media events in history (Felmlee, 2020).

Twitter was used by participants to organise and

coordinate the march, share information about logistics and transportation, and spread messages of solidarity and support. Many participants also used Twitter to share their personal stories and reasons for marching, highlighting the diversity of issues and identities represented at the event.

Twitter also played a significant role in amplifying the message of the Women's March beyond the physical event itself. The hashtag #WomensMarch trended globally on Twitter, reaching millions of people who were unable to attend the march in person. The hashtag was used to share photos and videos of the march, as well as to express support and solidarity with the participants. Twitter proved to be useful by allowing participants and observers to connect, share information, and amplify the message of the movement. Its use helped to make the event more accessible and inclusive, and it helped in raising awareness of the issues and goals of the Women's March beyond the physical event.

There are studies that examine different aspects of Twitter use during this march. The most common methodologies are sentiment analysis of tweets, role of place in formation of Twitter publics and the implications of social media advocacy.

A paper by Oosterhoff and Palmer (2018) examines how Twitter was used during the Women's March in 2017 and the #MeToo movement to reflect the changing landscape of feminism. The authors use content analysis to examine tweets related to the Women's March and #MeToo, focusing on themes related to intersectionality, solidarity, and resistance. They find that Twitter use during these events reflects a shifting feminist discourse, with greater emphasis on intersectionality and solidarity among women of diverse backgrounds. The authors argue that Twitter provides a platform for feminist activists to challenge dominant discourses and create new feminist narratives that centre on inclusivity and diversity. They conclude that the Women's March and #MeToo demonstrate the power of Twitter in amplifying the voices of groups and shaping the broader discourse around feminism (Oosterhoff, B., & Palmer, L. N., 2018).

As in their study on Black Lives Matter, Kitchin and Lupton (2018) examine the role of place in the formation of Twitter publics, focusing on the Women's March in 2017 as a case study. The authors argue that Twitter use during the Women's March was shaped by the physical locations of users, with users in different places engaging in different types of discourse. They used a mixed-method approach that included content analysis of tweets, network analysis of user connections, and interviews with users, to explore how places influenced Twitter use during the Women's March.

They found that users in urban areas were more likely to engage in political discourse and advocacy, while users in rural areas were more likely to focus on local community issues. The authors concluded that understanding the role of place in the formation of Twitter publics is important for understanding the diversity of perspectives and experiences within online communities (Kitchin, A. T., & Lupton, D., 2018).

In their paper, Yang et al. (2017) examine the sentiment expressed in tweets about the Women's March that took place in January 2017. The authors use a sentiment analysis approach to analyse a sample of over 10,000 tweets that contained the hashtag #WomensMarch. They classify each tweet as expressing positive, negative, or neutral sentiment, and further categorise the tweets based on the topics they addressed. The authors find that most tweets expressed positive sentiment, with focus on topics such as women's rights, equality, and social justice. However, they also identify some negative sentiment, particularly from users who opposed the Women's March or felt it was unnecessary. The authors conclude that sentiment analysis can provide valuable insights into public opinion and discourse around social and political events on Twitter (Yang, J., Liang, H., Li, Y., & Huang, C., 2017).

In a unique study conducted by De Choudhury et al. (2018), the authors investigate gender and power dynamics in hashtag campaigns and their implications for social media advocacy. The authors analyse three hashtag campaigns related to women's issues, including Women's March, and examine the patterns of participation, content, and language used by users. They find that women were more likely to participate in the campaigns, but men had a larger reach and impact on the conversation.

They also observe a power imbalance between men and women in the discourse, with men tending to dominate the conversation and frame the issues (De Choudhury, M., Sharma, S., Logar, T., & Eekhout, W., 2018).

Hong Kong Protests

Twitter has been used by pro-democracy activists in Hong Kong to share information about protests and to raise awareness about their cause. Hashtags such as #HongKongProtests and #FreeHongKong have been used to coordinate actions and to share information about police brutality and government repression.

During the Hong Kong protests in 2019, Twitter was used extensively by both protesters and observers to share information, express opinions, and organise events. Twitter was used to share information, amplify voices, and mobilise support around protest locations, schedules, and tactics. Protesters also used Twitter to share updates on police movements and to warn each other of potential dangers, to counter misinformation and propaganda from the Chinese government and its supporters. Activists used Twitter to fact-check official statements and to expose falsehoods. Affirming its role as a choreographer of assembly, Twitter was used to organise events and to coordinate protest actions. For example, protesters used Twitter to organise 'flash mob' protests, in which groups of people would quickly gather and disperse in different locations.

A study conducted by Chan C. K. in 2020 presents a big data analysis of public opinion on Twitter during the Hong Kong protests. Based on 6.8 million tweets and retweets collected during the two-month protest period, the study examines sentiments, topics, and key actors involved in the online discussions. The analysis reveals that Twitter was an important platform for the expression of pro-protest sentiment and a space for the formation of an online public sphere around the protests. The study also identifies key topics of discussion, including police violence, international support, and propaganda, and maps the network of users and hashtags involved in the discussion (Chan, 2020).

In the same year Fu, K. W., Chan, C. K., & Chau, M examined the credibility of social media sources for Hong Kong protest news by surveying a sample of Hong Kong residents (N = 1,004) during the 2019 protests. Results showed that, compared with traditional media, social media sources were perceived as less credible. Rumours, memes, and messages from unknown sources were seen as less credible, while messages from friends and family members were seen as more credible. Despite the low perceived credibility of social media sources, its use was found to be positively associated with political efficacy and protest participation. These findings suggest that social media played a complex role in the Hong Kong protests by providing alternative sources of information and mobilising support, but also by spreading misinformation and undermining the credibility of traditional media. The study provides insights into the challenges of assessing the credibility of social media sources including Twitter in the context of political conflict and highlights the need for media literacy education to help audiences navigate the complex media landscape (Fu, K. W., Chan, C. K., & Chau, M., 2020).

While Fu et al. studied all the social media Goh, D., & McLaughlin, E. examined the role of Twitter specifically in the 2019 Hong Kong protests. Based on a content analysis of 2,152 tweets posted by protest participants and journalists during the peak protest period, the study explores how Twitter was used to report, document, and comment on the protests. The analysis reveals that Twitter served as an alternative news source for protesters and a platform for the circulation of real-time information, images, and videos from the front lines of the protests. Twitter also provided a space for the expression of dissent, criticism of the authorities, and mobilisation of support for the protest movement.

The study argues that Twitter played a crucial role in shaping the protest narrative and influencing public opinion both within and outside of Hong Kong. The study concludes by discussing the limitations of Twitter as a platform for political mobilisation and the implications of the Hong Kong protests for the study of social media and political communication (Goh, D., & McLaughlin, E., 2020).

In the same year Jiang, M., Luo, X., & Zhu, H. conducted a comparative analysis about the usage of Weibo and Twitter in the Hong Kong protests, with focus on the structure and dynamics of the networked public sphere. Based on a comparative analysis of the two social media platforms, the study examines the characteristics of online discussions, the patterns of interaction among users, and the role of opinion leaders and media outlets in shaping public agenda. The analysis reveals that Weibo and Twitter played distinct roles in the protest movement, with Weibo being more tightly controlled and censored by the Chinese authorities, and Twitter serving as a more open and global platform for the expression of pro-protest sentiment. The study also identifies key differences in the use of hashtags, the structure of user networks, and the patterns of information flow on the two platforms. Overall, the study provides a comparative analysis of the use of Weibo and Twitter in the Hong Kong protests and contributes to the understanding of the role of social media in shaping public discourse and political conflict under authoritarian regimes (Jiang, M., Luo, X., & Zhu, H. , 2020).

Liu, Y., & Zhou, R. examined the use of Twitter during the Hong Kong protests from the perspective of communication ecology. Based on content analysis of 13,655 tweets posted by protesters and journalists during the peak protest period, the study explores the communication practices, content themes, and user roles on Twitter during the protests. The analysis reveals that Twitter served as an alternative news source for protesters and a platform for the circulation of real-time information, images, and videos from the protests. Twitter also provided a space for the expression of dissent, criticism of the authorities, and mobilisation of support for the protest movement. The study argues that Twitter played a significant role in facilitating communication and coordination among protesters, and in shaping the protest narrative and public opinion both within and outside of Hong Kong. The study also highlights the challenges of using social media in political conflicts, including the spread of misinformation, polarisation of public opinion, and surveillance by the authorities. The study concludes by discussing the implications of the Hong Kong protests for the study of communication ecology and social media in political conflicts (Liu, Y., & Zhou, R., 2020).

Global Climate Strike

The Global Climate Strike was a series of protests that took place in September 2019, in which millions of people around the world took to the streets to demand action on climate change. Twitter played a significant role in the organisation and promotion of the strikes, with hashtags such as #ClimateStrike and #FridaysForFuture being used to spread the word and mobilise support. Once again, Twitter was found useful as mentioned above.

The Global Climate Change protests are an example of how Twitter can create a large scale global protest. With media convergence, all media have the capacity to reach consumers the world over and therefore, platforms like Twitter are at the same time local as well as global. The entire protest was sparked by a tweet by environment activist Greta Thunberg in which Thunberg announced the start of the Global Climate Strike in September 2019. The tweet reads, 'Tomorrow we school strike for the right to a future. And we will continue to do so for as long as it takes. Adults are more than welcome to join us. Unite behind the science. #FridaysForFuture #ClimateStrike #SchoolStrike4Climate' (Thunberg, 2019).

A study by Middaugh, E., & Kim, Y., examines the use of Twitter and Instagram during the Global Climate Strike in September 2019, which involved millions of people around the world. Using content analysis and social network analysis, they examine the strategies used by climate activists on these platforms to mobilise support and engage audiences. Our findings suggest that Twitter and Instagram were effective in amplifying the voices of climate activists, sharing information and resources, and mobilising support for the Global Climate Strike. We also identify differences in the use of these platforms, with Twitter being more effective in facilitating direct communication and engagement with politicians and policymakers, while Instagram was more effective in engaging younger audiences and promoting visual activism. These findings have implications for the use of social media in climate activism and for the role of social media in shaping public opinion and policy (Middaugh, E., & Kim, Y., 2020).

The emergence of Fridays for Future (FFF) as a global climate activist movement has also been attributed, in part, to the power of social media. A case study by Leirvik, T., & Karlsson, M. explores how FFF has used social media as a platform for climate activism and communication. Drawing on the content analysis of FFF's Facebook, Twitter, and Instagram accounts, as well as interviews with FFF activists, the study identifies key themes and strategies in FFF's social media use. Findings show that FFF's social media presence is characterised by a strong focus on youth empowerment, mobilisation, and global solidarity. The movement has successfully utilised social media to mobilise participants for climate strikes and to communicate its message to a global audience. However, FFF's social media use also reveals challenges and tensions related to inclusivity, diversity, and representation. The study contributes to our understanding of the role of social media in environmental activism and highlights the opportunities and challenges of using social media for climate communication and advocacy (Leirvik, T., & Karlsson, M., 2020).

There is a historical pattern of media playing a pivotal role in mobilising protests and uniting the masses, from word of mouth to digital platforms. While recognising the significance of each medium in influencing its respective socio-political context, we acknowledge Twitter's current impact on society. Twitter's unique features, such as hashtags and retweeting, have democratised access to information, empowered marginalised voices, and facilitated global conversations, fostering collective action and challenging existing power structures. Understanding Twitter's influence is crucial in comprehending the evolving relationship between media and social mobilisation in our rapidly changing world.

This book focuses on two significant events that profoundly impacted the nation and drew individuals from diverse backgrounds onto a shared platform. It investigates the effective utilisation of Twitter in two pivotal events in India, namely the Nirbhaya Rape Case of 2012 and the Farmers' agitation of 2021, which occurred nearly a decade apart. Through a rigorous analysis, this research explores the ways in which Twitter played a significant role in both events, examining its impact, influence, and effectiveness as a platform for disseminating information, organising collective action, and mobilising public support.

Many studies have been conducted on the same aspect over the years. I am trying to put together some of them in the following pages.

Nirbhaya

The Nirbhaya case, also known as the Delhi gang-rape case, was a heinous incident that took place in 2012 in Delhi, India. It involved the gang-rape and murder of a twenty-three-year-old woman who was traveling with a friend on a bus in Delhi. The incident sparked nationwide protests and highlighted the issue of women's safety in India.

In the context of this book, Nirbhaya can be viewed as an example of a modern middle-class urban girl with high ambitions and aspirations. She is seen as hardworking and capable and knows how to live within her means. It was this symbolism that led to most urban youngsters to identify with her and feel her pain. India has seen bigger stories of both gruesome crime and heroic confrontation with authority such as the Bhanwari Devi Rape Case, but the symbolism around Nirbhaya makes her a daughter, a sister, and a friend in the urban setting. It is the urban setting, indeed the capital of the country, that highlighted her case even more. The urban youngsters used the forum they knew best and filled social media with expressions of shock, grief, anger, and outrage. Their collective cry was loud and reverberated in the cyber world.

Social media mirrors the real world and is all about conversations. Social media facilitates the interactive web by engaging users to participate comment and create content as a means of communicating with a specific social graph, and involves other users, and the public at large (Kaur, 2013). The social media revolution in the Indian political space is real, tangible, and accelerating. Social media was central to connecting and bringing awareness among people in the aftermath of the rape case. The Nirbhaya case was a watershed moment in the way the public made use of social media to not only draw attention to the intensity of the crime, but to the issue of gendered violence plaguing the Indian society. Contemporary protesters engage in mediation processes and develop media practices with respect to media environments at local and transnational levels covering both online and offline contexts as well as mainstream and alternative media. Mediation and protest movements explore the nature of the relationship between protest movements, media representations, and communication strategies and tactics (Bart Cammaerts, 2013).

Debolina Dutta and Oishik Sircar in their article *India's Winter of Discontent: Some Feminist Dilemmas in the Wake of a Rape* discuss the Nirbhaya case with reference to the previous rape cases in India. The reaction of middle-class India to the Nirbhaya case with around-the-clock news media coverage and a rush of commentary on Facebook and Twitter seemed to have the effect of erasing history. The authors believe that the Nirbhaya event was rendered exceptional by the manner in which it erased the memories of equally brutal experiences of sexual violence against women from marginalised communities. Location and identity thus seem to be essential qualifiers in determining whose rape is worth being the subject of urban, middle-class concern, and rage (Sircar, 2013).

Corroborating the importance of public participation in online movements and in the wake of the internet playing a crucial role in social movements like Anna Hazare's India Against Corruption Movement, 2011 and Nirbhaya's Delhi Gang Rape case of 16 December 2012, N. Usha Rani talks about the flexibility of the communication technology in transforming society through a political empowerment of ordinary people. Democratisation of media has created a space for public opinion that has evolved through intense participation and commitment of the masses. The recent social and political engagements of ordinary citizens of India endorse the view that social media like Twitter, Facebook, and blogs have become the mainstay for activists around the world to share information and organise protests (Rani N., 2013).

This relatively recent phenomenon has also changed the way women participate in the public sphere. Sumaiya Nasir's thesis discusses the role of social media in the lives of women, particularly after the 2012 'Delhi gang rape'. It explores the appropriation of Facebook and blogs by women in India, and how these media enable participation in the online public sphere. This participation is evaluated by establishing an online public sphere framework and its replication in these two Web 2.0 enabled platforms. By analysing Facebook and blogs, Nasir explores the manner of women's online participation, and also asks to what extent these platforms appear to be contributing to a new 'public sphere' online. She found that women who choose to speak online often face harassment and bullying, called 'trolling' in digital parlance (Nasir S., 2014).

As more and more people want to be 'part of' this, the power of social media has surfaced as a critical benchmark for change. The nation recorded a large number of rallies and protests on the streets, people created pages on social media to highlight this incident, many voiced their thoughts through Twitter and Facebook, connected at public locations by coordinating and organising meets using social media. 'Nirbhaya' was the top trend on Twitter India while people across the world expressed shock and disgust, and demanded reforms ensuring the safety of women in India. It is however with the emergence of new media and media convergence that recent practices of an interactive 'public' became possible (Chopra S., 2014).

A significant convergence of the political mood of the 'public' and the technological possibility for enhanced public interactivity took place. The spontaneous outburst was triggered by what happened to Nirbhaya. Activism prevailed to a great extent in an emerging digital public sphere represented by online discussion fora, blogs and social media platforms such as Twitter and Facebook (Titzmann F., 2014).

India's Facebook, Twitter, and blog spheres spread news and opinions, as well as gave calls for demonstrations, asked for the castration of rapists, and brought about a political revolution. The question arises whether the social media mobilisation of protests generated by the Delhi rape case can be termed as 'the Indian Spring' in the style of the so called 'Arab Spring', in Tunisia, Egypt, and the Middle East.

The Delhi case resembles Castells' common patterns of networked social movements in many ways. Consider the first point of multimodal networking: the Delhi gang rape facilitated a coalition between long standing activist movements, regular citizens, celebrities, and global supporters. The emerging pyramid mobilisation of protesting crowds via online and offline channels further linked the cyberspace to real life street protests and bridged the dichotomy between virtual and 'real' spaces (Titzmann N. C. S. M., 2014).

A notable change in discourse took place in the broader socio-legal context with the subsequent formation of the Justice Verma committee. Shalu Nigam explores the changes in the discourse on gender violence. Though, this was not the first case of gang rape in India, yet it compelled the government to take measures which it hadn't taken before. The power of such a vibrant social revolution cannot be ignored or underestimated. Nigam also asserts that these rapists inhabited an environment in slums where brutality is the custom and where sexual and physical violence takes place every day. Men and women in this hostile situation feel helpless, excluded, marginalised, and oppressed. Extreme degradation, destitution, and viciousness lead them to believe that brutalisation is a norm. Furthermore, marginalisation generates despair, anger, fury, frustration, and a sense of desperate rejection which inevitably leads to criminal activity or behaviour (Nigam S., 2014).

Social media use and protest behaviour in the context of growing social unrest among the younger population indicate that both Facebook and Twitter significantly affect the likelihood of protesting, although these effects vary across time and platforms. Studying the 2011 student demonstrations in Chile, the researchers explain the differences in terms of the protest cycle and the strong-tie versus weak-tie network structures that characterise Facebook and Twitter. Furthermore, the findings highlight the value of studying the time dynamics of the social media–protest relationship (SebastianValenzuela, 2014).

In one of the studies conducted on the media coverage of the Delhi gang rape case, Phillips et al., (2015) found that the reports of the rape incident in mainstream media were classified into five different categories – 1) Description of the event 2) Description of victim's health condition or medical decisions 3) Description of protests as a result of the event 4) Testimonies (victim, victim's friends, witnesses, accused or family members) 5) General public's response to the event (excluding protests). The study showed that the news of the gang-rape in Delhi on 16 December 2012, spread globally through professional media sources within two days.

This transition followed a pattern in which Indian news sources provided the first reports and international reports were delayed by a day. By 18 December 2012, the news of events in Delhi was globally distributed (Mark Phillips, 2015).

In a study presented at an international conference in Singapore I employed semiotics to analyse the public outcry following the Nirbhaya case. The study examined tweets related to the case, focusing on factors such as hashtags, retweets, and organisational backing to understand the extent of public involvement. It also explored the role of media in shaping public perception and agenda setting. The semiotic analysis revealed the cultural nuances and individual perspectives embedded in the tweets, emphasising their local nature despite the global reach of Twitter (Singh A. R., 2015).

Viswanath, S., & Banerjee, B. in their 2019 paper explore how Twitter is being used as a platform for public deliberation on sexual violence in India, focusing on the #Rape hashtag. Drawing on content analysis and interviews with activists and scholars, the paper examines the ways in which Twitter is being used to raise awareness about sexual violence, provide support to survivors, and mobilise social and political action.

The paper also analyses the challenges and limitations of using Twitter for such purposes, including issues of access, representation, and accountability. Despite these challenges, the paper argues that Twitter can serve as a valuable tool for public deliberation on sexual violence, helping to create new spaces for dialogue and action in a context where traditional media channels are often closed or compromised (Viswanath, S., & Banerjee, B., 2019).

Farmer's Protest

India has witnessed several farmer protests over the years. The protests have drawn attention to the challenges faced by farmers in India, some of them being low crop prices, lack of access to credit and technology, and the impact of climate change on agricultural productivity. The origins of the farmer protests in India can be traced back to the country's Green Revolution in the 1960s and 1970s, which was aimed at increasing agricultural productivity through the use of high-yielding varieties of seeds, fertilizers, and irrigation. While the Green Revolution led to significant increases in crop yields, it also had unintended consequences, including the concentration of land ownership among a small number of farmers, the displacement of rural communities, and the emergence of a debt crisis among farmers. The debt crisis was exacerbated by the liberalisation of India's economy in the 1990s, which led to a reduction in government support for agriculture and a shift towards market-based policies. However, none of the previous farmers' protests made it to mainstream participation as the one in 2020.

The latest wave of farmer protests began in 2020, following the passage of three controversial agricultural laws by the Indian government. The laws have been described in the coming pages. The laws aimed to liberalise the agricultural sector by allowing farmers to sell their crops directly to buyers, including private companies, rather than through government-regulated markets. Supporters of the laws argue that they would create more competition and better prices for farmers, while critics argue that they are likely to benefit large corporations at the expense of small farmers and exacerbate inequality in the agricultural sector.

The protests were characterised by their size and scope, with hundreds of thousands of farmers participating in marches, sit-ins, and roadblocks across the country. The protests highlighted the deepening divide between rural and urban India, and the challenges faced by marginalised communities in accessing political power and resources. The consequences of the farmer protests in India are still unfolding, but they have already had significant political and social implications. The protests galvanised a diverse coalition of farmers, labour unions, and civil society groups, and sparked a wider conversation about the role of agriculture in the Indian economy and the need for reform. The protests also put pressure on the Indian government to address the concerns of farmers and led to the suspension of the agricultural laws. However, the protests also exposed the limits of democratic participation and freedom of expression in India and raised concerns about the erosion of civil liberties and democratic institutions. The farmer protests are a complex and multifaceted phenomenon that reflect the challenges facing rural communities in a rapidly changing economic and political landscape. The protests highlighted the need for more equitable and sustainable agricultural policies that would consider the needs and aspirations of farmers, and promote social and economic justice. The protests also raise important questions about the future of democracy and civil liberties in India, and the role of citizens in shaping their own destinies.

During the agitation Twitter was used to share information about the protests, including updates on the status of negotiations with the government, reports of police violence against protesters, and accounts of solidarity actions by activists and supporters. Twitter has also been used to amplify the voices of farmers themselves, who have used the platform to share their stories and demand justice. Another important use of Twitter during the farmers' agitation was to mobilise support for the protests. Hashtags such as #ChakkaJam, #FarmersProtest, #IndiaAgainstPropaganda, and #IStandWithFarmers have trended on Twitter, with users sharing messages of support, expressing solidarity, and giving out calls for action. Twitter has also been used to coordinate offline actions, such as protests, rallies, and marches, as well as online campaigns, such as petitions and letter-writing. It has played a role in challenging the government's narrative on the farmers' agitation. Supporters of the protests have used Twitter to push back against government claims that the agitation is being orchestrated by foreign interests, and to demand that the government engage in meaningful dialogue with farmers. It has also been used to hold the media accountable for their coverage of the protests, with users calling out biased reporting and demanding a more balanced and accurate coverage. However, the use of Twitter during the farmers' agitation has not been without controversy. The government accused Twitter of failing to comply with its new social media guidelines, which require platforms to remove content deemed to be illegal or harmful within 36 hours. Twitter has pushed back against these accusations, arguing that it is committed to protecting the freedom of expression of its users while also complying with local laws.

The use of Twitter during the farmers' agitation in India in 2020 has been an important and dynamic aspect of the protests. Twitter has been used to share information, mobilise support, challenge the government's narrative, and hold the media accountable. While the use of social media has been an important tool for activists and supporters of the protests, it has also raised questions about the role of technology platforms in facilitating political dissent and the limits of free expression in the digital age. Some recent studies related to the Farmers' agitation in India are discussed below.

A study was conducted by Ashwin Sanjay Neogi, Kirti Anilkumar Garga, Ram Krishn Mishra and Yogesh K Dwivedi as the agitation was still going on. They gathered data from Twitter concerning farmers' protest to understand the sentiments that the public shared on an international level. They used models to categorise and analyse the sentiments based on a collection of around 20,000 tweets on the protest. They conducted a sentiment analysis using Python based machine learning tools for big data analysis, which gives us the positive, neutral and negative sentiments of the users based on the content of their tweets. With the increasing use of AI, and the availability of state-of-the-art machine learning and natural language processing algorithms, it is possible to analyse the emotions of the conversations on social media platforms. The researchers used four such tools and found that the bulk of the tweets are neutral (8000+ tweets, i.e. 46 per cent) followed by positive tweets (5000+ tweets, i.e. 29 per cent) and the negative tweets were least in number (3000+ tweets, i.e. 17 per cent) (Ashwin Sanjay Neogi, 2021).

Mehta D and Sharma R in their recent study examine the use of social media, particularly Twitter, in the #FarmersProtest, and its impact on political communication in India. The study uses a mixed-method approach, which included content analysis of tweets related to the #FarmersProtest, and interviews with social media users and experts. The analysis found that Twitter has been a key tool for political communication during the #FarmersProtest, with users sharing information, expressing opinions, and mobilising support. The study also identifies several key themes in the tweets related to the #FarmersProtest, including calls for justice, demands for accountability, and expressions of solidarity. The study argues that social media has played a significant role in shaping public discourse around the #FarmersProtest and has provided a platform for marginalised voices to be heard. The study identifies some challenges and limitations of social media as a tool of political communication, including the spread of misinformation and the potential for polarisation and division (Mehta, D., & Sharma, R., 2021).

Conducted by Kumar and Vaidya, a network analysis approach is used to investigate the utilisation of Twitter during the farmers' protests. Focusing on the identification of key actors and their interconnections within the network, the research examines a sample of tweets associated with the protests. The analysis delves into the network structure of the tweets, encompassing patterns of retweets, mentions, and replies. It successfully identifies the prominent actors involved, encompassing farmers, journalists, politicians, and activists. The findings underscore the pivotal role of Twitter as a political communication tool during the farmers' protests, facilitating information sharing, mobilisation of support, and challenging the government's narrative. The network structure of the tweets exhibits a core-periphery configuration, with a central group of influential users and a larger peripheral group of less influential users. The study asserts that social media, particularly Twitter, has significantly influenced public discourse regarding the farmers' protests, amplifying marginalised voices. Nonetheless, the research acknowledges the limitations and challenges of social media in political communication, including the dissemination of misinformation, polarisation, and the formation of echo chambers (Kumar, A., & Vaidya, A., 2021).

Framing analysis approach has been used by Saha and Sanyal (2021) to examine the use of Twitter during the farmers' protests, with focus on identifying key frames and their associations with different actors and ideologies. The study analyses a sample of tweets related to the farmers' protests and identifies the key frames used to frame the protests, including those related to farmers' rights, government policies, and media coverage. The study also examines the associations between these frames and different actors and ideologies, including farmers, political parties, media outlets, and individual users (Sanyal, S., & Saha, S., 2021). The findings are similar to the previous review.

Discourse analysis approach to examine the use of Twitter during the farmers' agitation, with focus on identifying the dominant discourses and their implications has been used by Bhattacharya & Banerjee (2021). The study analyses a sample of tweets related to the farmers' agitation and identifies the dominant discourses in the tweets, including those related to farmers' rights, government policies, and media coverage. The study also examines the implications of these discourses for the farmers' movement and the broader political landscape in India. The study finds that the dominant discourses on Twitter are characterised by a strong sense of solidarity among the protesters, as well as a critique of the government's policies and actions (Bhattacharyya, R., & Banerjee, S., 2021).

Twitter discourse has been examined in a study by Sarwar & Saleem (2021) and aims to identify the dominant themes, sentiments, and actors involved in online conversations. The study uses machine learning techniques to conduct a social network analysis to identify the dominant themes and sentiments in the tweets. The study finds that dominant themes in the tweets were related to the farmers' demands for fair prices and the government's response to the protests. The study identifies a range of actors involved in the Twitter discourse, including farmers, politicians, activists, journalists, and ordinary citizens. The study also finds that there were different clusters of users in the Twitter network, with some clusters being more influential and engaged than others (Sarwar, M. S., & Saleem, H., 2021).

Singh (2021) used content analysis method on a sample of tweets related to the farmers' protests to identify the dominant themes and sentiments in the tweets. The study finds that the sentiment in the tweets was overwhelmingly supportive of the farmers' protests, with users expressing solidarity and sharing information about the movement. The study suggests that social media can be a powerful tool for activism and political engagement, particularly for marginalised groups. However, the study also identifies the challenges and limitations of social media, including the potential for misinformation, polarisation, and the spread of hate speech (Singh, 2021).

Another study aimed at examining public opinion related to the farmers' protests in India using Twitter as a data source was conducted by Sharma and Narayan. The study analyses a sample of tweets related to the farmers' protests and uses sentiment analysis and topic modelling techniques to identify the dominant sentiments and themes in the tweets. The study identifies several dominant themes in the tweets, including concerns about the impact of the protests on the economy, criticism of the government's handling of the protests, and calls for justice for the farmers. It further explores the relationship between sentiment and topics in the tweets, finding that positive sentiment was most closely associated with themes related to support for the farmers and their demands, while negative sentiment was associated with concerns about the impact of the protests on the economy (Sharma, R. K., & Narayan, R., 2021).

One finds that the literature review discusses relevant topics directly related to the present study, highlighting the integration of new media into future lifestyles and the steady increase in social media usage. It demonstrates that earlier studies expressed concerns about the introduction of the internet into mainstream society, the involvement of journalism with social media, and the evolving dynamics between organised structures and collectives. During the period of 2010-2014, initial attempts were made to comprehend these phenomena and their consequences. Subsequently, the review focuses on studies conducted during the 'Twitter Revolutions' that took place, showcasing the successful utilisation of Twitter by activists in various protests since 2010. The review includes studies from the decade spanning 2010-2020, with some flexibility. Additionally, it reveals the interdisciplinary interest among scholars from various fields, including sociology, public administration, computer science, political science, and mass communication, in exploring the utilisation of social media for creating, altering, and influencing public opinion. It also shows the variety of methodologies that have been used to study the tweets. However, several studies that have specifically used sentiment analysis on tweet corpora have got good results.

Ahmad et al. conducted a sentiment analysis of Tweets during the Nirbhaya issue and found that the importance of anger and anxiety in stirring the collective conscience was highlighted during the protest event (Ahmed,S.,et al, 2017) and during the Covid lockdown Gupta et al. conducted a sentiment analysis and found that majority of Indian citizens supported the decision of the lockdown implemented by the Indian government during the corona pandemic (Gupta, P., et al 2021). A sentiment analysis about opinion mining was conducted by Mishra et al and they collected opinions as positive, negative, and neutral (Mishra,P., et al, 2016). Therefore, I decided to work with a corpus of tweets collected through reliable sources.

Unearthing Digital Footprints in Social Activism
Methodological Insights

> *Research is something that everyone can do, and everyone ought to do. It is simply collecting information and thinking systematically about it.*
> -Raewyn Connell, Sociologist

THE CURRENT STATE of research as depicted by the review of literature on the use of Twitter in India and elsewhere, suggests that the focus has primarily been on crisis situations, particularly those in Egypt, Iraq, Mumbai blasts, and Tsunami and also on political communication as in elections. Use of Twitter by the common man, media organisations and influencers for the purpose of choreography of assembly and collective action in social movements in India, warrants further attention and investigation.

Overall, social media has emerged as a powerful tool for political communication and mobilisation in recent years. Twitter, in particular, has been used extensively by activists, journalists, and citizens to voice their opinions and engage in political discourse. It is acting as a crucial platform for organising and mobilising around major socio-political events. These two cases under discussion are almost a decade apart but have used the medium to its full capacity. These are the Nirbhaya Rape Case of 2012 and Farmers' agitation of 2020-21. The Nirbhaya case involved the brutal rape and murder of a young woman in Delhi in 2012, while the Farmers' agitation was a nationwide protest against the new farm laws introduced by the government in 2020.

As the literature review has shown, there exist research papers employing sentiment analysis and big data tools to analyse tweet corpora in the cases under discussion. However, there is a lack of consolidated resources that offer a comprehensive overview and analysis, allowing for a deeper understanding of the role of Twitter in social mobilisation and activism that would serve as a valuable resource for researchers, policymakers, and activists interested in harnessing the potential of social media for societal change. The Indian context presents unique socio-political dynamics and challenges, and examining Twitter's impact within this context would enrich the discourse on the transformative potential of social media in India.

This book contributes to the ongoing scholarly dialogue on digital activism. It sheds light on the effectiveness of Twitter as a platform for mobilising support, disseminating information, and challenging dominant narratives, thereby expanding our understanding of the role of social media in contemporary social movements. By demystifying the content of the tweets, focusing on the sentiment of the users, identifying the most prolific users and consolidating the findings, insights, and lessons learned from these specific cases, would provide an accessible reference material for both academic and practical purposes.

Using two corpora of tweets through sentiment analysis generated by www.topsy.com and www.twitterbinder.com, both being data analytics websites, the tweets related to these events have been collected and studied for the patterns of communication and discourse on the platform. Since there is a gap of nine years it is easy to assume that although Twitter was instrumental in both events, the nature of discourse and engagement would differ. The Nirbhaya case generated a greater sense of outrage and mobilisation, while the Farmers' agitation was characterised by more nuanced and complex discussions. During the Nirbhaya case, there was a large number of tweets expressing anger and demanding justice for the victim. The discourse was dominated by a few key themes, such as women's safety, patriarchy, and the justice system. There was an overall agreement across class, region, gender, and political lines as the issue left everyone appalled. In contrast, the Farmers' agitation was not dominated by any single theme, but rather reflected the diversity of perspectives and opinions on the issue. There were tweets expressing support for the farmers, criticism of the government's policies, and debates on the economic implications of the new laws. The discourse also reflected the polarisation and politicisation of the issue, with tweets from both sides of the political spectrum.

Research questions

1. What was the nature and substance of the tweets posted on the topic under investigation?
2. Which individuals garnered the highest level of popularity in terms of mentions, retweets, and overall engagement on the topic under investigation?
3. Which organisations or institutions were the most active in tweeting about the topic under investigation and what was the content of their tweets?
4. Did any influencers, politicians, or public figures engage in the conversation surrounding the topic under investigation?

5. What was the overall sentiment expressed in the tweets posted on the topic under investigation, and how did this sentiment evolve over time?
6. Do the photographs say something?

Based on these research questions the objectives are:
1. Analyse a large sample of tweets on the Nirbhaya Rape Case and the Farmers' agitation to determine the nature and substance of the discussion.
2. Identify the individuals who garnered the highest level of popularity in terms of mentions, retweets, and overall engagement on the topic under investigation.
3. Determine the level of activity and the content of tweets from media organisations or institutions.
4. Identify any influencers, politicians, or public figures who engaged in the conversation surrounding the topic under investigation.
5. Determine the overall sentiment expressed through the tweets posted on the topic under investigation.
6. Provide an analysis of top tweeted photographs

Methodology

The method used here is a big data analysis of the corpora of Tweets related to the two cases under observation. Analysis of a corpus of tweets is a useful way to gain insights into how people use Twitter and what they use it for. Using inductive reasoning an effort is made to garner specific observations that have the potential to move from specific instances to broader generalisations through the data collected and analysed with the help of the two websites. A computerised computer-mediated text analysis through the online tool of www.topsy.com and www.twitterbinder.com is employed to identify volume and content patterns, topics, and prominent influencers from the Twitter posts. Hashtag has been used as the unit of analysis and thereby three hashtags per case have been identified for the purpose of collecting the tweets. Analysing a corpus of tweets using hashtags as the unit of analysis can provide valuable insights into trending topics, conversations, and user engagements.

Steps Taken

Data collection was conducted using third-party tools that provide access to historical tweet data. The tweets are extracted as per the most popular hashtags. Hashtags are typically denoted by the "#" symbol followed by a word or phrase without spaces. Frequency Analysis by counting the occurrences of each unique hashtag in the dataset and Sentiment Analysis to gauge the overall sentiment surrounding particular topics was conducted involving natural language processing techniques to classify tweets as positive, negative, or neutral in the case of Farmers' agitation. Finally, interpretation and insights from the data is conducted and conclusions drawn.

Top tweeted photograph is analysed by using a method of visual social semiotics as the theoretical framework for examining how images convey meaning. There are many methods for conducting such analyses, such as Gestalt theory, art history, psychoanalytical image analysis, and iconography, to name a few (Harrison, 2003). Chandler explains three important principles when analysing a semiotic system such as language or imagery and this study uses them as its basic premise.

1. Semioticians believe all people see the world through signs which are related to the signified by social conventions.
2. The meaning of signs is created by people and does not exist separately from them and the life of their social/cultural community. Therefore, signs have different meanings in different social and cultural contexts.
3. Semiotic systems provide people with a variety of resources to create meaning. Therefore, when they make a choice to use one sign, they are not using another (Chandler, 2001).

It was felt that analysis of the photograph is important as it plays a big part in popularising a tweet. Photographs are impactful in increasing the reach and engagement of a tweet by increasing their visual appeal. Photographs catch the attention of Twitter users as they scroll through their feeds. Eye-catching visuals have a higher chance of capturing users' interest and encouraging them to stop and engage with the tweet. As they say, a picture speaks a thousand words, the photographs can convey a story or evoke emotions more effectively than text alone, making the latter more engaging and shareable. Tweets with appealing photographs tend to attract more retweets and shares. Visual content is more likely to be shared by users who find it interesting, relatable, or valuable. This can lead to increased visibility and a broader reach. In the presence of numerous tweets that are posted every second, including a photograph helps the tweet to stand out amidst the constant stream of text-based content, increasing the chances of user engagement by clicking, liking or retweeting.

Visual social semiotics is a new field of study (originating in the 1990s) that is for the purpose of analysing pictures and other visual content. It has been defined by Jewitt and Oyama as involving 'the description of semiotic resources, what can be said and done with images (and other visual means of communication) and how the things people say and do with images can be interpreted' (Oyama, 2001). This analysis uses the Kress and van Leeuwen framework which recognises that an image simultaneously performs, three kinds of meta-semiotic tasks to create meaning. These tasks are called 1) Representational meta-function, 2) Interpersonal meta-function, and 3) Compositional meta-function (Leeuwen, 1996).

This study uses elements from each of the meta-functions to arrive at an analysis of the pictures.

The basic structure and processes of Representational meta-function are:

Structure could be narrative, which allows viewers to create a story about the Representative Personality/ies (RP) and the images include vectors of motion. They could be conceptual which include images that do not include vectors. Rather, RPs tend to be grouped together to present viewers with the 'concept' of who or what they represent.

The Processes are Action, Reactional, Analytical, and Symbolic. In the Action process, the narrative is created by vectors that can be bodies, limbs, tools, weapons, roads, and so forth, 'Reactional' where the narrative is created by eye lines (acting as vectors) between RPs and 'Classificatory' where RPs are associated with something or some group (that is, they are members of the same class). Advertisements for beauty products often have classificatory images such as a group of models (for instance, Revlon models). The process could be Analytical also where the RPs are displayed in terms of a 'parts-whole' structure. The 'whole' is a Carrier who possesses "parts" called Attributes. A pie chart is an analytical image in which the chart is the Carrier and its segments are Attributes. Diagrams are also analytical processes. In a Symbolic process, the RPs are important for what they 'mean'. A motorbike in an advertisement can, for example, be analytical (that is, asking the viewer to check out its attributes), but it is also symbolic of virility. Abstract shapes such as triangles, squares, and circles also fall in this category.

Structure and processes of Interpersonal meta function are Features, Image Act, and Gaze.

The image act involves the eye line of the RP(s) in relation to the viewer. Social Distance and Intimacy come into play because social distance is determined by how close do the RPs in an image appear to the viewer, thereby resulting in feelings of intimacy or distance.

Similarly, the Perspective plays a role in the perception of the picture such as—the Horizontal Angle and Involvement: this angle refers to the relationship between the position of the RP(s) and the viewer. The Vertical Angle and Power: There are two possible vertical-angle relationships: 1) That of the RP(s) and the viewer, and 2) that between RPs within an image.

Feature Processes are Demand where the RP is looking directly at the viewer. A demand generally causes the viewer to feel a strong engagement with the RP. The second feature is Offer where the RP is looking outside the picture or at someone or something within the image. In this case, the RP becomes an object of contemplation for the viewer, creating less engagement than that of the demand. The viewer can see RP in six different ways:

- Intimate distance: The head and face only
- Close personal distance: The head and shoulders
- Far personal distance: From the waist up
- Close social distance: The whole figure

- Far social distance: The whole figure with space around it
- Public distance: Torsos of several people
- The frontal angle: When an RP is presented frontally to the viewer. This angle creates stronger involvement on the part of the viewer as it implies that the RP is 'one of us'.
- The oblique angle: When an RP is presented obliquely to the viewer. This angle creates greater detachment since it implies that the RP is 'one of them'.
- High angle: The RP 'looking down' has less power.
- Medium angle: The RP 'looking horizontally' has equal power.
- Low angle: The RP 'looking up' has less power.

The basic structure and processes of the compositional meta-function are System Information Value which depends on the placement of RPs and allows them to take on different information roles.

Elements

- Left/Right: RPs on the left side of an image have the value of being 'given' knowledge while RPs on the right are 'new'.
- Given = familiar, common-sense
- New = an issue, a problem, a solution (Note: This value is based on how we read from left to right. This does not necessarily apply to cultures in which reading occurs from right to left or in columns).
- Top/Bottom: RPs at the top of an image have the value of being 'ideal' while RPs below represent the 'real'.
- Ideal: emotive, imaginary and what might be; often the pictorial elements of an image.
- Real: factual, informative, down to earth, practical; often textual elements in an image.

- Centre/Margin: RPs in the centre provide the nucleus of information to which surrounding elements are subservient.
- Salience: The ability of an RP to capture the viewer's attention.
- Size: The larger the RP the greater the salience.
- Sharpness of focus: Out-of-focus RPs have less salience.
- Tonal contrast: Areas of high tonal contrast have greater salience.
- Colour contrast: Strongly saturated colours have greater salience than 'soft' colours.
- Foreground/Background: An RP in the foreground has greater salience than an RP in the background.
- Flow chart: is presented below to bring clarity to the methodology.

Meta-Functions Analysis Flowchart
(Gunther Kress and Theo van Leeuwen, 1996)

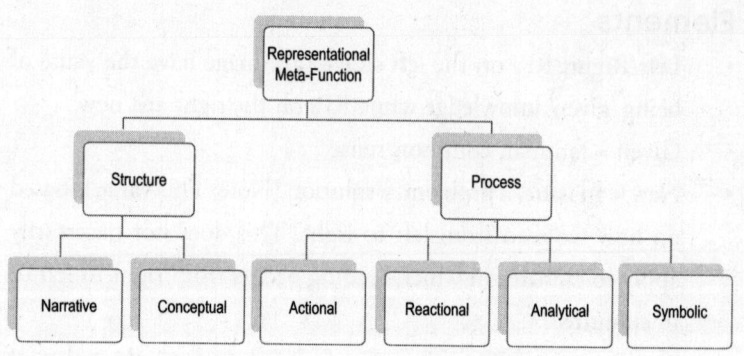

Figure 4: Representational Metafunction

Methodological Insights 123

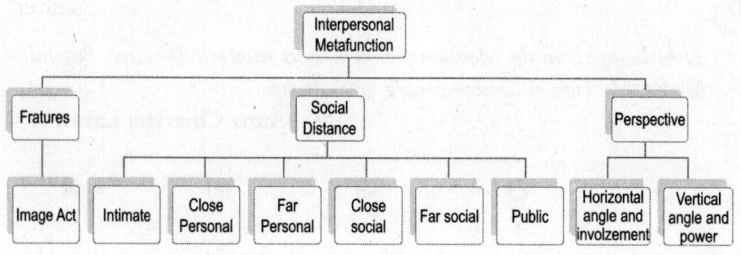

Figure 5: Interpersonal Metafunction

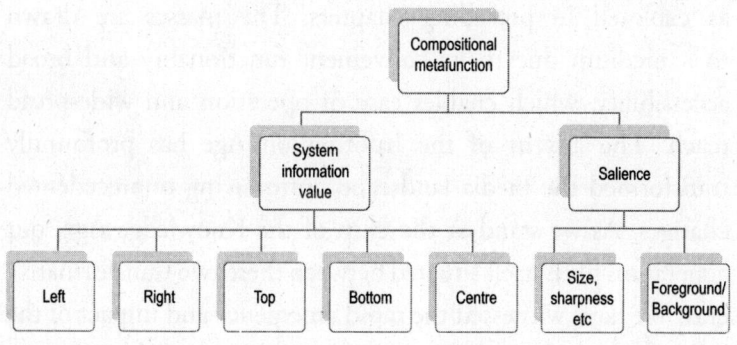

Figure 6: Compositional Metafunction

Medium, Message, and Masses
Decoding the Data

> *The Message is in the Medium for the Masses Associate Director, Digital Media, Museum of Contemporary Art, Chicago*
> —Anna Chiaretta Lavatelli

THE INTERRELATIONSHIP AMONG the three entities, namely the medium, message, and masses, is deeply intertwined, as explored in preceding chapters. The masses are drawn to a medium due to its convenient functionality and broad accessibility, which enables ease of operation and widespread reach. The advent of the Information Age has profoundly transformed the media landscape, introducing unprecedented changes. As we stand at the cusp of the Knowledge Age, our generation finds itself situated between these two transformative eras. We have witnessed the rapid emergence and impact of the Information Age, grappling to adapt to its remarkable changes, getting prepared to now confront the impending Knowledge Age and the advancements in artificial intelligence.

Evolving technology has metamorphosed media into a ubiquitous entity. Consequently, journalism finds itself more fragmented and filled with competition from non-traditional sources (Willis, 2003). The Internet has provided a forum for discussion and has also provided the tools for discussion in the form of various websites ranging from the most general to the most specialised. Marshall McLuhan's aphorism 'The Medium is the Message' pointed towards the impact of media through its structure rather than its content. (Gordon, 2003). McLuhan's philosophy predicted that the medium was powerful enough to impose a mindset such as linear and sequential for print and for radio, which he believed to have returned to the oral and musical tradition of the tribal societies, with the only difference being the global reach, suggesting the emergence of a global village. Since the coming of smart phones, the global village is encapsulated in a small gadget and is available in the pockets of most people around the world. McLuhan also talked about the medium being the message implying that the medium changes the structure and the format of the message to suit its technical requirements.

Twitter has reduced every message to 280 characters. However, as explained in Chapter II, the messenger has a lot to do with the message. The medium has an influence, but the messenger exerts his influence too. In fact, the messenger forms a big part of the message which is not only a reflection of the medium but also of the messenger and the circumstance. Tweets as a medium for a variety of messengers is being studied here.

In India, Twitter attracted the attention of the media and the common man alike when it was used extensively during the elections. Much debate about the social media cells of political parties have been doing the rounds and certainly no political campaign is complete without social media interventions. However, the power of the medium can not only be capitalised by the political bigwigs but also by the common man. Twitter has proven to be a powerful tool for advocacy and activism, providing a platform for the common man to raise awareness about social issues, rally support, and initiate change. Through hashtags and retweets, important causes gain visibility and attract the attention of a broader audience. The platform has played a significant role in various social movements, such as #BlackLivesMatter, #MeToo, and #ClimateAction, giving individuals the ability to contribute to meaningful societal change. Twitter enables the common man to connect with professionals, experts, and organisations in their fields of interest. By engaging with influencers and thought leaders, individuals can expand their networks, seek mentorship, and access opportunities they may not have otherwise encountered. This democratisation of networking provides a level playing field where talent and ideas can be discovered and acknowledged, regardless of social background or geographical location. From amplifying voices and building communities to accessing information, fostering advocacy, and enabling networking, Twitter offers individuals a unique platform to connect, engage, and make a difference. In a world where the digital realm increasingly shapes our lives, harnessing the potential of Twitter can lead to a more inclusive, informed, and connected society. It is up to individuals to seize this opportunity and use this powerful tool to create positive change, one tweet at a time.

The fact that Twitter has been used for over a decade for social activism has been studied in academic journals for scholarly purpose but in this book, I am trying to reveal the power of a medium like Twitter for the students of mass media and anyone interested in being media literate about the uses of media platforms. I am therefore concentrating on two cases that broke through the boundary between online and offline activism. The cases are closer home as we have witnessed them in India. The two cases are different in their socio-political context but the role of Twitter in the two cases can be seen as crucial. Separated by nearly a decade, diverse in terms of content and context, both the cases are stark examples of the kind of online activism never witnessed before.

The Twitter users, mostly youth, took to social media to not only voice their anger but also to condemn, console, plan and strategise. Information spread like wildfire and sometimes there was a coordination between what was happening on the streets with what was being said on Twitter, compelling one to believe that it was infact an example of Choreography of Assembly as described by dance historian, Foster Susan Leigh in 2003 and popularised by sociologist Paolo Gerbaudo in 2012. It also showed the importance of plaza protests and the growing popularity of digital media. These two events witnessed the Twittersphere go turbulent with outrage and the angst spilling over onto the streets.

Case I: Nirbhaya

The first case that I am discussing is the Nirbhaya Rape Case of 16 December 2012. This case shocked the nation. It numbed the senses and brought blood to boil at the same time. There was anger, outrage, disbelief, and shame filling the minds. As the news of a young girl was broken by the print media on 17 December, tweets about her started to fill the cyberspace.

Nirbhaya was the victim of a brutal gang rape that occurred on 16 December 2012 in a moving bus in New Delhi. The crime shook the nation. Government got down to creating more stringent laws, young boys and girls came out onto the streets of New Delhi, women's groups demanded immediate action while social media was swamped with streams of comments; the anger among Indians was palpable. The Twitter sphere was abuzz with condemning tweets, demands for justice for the victim and calls for collective action against the rapists. The country came together in their effort to seek justice for the young physiotherapist.

While government made laws and took other measures for safeguarding the rights of women and addressing this case, the concerned netizens laid bare their sentiments on social networking sites. The effort may not have been fruitful immediately but as is the case with most media effects, the online barrage of tweets and updates did not reap instantaneous success. The fact remains that the country came together to raise its voice in support for a cause.

The accused were apprehended and charged with sexual assault and murder. One of the accused, Ram Singh, died in police custody on 11 March 2013. The rest of the accused went on trial in a fast-track court; the prosecution finished presenting its evidence on 8 July 2013. The juvenile was convicted of rape and murder and given the maximum sentence of three years' imprisonment in a reform facility. On 10 September 2013, the four remaining adult defendants were found guilty of rape and murder and three days later were sentenced to death by hanging.

On 13 March 2014, Delhi High Court in the death reference case and hearing appeals against the conviction by the lower court upheld the guilty verdict and the death sentences (Vallinyagam, 2013). Eventually, in March 2014 Delhi High Court also upheld the penalty.

Following is the chronology of events in the Nirbhaya gang-rape and murder case:

Date	Activity
16 December 2012	Paramedical student gang-raped and brutally assaulted by six men in a private bus and thrown out of the moving vehicle along with her male friend. Duo admitted to Safdarjung Hospital
17 December 2012	Widespread protests erupt demanding strict action against the accused
17 December 2012	Police identify four accused - bus driver Ram Singh, his brother Mukesh, Vinay Sharma and Pawan
18 December 2012	Ram Singh and three others are arrested
20 December 2012	Victim's friend testifies
21 December 2012	Delinquent juvenile nabbed from Anand Vihar bus terminal in Delhi. The victim's friend identifies Mukesh as one of the culprits. Police conduct raids in Haryana and Bihar to nab the sixth accused, Akshay Thakur
21-22 December 2012	Thakur was arrested in Aurangabad district of Bihar and brought to Delhi. Victim records statement before the SDM in hospital
23 December 2012	Protesters defy prohibitory orders, take to the streets. Delhi Police Constable Subhash Tomar, on duty to control protests, rushed to hospital with serious injuries
25 December 2012	The girl's condition declared critical. Constable Tomar succumbs to injuries
26 December 2012	Following a cardiac arrest, the girl is flown to Singapore's Mount Elizabeth Hospital by the government
29 December 2012	The girl succumbs to injuries and other medical conditions at 2:15am. Police add murder charge in the FIR

2 January 2013	The then Chief Justice of India Altamas Kabir suggests Fast Track Court (FTC) for speedy trial in sexual offence cases
3 January 2013	Police file charge-sheet against five adult accused for offences including murder, gang-rape, attempt to murder, kidnapping, unnatural offences and dacoity etc.
5 January 2013	Court takes cognisance of the charge sheet
7 January 2013	Court orders in-camera proceedings
17 January 2013	FTC starts proceedings against the five-adult accused
28 January 2013	JJB says minority of juvenile accused is proved
2 February 2013	FTC frames charges against the five-adult accused
28 February 2013	JJB frames charges against the minor
11 March 2013	Ram Singh commits suicide in Tihar jail
22 March 2013	Delhi HC allows national media to report trial court's proceedings
5 July 2013	Inquiry (trial) in JJB against juvenile in gang-rape-cum-murder case and robbery concludes. JJB reserves verdict for July 11
8 July 2013	FTC completes recording of testimonies of prosecution witnesses
11 July 2013	JJB holds minor guilty of illegally confining and robbing a carpenter on December 16, night before allegedly taking part in the gang-rape. Delhi High Court allows three international news agencies to cover the trial in the case
22 August 2013	FTC begins hearing final arguments in trial against four adult accused
31 August 2013	JJB convicts the minor for gang-rape and murder and awards three-year term at a probation home

3 September 2013	FTC concludes trial. Reserves verdict
10 September 2013	Court convicts Mukesh, Vinay, Akshay, Pawan of 13 offenses including gang-rape, unnatural offense and murder of the girl and attempt to murder her male friend
13 September 2013	Court awards death to all four convicts
21 September 2013	High Court decides to hear the death sentence reference on a day-to-day basis
23 September 2013	Delhi High Court begins hearing the convicts' death sentence reference sent to it by the trial court
7 October 2013	Convicts Vinay Sharma and Akshay Thakur file appeal against conviction and sentence
12 November 2013	Supreme Court asks HC not to rush through with the December 16 gang rape case
3 January 2014	HC reserves verdict on convicts' appeals
13 March 2014	HC upholds death penalty awarded to the four convicts
20 March 2020	Mukesh Singh (32), Pawan Gupta (25), Vinay Sharma (26) and Akshay Kumar Singh (31) were executed at 5.30 am

Figure 7: Chronology of the Nirbhaya case (Zee, 2014)

For eight long years the case continued, and media did not let the nation forget Nirbhaya. While legacy media highlighted the case every time there was a new development, Twitter had already set the momentum in the initial period of the protests. Twitter is often described as a transient medium because tweets are visible for a limited period and are then lost in the maze of new tweets as the timeline continues to be updated. However, Twitter can also have a lasting impact. For example, tweets have been used to spread news and information, to raise awareness of important issues, and to mobilise people to act. In 2011, for example, Twitter was used to spread news of the Arab Spring uprisings.

Tweets from activists and journalists helped to raise awareness of the protests and to rally support for the protesters. Twitter was also used to coordinate protests and to organise the distribution of food and medical supplies. In 2017, Twitter was used to raise awareness of the #MeToo movement. Tweets from survivors of sexual assault and harassment helped to break down the silence around these issues and to encourage others to come forward. Twitter was also used to organise protests and to demand action from law enforcement and policymakers. These are just two instances of the many more where Twitter has been used proactively.

This chapter examines archives of tweets related to three hashtags #Nirbhaya, #delhigangrape, #Delhirape obtained from the online archive service www.topsy.com for capturing public timelines of tweets from Twitter. The analytics received from the archivist site gives 'all time influencers', 'exposure', 'sentiment' and 'top links'. The discovery as per acceleration, peak, and momentum gives the top keywords used in the tweets. The tweets are analysed as per the most influential words that are processed and presented by the archive. The volume and content patterns, topics, and prominent Tweeters in the Twitter posts during the selected period are outlined in the following pages.

The time period covers one month from the date of the incident of Delhi Rape i.e., 16 December 2012 to 16 January 2013. (Henceforth called as the Nirbhaya case). The study follows the asynchronic communication of the news feeds on Twitter by concerned individuals, journalists and news organisations.

The total activity related to the three sample hashtags during the selected month approximately amounted to 168K tweets from India.

Location	Tweets	% Activity
World	335,528	0.002%
India	168,518	0.509%
United States	161,253	0.004%
United Kingdom	23,157	0.005%
United Arab Emirates	14,165	0.022%
Canada	7,665	0.005%
Australia	4,446	0.009%
Brazil	3,128	0.000%
Indonesia	2,767	0.000%
Pakistan	2,262	0.027%
Spain	2,110	0.000%
South Africa	1,709	0.005%
Italy	1,675	0.002%

Figure 8: The total activity related to three hashtags during the month from 16 December 2012 to 16 January 2013 as per primary data collected from www.topsy.com

Nirbhaya was an important case for India that is why Indians provided half the activity on Twitter. Yet, the fact that tweets were being generated from other countries did speak of the worldwide impact of the story. Globalisation has a hand in turning geographical proximity into emotional proximity. All those who had any affinity towards India and any animosity towards the incident reacted through their tweets from all parts of the world.

The tweets started to pour in on 17 December 2012 and kept on accelerating, reaching their peak between 20 and 28 December. This was a crucial week as Nirbhaya was shifted to Singapore for treatment where she subsequently died. Tweets reflected the public sentiment. Tweets have been used as an outlet to vent out collective fury in big and small ways across the globe and the angst poured on Twitter against this incident further reinforced the medium's relevance to the cause as the review of literature has proved. At times, it was felt that justice was being democratised through the inclusion of the common man in the discussion via tweets. They also appear to be great equalisers where both the celebrity and the common man can be on the same platform and share their viewpoints without the barriers of their status. However, public attention and involvement with the issue often does not last long as other events take over. The effect, however, is long lasting as the movement transfers itself offline.

This is visible in the graph in Figure 9. The issue frizzled off by the 9 of January 2013.

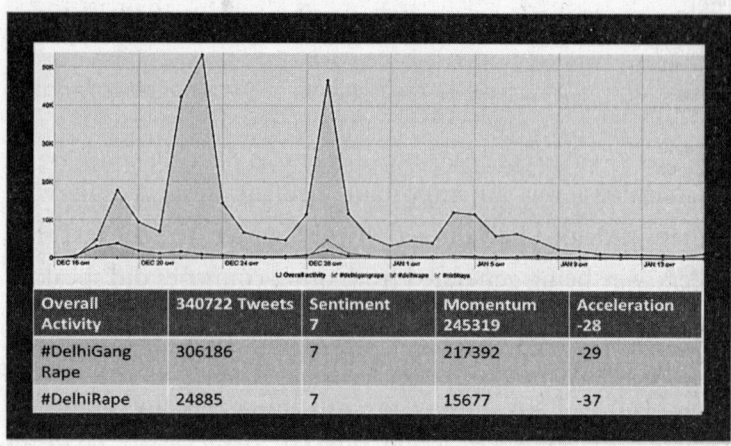

Overall Activity	340722 Tweets	Sentiment 7	Momentum 245319	Acceleration -28
#DelhiGangRape	306186	7	217392	-29
#DelhiRape	24885	7	15677	-37

Figure 9: Overall activity of three hashtags

As is evident from Figure 9 the two hashtags of #nirbhaya and #delhi rape lose out in terms of activity in comparison to #delhigangrape. A relook at the three nomenclatures shows us that the word that stands out is 'gang rape'. Nirbhaya at that time was not a very common name and did not have a universal meaning. On the other hand, 'gang rape' was being viewed as a heinous crime than just rape. As per Figure 9, from amongst the total of 340,722 tweets, #delhigangrape has 306,186 tweets attributed to it.

When it comes to peaks and lows the three hashtags behave similarly and follow the same pattern. It is evident that regardless of the hashtag nomenclature used by the Tweeters, their sentiments were the same.

The Messengers

The entities that made their place amongst the all-time influencers were both organisations as well as individuals.

Figure 10: All-time influencers

Figure 11: All time influencers

The prominent participant data is as follows:
1. Media organisations: 4
2. Media persons: 6
3. Celebrities: 3
4. Social organisations: 2
5. Individuals: 6

The participant data is an eye-opener. For one, the common man is standing tall along with the media organisations for a place among the top influencers. Media persons have not been counted as media organisations because when they tweet from their individual handle, they put forth their opinion and not the opinion of the organisation. Yet, media people have their following based on their performance as professionals. In fact, @raheelk was the head of Twitter India @VikramChandra the CEO of NDTV, and @Rahulkanwal the executive editor of Headlines. The trio were highly influential in journalistic circles in that their tweets were likely to not only influence their own media organisation but also journalists from other media groups. They are opinion makers and creators of viewpoints. The tweets by media persons can be confused as they represent not only their individual viewpoint but also that of the organisational agenda of the media house to which they belong. Media persons are a very good source of news for other journalists and the common man that follows them.

The media organisations amongst the top influencers include only one newspaper 'Hindustan Times' while all the others are prominent news channels. The presence of news channels on Twitter in such an influential manner does point towards their role in affective news. The concept of affective news streams is used by Z. Papacharissi & M. de Fatima Oliveira, in their analysis of #Egypt where they describe it as the manner in which news is collaboratively constructed out of subjective experience, opinion, and emotion within an ambient news environment. Characterised by pre-mediation, affective news streams are filled with anticipatory gestures that are not directly predictive of the future but instead communicate a predisposition to frame it, and in doing so, lays claim to latent forms of agency that are also affective and networked. Affective news also points towards the coming together of the medium, masses, and message as one big whole. The three influence each other and in doing so, adopt each other's identity.

In the case of Twitter, the tweet is the message that is encoded by one individual and transmitted by him based on his perception and level of understanding of the issue. It passes through the channel of Twitter and is received at the destination where the individual's 'followers' are. They are the ones who see it. The system of 'following' is based on independent decisions taken by the users. One 'follows' another individual, celebrity, or organisation one feels affiliated to, either personally or professionally. The relationship could also be ideological. Nonetheless, at a given time Twitter is a forum where like-minded people come together either by following or by being followed.

Given this perspective, a safe assumption would be that the media persons, organisations, and celebrities together create a space laden with viewpoints. The collaborative construction is more with the elite where the first rung of elitism points, in the Indian context, to the use of social media. Twitter and the second rung highlights the status that the elite already enjoy in the real world, which is translated on the virtual world too. This real and virtual status gives them the power to rise on the influencers' list leaving behind the rest of the Tweeters. Please note that all the data mentioned in this section pertains to the time between 2012-2013 because the event is located in that period.

The Common man in the uncommon circle: A closer look at the identity of the individuals who are members of this elite circle of influencers gives us the following information:

1. @amishra77: Akhilesh Mishra was the Director of MyGov.in. He declared on his profile that all views were personal. He had 42.4K followers and exerted considerable influence. He blogged and referred to his blog in his tweets. He had tweeted 60.5K times. He had 94 tweets and 76 retweets in the Nirbhaya story.

2. @Vidyut: Available on the site as Wildcat Vidyut. She had 23.2K followers and 243K tweets and she was second to Akhilesh Mishra in terms of popularity. She was a blogger, a human rights activist, for women's empowerment, child rights, homeschooling, and political accountability. On her profile,

she declared that 'the next freedom struggle will be of the mind'. She interacted with media persons, followed prominent personalities, and kept track of her own Twitter performance with the help of apps. During the period, she had 106 tweets about Nirbhaya with 54 retweets.

3. @gsurya: Suryanarayan Ganesh. With 18.7K followers and 282 K tweets, he claimed to be a Secular Nationalist Indian with Centre-Left-Liberal leanings. He was a supporter of INC and social worker, entrepreneur, technocrat, traveller and photographer in that order. He wrote 96 tweets and received 53 retweets on Nirbhaya.
4. @yearning4d_sky: Serendipity, claimed to be 'a little poetic' wrote haikus/micro-poetry. She did not give her name and identity but had added a picture of a middle-aged urban woman as her profile picture. She had 6910 followers but interacted with a closer circle by name. She had 100K Tweets to her credit with 31 tweets and 17 retweets pertaining to the Nirbhaya story.
5. @against_pseudos: Did not give a name but described himself as Extreme Right. A profile picture showed a serious-looking young man. He had a total of 82.2K Tweets to his credit and had 4,903 followers. He tweeted 89 times on Nirbhaya and had 43 retweets.
6. @nkumar: Nitish Kumar. He had 2318 followers and 254K tweets. He described himself as a movie maniac, techy, political, family man. He declared that he trolled fake intellectuals and warned others in TL (Timeline) = riot, Abuse = block. With reference to the Nirbhaya story, he had 441 tweets and 3 retweets.

A deeper search for the prominent tweeters on the Nirbhaya case revealed that they were all established professionals and reacted strongly about the issues they tweeted about. In fact, 46-year-old IT consultant Suryanarayan Ganesh (@gsurya) featured in the list of the most influential all-time tweeters in India (Sruthijith, 2013). Akhilesh Mishra worked for MyGov, which was a Government of India's online citizen engagement platform. The principal aim of the platform was to achieve the following purposes: a) Pro-active citizen participation in policymaking; b) Citizen participation in governance tasks; and c) Volunteer participation to achieve synergy in the ideas and discussions in the online world with action on the ground. The presence of persons from different political affiliations provided the platform an unbiased character but the fact remains that the deeply political viewpoints had their own biases. These got played up or down as the situation demanded, and created public opinion thus fulfilling the agenda that these two individuals with the highest following had in mind.

The Organisations:

1. @avaz was an organisation that had 41,818,815 members all over the world and a global web movement that aimed to bring people-powered politics to decision-making everywhere as per its website http://www.avaaz.org/en/about.php. It provided the public a forum to start their own petitions with a click of a button which said, 'Have an issue you'd like to get support on? Start your own petition with Avaaz Community Petitions!'. It cited its mission as providing 'Avaaz—meaning 'voice'—in several European, Middle Eastern, and Asian languages. It was launched in 2007 with a simple democratic mission: organise citizens of all nations to close the gap between the world we have and the world most people everywhere want. The Avaaz community campaigned in 15 languages, served by a core team on six continents and thousands of volunteers. They acted—signing petitions, funding media campaigns and direct actions,

emailing, calling, and lobbying governments, and organising 'offline' protests and events—to ensure that the views and values of the world's people informed the decisions that affected them. It had a total of 2,721 tweets and 765K followers. For the Nirbhaya issue, it had 6 tweets and 6 retweets.

2. @janlokpal had the national flag as the profile and cover pictures. It was in favour of a Jan Lokpal bill. The page said, 'People power won, Lokpal is a law now. Let's ensure its implementation in letter and spirit. We tweeted about issues of public interest'. It had 266K followers and 31.5K Tweets. For the Nirbhaya issue, it had 100 tweets and 9 retweets.

The Media Organisations:

1. @ndtv: The profile read 'Breaking news alerts from India' and it had 202K tweets and 4.67 M followers. The channel followed only 32 people. On the Nirbhaya issue, it tweeted 126 times and got 100 retweets. The persons it followed were its own correspondents such as @bdutt, politicians like @BarackObama, @arunjaitley, and its own subsidiaries such as @NDTVAuto, @GadgetsHindi, @ndtvindia, @moviesndtv @NDTVFood and @PrannoyRoyNDTV. Prannoy Roy was its co-founder.

2. @httweets: This was the only newspaper amongst the media organisations. It had 196K tweets till date with 2.25 million followers. The paper followed 797 people only. It declared in its introduction that it was 'one of India's largest media companies'. It carried the latest news from around the world. Retweets are not endorsements. On the Nirbhaya case, it had 208 tweets and 99 retweets. Amongst the people it followed were its own subsidiaries such as @htpunjab or @htentertainment, besides, its reporters who brought direct news from locations/beats. It also conducted chat sessions with its reporters.

3. @zeenews: On its colourful cover page, the channel advertised an astrologer with his picture. In the profile, it provided such details as '10 Channels, India's Largest News Network, 140 mn viewers, Breaking News alert from India & world. Download Zee Media Apps'. It had 147K tweets and 1.26 million followers. In the Nirbhaya episode, the channel tweeted 119 times and had 78 retweets. The channel followed 98 people only.
4. @TimesNow: called itself India's most watched English news channel and had tweeted 94.3K times with 2.73 million followers. The channel followed 142 persons. On the Nirbhaya case, it had tweeted 197 times and retweeted 100 times. The people and organisations it followed were other media organisations like BBC and social organisations like India Trends. It also followed politicians and people who were in the news, such as Shivraj Chouhan, P. Chidambaram, Vasundhara Raje, and political parties like the Indian National Congress.

The Media Persons:

1. @adityarajkaul: Aditya Raj Kaul was a journalist with Times Now. He described himself as a political and conflict reporter, and a Kashmiri in New Delhi who loved mountains and deserts. He had tweeted 33K times and had 38.1K followers. On the Nirbhaya issue, he had tweeted 90 times and had 85 retweets.
2. @kanchangupta: Kanchan Gupta was a writer, conservative, and a Brahmo. He had 79.5K tweets to his credit and 128K followers. He followed 705 people. On the Nirbhaya issue, he had tweeted 37 times and had 36 retweets. He wrote on national and regional politics, international affairs, and security issues. His weekly column, Coffee Break, used to appear in The Pioneer every Sunday. Among the people who followed him were politicians such as Arun Jaitley and Narendra Modi, journalists such as

Rahul Kanwal and Shekhar Gupta, and organisations such as The Caravan, ABP News TV, and CNN-IBN.

3. @rahulkanwal: Rahul Kanwal was the Managing Editor of India Today and Aajtak, and an anchor for Newsroom and Seedhi Baat. He had 17.8K tweets to his credit and 864K followers. He followed 2,087 people. On the Nirbhaya issue, he had tweeted 13 times and had 12 retweets. Many famous personalities, including politicians, actors, and journalists, used to follow him.

4. @raheelk: Raheel Khursheed was the Head of News, Politics, and Government at Twitter India. His profile stated that he served users and partners, coordinated InCrisisRelief.org, cycled, ran, and cooked. He had 60K tweets to his credit and was followed by 42.1K people, while he followed only 692. On the Nirbhaya case, he tweeted 11 times and had a 100% retweet rate. He was followed by many politicians, journalists, and media organisations. The most prominent person to follow him was Barack Obama.

5. @vikramchandra: Vikram Chandra was the CEO of the NDTV Group and the anchor of The Big Fight, Gadget Guru, and special shows like The Greenathon and Save Our Tigers. He had 11.4K tweets and 615K followers. He followed 139 people, who were mostly journalists, media, and political organisations. On the Nirbhaya issue, he tweeted 4 times and was retweeted every time.

6. @asher_wolf: Asher Wolf was an award-winning journalist and social media consultant. She was a Melbourne-based journalist, internaut, information activist, and gonzo political theorist. On weekends, she used to fly drones at the park with her three-year-old son. She was the Pirate Party Australia social media officer for the Griffith 2014 by-election. Using this pseudonym, she built up a following on Twitter by tweeting news about WikiLeaks and the Occupy movement and those

who care deeply about online privacy. She had 334K tweets to her credit and was followed by 37K people, while she herself followed 18.4K people. On the Nirbhaya case, she tweeted 316 times out of which 15 were retweeted.

The Celebrities:

1. @kamaalrkhan, who called himself an Actor/Producer/Critic on his profile, gained fame in the mainstream with his stint in the television reality show 'Big Boss'. He had a total of 18.6K tweets and 1.05M followers. He followed 11 people who were film stars such as @SrBachchan and @juniorbachchan and some film makers and trade analysts and one writer @chetan_bhagat. He tweeted 34 times for Nirbhaya and got retweeted 33 times.
2. @ayeshatakia, who said 'Following my Bliss......' on her profile, was a film actor who started her career with the Complan advertisement as a child. She tweeted nearly 16.2K times and had 383K followers. She followed 166 persons. She tweeted mostly about women's issues, weight watching, and vegan food. For Nirbhaya, she tweeted 14 times and got retweeted only once.
3. @gulpanag, tweeted 14 times about Nirbhaya and received 3 retweets. She had 89.4K tweets to her credit and 1.32M followers. She followed 1,322 people and described herself as an activist, actor, aviator, animal lover, adrenalin junkie, adventurer, avid traveller, automobile and fitness enthusiast, biker, entrepreneur, student, writer #AAP. Her tweets often talked about exercising and fitness.

Identifying the influential tweeters is not the same as identifying the most influential tweet. The above are the individuals and organisations that already commanded a status and following in the real world. Whatever they say is followed by millions of people and they have the ability to set an agenda. Some of them, as we have seen are followed by presidents and prime ministers besides journalists and other opinion leaders of the society. Such tweeters influence policy making with their opinions as they directly affect the policy makers.

There are tweets that come out of nowhere and make a place for themselves due to maximum acceleration and momentum. Some reach an all-time peak. Such tweets are different from those emanating from the All-time influencers. The tweets that accelerate are not due to an individual or his standing in society but due to the content of the tweet.

Discovery as per acceleration: The tweets that had the maximum acceleration in the twittersphere were the ones identified under this head. Total tweets in this category are 12 with keywords such as 'Asarambapu, Northandrew, bhawalpur, campaign, impassioned, @bbchindi, @bbcbreaking, mindsets, @yogital, #petition,@dr_black, #mindset'.

Asaram Bapu, a self-styled godman, made outrageous comments about the case blaming the victim as much as the perpetrators. According to a report broadcast on *CNN-IBN*, Asaram Bapu made the following observations about the Delhi gang-rape.

'Jinone galti ki... sharabi they. Agar us kanya ne saraswati mantra liya hota, guru diksha li hoti.. toh boyfriend ke saath picture dekh kar jis kisi bas mein ghusti nahin. Agar ghus bhi gayi.. toh 6 sharabi the... Bhagwan ka naam leti aur ek ka haath pakadti "Tere ko toh mai bhai maanti hoon." Do ko bolti "Bhaiya! Main abla hoon. Tum mere bhai ho. Dharam ke bhai ho." Bhagwan ka naam lekar haath pakadti, pair pakadti.. itna durachar nahi hota. Galti ek taraf se nahi hoti.'

The above remarks could be paraphrased thus: 'Those

who were at fault were drunk. Had she taken guru diksha and chanted the Saraswati Mantra, she would not have boarded any random bus after watching a movie with her boyfriend. Even if she did, she should have taken God's name and asked for mercy. She should have called them brothers, fallen at their feet, and pleaded for mercy. Had she said, "I am a weak woman, you are my brothers", such brutality would not have happened.' The self-proclaimed godman also said he was against harsher punishments for rape accused as such laws could be misused (Singh, 2013). The remarks were so scandalising that the tweets accelerated through the month.

Twitter feeds tell us that it is not the politically correct or righteous tweets that get retweeted. The comment that affects maximum number of persons goes viral.

Andrew North was the BBC correspondent covering the Nirbhaya case. His tweets along with @BBC's tweets raced the twittersphere. Pakistan witnesses a rape of a nine-year-old at a place called Bahawalpur and the twitterati began the comparison with the Nirbhaya case.

Discovery as per momentum: Some tweets rise faster than others and the movement of a tweet mass that moved at the fastest speed is discovered as below. The dominant sentiments are 'violence', 'democracy', 'fearless', 'women', 'shame', 'rape', 'identified', 'protestors'. These were the sentiments that became most popular the fastest. The medium of Twitter is about speed, and it is a yardstick to measure the sentiment of the people with the speed with which they act and react. These tweets rose the fastest in terms of popularity. Most of the tweeters in this case were social and media organisations such as @50millionmissing and @wsj.

"Asaram Bapu"	@Northandrew	#Bhawalpur	"Campaign"
"impassioned"	@BBCHindi	@BBCbreaking	"Mindsets"
@yogital	#petition	@dr_black	#mindset

Figure 12: Discovery as per Acceleration

Violence Related to #delhigangrape #delhirape @hallabol Police Violence and a government in hiding December 25, 2012	#photo Related to #Delhigangrape, #Nirbhaya @Rita_ Banerji #Nirbhaya (FEARLESS) #India's @Women's Freedom anthem a #photo and a #poem salute to the #Delhigangrape uprising January 8, 2013	Democracy Related to #Delhigangrape @Prashant1280 Prashant Mehrota No female cops at India Gate, female protestors manhandled by male cops… pathetic Delhi police… sad day for democracy #Delhigangrape December 23, 2021	#India Related to #Delhigangrape, #Delhirape, #Nirbhaya @Muthukish7 Muthu Krish #Delhigangrape, #Nibhaya, #gangrape Will the rapist go scot fee? The law is an ass… they say, I now know why? January2, 2013
1M Tweets 1 M Momentum -6 Accelerations	495 K Tweets 55 K Momentum 4 Acceleration	479 K Tweets 503 K Momentum 5 Acceleration	44 K Tweets 470K Momentum 5 Acceleration
Fearless Related to #Delhigangrape, #Nirbhaya #50MillionMissIn in 50 Million missing #Delhigangrape, #Nirbhaya #Fearless, #India, #Women, #Violence, #Gendercide, #Fightback January 3, 2013	#dt Related to #Delhigangrape, #Nirbhaya @MarySarahMusic Mary Sarah RIP Nirbhaya December 29, 2012	@wsj Related to #Delhigangrape, #Nirbhaya @paulwsj Paul Beckett "We could all try to do a better job of frightening what sometimes feels like an army of gropers" December 31, 2012	#women Related to #Delhigangrape, #Nirbhaya #50MillionMissIn in 50 Million missing #Delhigangrape, #Nirbhaya #Fearless, #India, #Women, #Violence, #Gendercide, #Fightback January 3, 2013
319K Tweets 310K Momentum -3 Acceleration	260 K Tweets 266 K Momentum 2 Acceleration	171 K Tweets 180 K Momentum 5 Acceleration	152 K Tweets 156 K Momentum 3 Acceleration
#shame	#rape	Identified	Protestors

Figure 13: Discovery as per Momentum

Discovery as per peak: The tweets that peaked the graph are the ones that reached an all-time high.

Violence	@dr_black	Identified	@bbcbreaking
democracy	#mindset	#photo	impassioned
Fearless	#Petition	@Indiatoday	#women

Figure 14: Discovery as per peak

As is visible from Figure 14, the tweets that peaked had the same signs as the ones that moved/became popular the fastest.

Overall Exposure

Figure 15 depicts the highest exposure that the tweets received over the selected duration of time. The links that were most popular were bbc.co.uk, mirror.co.uk, online.wsj.com and causes.com. Firstly, none of the top links is an Indian entity and secondly three of them are media organisations while www.causes.com is a website that helps people to come together for a cause and support either a person or an event by creating a campaign. In its profile it says, 'The place to discover, support and organize campaigns, fundraisers, and petitions around the issues that impact you and your community.' The tweeters whose tweets got overall exposure were @historyneedsyou, @youranonnews, @shellylakhani and @wajahatali.

Top Tweets	Top Links
@historyneedsyou Mathew Ward Listen to the women of India. Don't stop your daughter from going out. Teach your son how to behave. #Delhigangrape Dec 29,2012 0:48 GMT 1K Tweets	Charges for Delhi Rape suspects Bbc.co.uk Jan 7,2013 7:33 GMT 1K Tweets
@youranonnews Anonymous Way to protest the rape in #India. "Men, don't skirt the issue, speak up & support women" #Delhigangrape Jan 16,2013 5:26 GMT 372 Tweets	India gang rape victim's father reveals daughter's name is Jyoti Singh - Mirror Online Mirror.co.uk Jan 5,2013 21:00 GMT 17 K Tweets
@shellylakhani Shelly Lakhani Don't stop your daughter from going out. Teach your son how to behave... #Delhigangrape,#Delhoprotests,#India Dec 29, 2012, 14:26 GMT 1K Tweets	India Rape Case: New Delhi Attack The victim;s story-WSJ.com Online.wsj.com Jan 8,2013 3:44 GMT 2K Tweets
@Wajahatali Wajahat Ali Don't stop your daughter from going out. Teach your son how to behave... #Delhigangrape Dec 29, 2012 4:10GMT 1K Tweets	How India treats its women Bbc.co.uk Dec 29,2012 11:48GMT 2K Tweets

Figure 15: Overall exposure

Photographs

The photographs that touched a chord in the hearts of most of the tweeting public were also the ones that shook the conscience of everyone who saw it. **'Listen to the women of India: Don't stop your daughter from going out, teach your son how to behave'** showing Indian girls carrying a placard. In another picture that was retweeted repeatedly was the one where a group of men wore skirts and the caption read, **'Way to protest against rape in India: Men don't skirt the issue, speak up and support the women.'** The photographs and captions were so powerful that they caught the imagination of the people and were shared on most social platforms. The unique aspect about these photographs is that although they were in protest against the Nirbhaya rape case, they did not pointedly refer to her. The references were generic and showed the anger of the public against the crime. The people of India, on Twitter and otherwise, seemed to be uniting in favour of a cause.

The visual analysis of the top picture is being conducted using Kress and van Leeuwen framework. This framework recognises that an image simultaneously performs, three kinds of meta-semiotic tasks to create meaning, as explained earlier. These tasks are called the representational meta-function, interpersonal meta-function, and compositional meta-function (Gunther Kress and Theo van Leeuwen, 1996). This study uses elements from each of the meta-functions to arrive at an analysis of the pictures.

Semiotic analysis is a powerful method for gaining a deeper understanding of visual imagery, particularly photographs. By analysing the various signs, symbols, and codes present within an image, semiotic analysis allows researchers to uncover hidden meanings and interpretations that might not be immediately apparent upon first glance.

One of the key strengths of semiotic analysis is its ability to reveal the cultural and historical context in which an image was created. This can be particularly useful when examining photographs from different eras or cultural backgrounds, as the symbols and codes present within an image may hold different meanings depending on the time and place in which they were produced.

Another important aspect of semiotic analysis is its focus on the relationship between the signifier (the physical form of the image) and the signified (the underlying meaning or concept that the image represents). By examining this relationship in detail, researchers gain a more nuanced understanding of how images are constructed and how they function within broader cultural contexts.

	Listen to the women of India: Don't stop your daughter from going out. Teach your son how to behave. #Delhigangrape	3K Tweets
	Don't stop your daughter from going out. Teach your son how to behave. #Delhigangrape #Delhiprotests #India	1K Tweets
	Way to protest rape in #India. "Men don't skirt the issue, speak up and support women." #Delhigangrape	410 Tweets

Figure 16: Top Photographs

In order to conduct a semiotic analysis of photographs Barthes (Barthes, 1970) points out that no picture contains information in itself or, alternatively, that it contains so much contradictory information that a verbal message is needed to fix its meaning. Barthes had studied the pictures in a very strongly organised communication context such as advertisements and press photographs. Barthes became convinced of the leading part played by verbal language even in the understanding of pictures. Researchers believe that neither art photography nor scientific photographs would seem to be determined linguistically to a comparable extent, though their interpretation certainly requires them to be inserted into some more general background frame, that is to say, assimilated to a selected set of interpretational schemes (Sonesson, 1989). The photographs being chosen in this research have very strong context and are therefore required to be studied along with the verbal aspect to derive the meaning.

Figure 17: Original photo posted by @WajahatAli Retrieved from https://twitter.com/search?q=wajahat%20ali%20%23Delhigangrape&src=recent_search_click

Origin of the Tweet: The tweet was first posted by Wajahat Ali, who as described on his Twitter account is 'Co-hosting Al Jazeera America's AJAMStream; Frequent Writing; Occasional Lawyering; Perpetual Chai Drinking; RT's aren't endorsements; Opinions my own' (Source: www.twitter.com). His tweet was re-tweeted 1246 times. The source of the tweet was a popular media figure with 20.3K followers.

Grammar of Communication: It is pertinent to mention that in the original tweet, the phrase 'Listen to the women of

India' is missing. The phrase was added in subsequent RTs. The text used by the tweeter does not use the chat abbreviation 'ur' which is being used by the text in the poster. The initial phrase 'Listen to the women of India' is an assumption that women of India are raising their voice making the men redundant in the process. Directing the statement to the parents of young people in the country, the statement acknowledges the differential parenting accorded to girls and boys and advises correct parenting behaviour towards both genders.

Contextual meaning: As is visible from the visual analysis, patriarchal society leaves its trace on the way the message has been drafted and subsequently re-tweeted by many. Motherhood, in a patriarchal society, is what mothers and babies signify to men. Dominant paradigms, predefined concepts that exist as unquestionable, unchallengeable, are transmitted to us through the culture which is made by those in power i.e. men. Men make the rules and laws; women transmit them (Evelyn Nakano Glenn, Grace Chang, Linda Rennie Forcey, 1994). In fact, in feminist literature 'rape' has been called the foundation of patriarchy. Rape has been used as a means of social control over women by men (Brownmiller, 1993). The message in the tweet is addressed by 'Women of India' to all parents, young and old as discussed earlier. However, only one half of the parent is the 'Mother' or 'Woman'. In effect, the message is directed at Indian women and men who both share the responsibility of raising children, whether sons or daughters. The contradictions that permeate women's lives create the potential for both alienation and liberation (Westkott, 2012). In the present tweet both alienation and liberation are evident. As the tweet changed hands and got re-tweeted, nuances were added to it. The text underwent a change although the picture remained. The photograph caught the imagination of the re-tweeters.

The Meta-Semiotic Analysis of the Photograph Shows the Following:

The image is a narrative because the vectors of motion are present. The narrative is created by the vectors as they are facing front and their bodies being in motion create a story. They can be classificatory because they belong to a 'group' of protestors and are present in the picture in the same identity. The demand for the viewer is great because the Representative Participant (RP) is looking at the viewer and this kind of demand generally causes the viewer to feel a strong engagement with the RP. The distance from the viewer is personal and within public distance are several other persons. The RP is 'looking horizontally' and has equal power as the viewer. This helps the viewer to identify with the RP in the picture. RP is on the left side of the image and hence has the value of being 'given knowledge' i.e. familiar or common sense. With RP being in this position, the viewer feels familiar to the RP and not alienated. The RP is in the centre of the page, neither up nor down and hence they provide the nucleus of information to which surrounding elements are subservient. The RP is large, in focus, and has high tonal contrast. The fact that RP is in the foreground of the picture gives it more salience.

It is no surprise that the picture occupies the top slot among the tweeted photos. It is very powerful and hence more likely to be remembered. The effectiveness of the RP gives prominence to the picture and helps it to leave a lasting impression.

The tweets have revealed that both the common man and celebrities participated in the movement and the most popular tweet did not really need a celebrity. Analysing tweets has opened a whole new area of knowledge as it floats through cyberspace. Much of Twitter content is devoted to news, mainstream news networks frequently poll the Twitterverse for public opinion, independent bloggers use it to promote their own or other content, and journalists use it to supplement their own reporting. In this case Twitter brought the issue into public consciousness by providing a platform for gathering dissenting voices, circulating stirring group images and affects, and collectively mobilising the public into action. They are, as Zizi Papacharissi contends, expressions of emerging 'structures of feeling' (Papacharissi, 2015). The structures of feeling take the form of a collection of bodies as they move in plaza protests creating mass movements. Together they can bring issues to light and command action.

Case II: Farmer's Agitation

The Indian Parliament passed three agriculture acts—Farmers' Produce Trade and Commerce (Promotion and Facilitation) Act 2020, Farmers (Empowerment and Protection) Agreement of Price Assurance, Farm Services Act 2020, and the Essential Commodities (Amendment) Act, 2020—during its monsoon session culminating on 23 September 2020. The bills were signed by the President of India on 27 September 2020.

A few key points from each act that explain the changes proposed by them to the existing agriculture laws in the country are given below:

1. Farmer's Produce Trade and Commerce (Promotion and Facilitation) Act, 2020

This act allows farmers to engage in trade of their agricultural produce outside the physical markets notified under various state Agricultural Produce Marketing Committee laws (APMC acts). Also known as the 'APMC Bypass Bill', it will override all the state-level APMC Acts.

- Promotes barrier-free intra-state and inter-state trade of farmer's produce.
- Proposes an electronic trading platform for direct and online trading of produce. Entities that can establish such platforms include companies, partnership firms, or societies.
- Allows farmers the freedom to trade anywhere outside state-notified APMC markets, and this includes allowing trade at farm gates, warehouses, cold storages, and so on.
- Prohibits state governments or APMCs from levying fees, cess, or any other charge on farmers produce.

2. Farmers (Empowerment and Protection) Agreement of Price Assurance and Farm Services Act, 2020

The Act seeks to provide farmers with a framework to engage in contract farming, where farmers can enter into a direct agreement with a buyer (before sowing season) to sell the produce to them at pre-determined prices.

- Entities that may strike agreements with farmers to buy agricultural produce are defined as 'sponsors' and can include individuals, companies, partnership firms, limited liability groups, and societies.
- The Act provides for setting up farming agreements between farmers and sponsors. Any third parties involved in the transaction (like aggregators) will have to be explicitly mentioned in the agreement. Registration authorities can be established by state governments to provide for electronic registry of farming agreements.

- Agreements cover mutually agreed terms between farmers and sponsors, and the terms cover supply, quality, standards, prices, as well as farm services. These include supply of seeds, feed, fodder, agro-chemicals, machinery and technology, non-chemical agro-inputs, and other farming inputs.
- Agreements must have a minimum duration of one cropping season, or one production cycle of livestock. The maximum duration can be five years. For production cycles beyond five years, the period of agreement is mutually decided by the farmer and sponsor.
- Purchase price of the farming produce—including the methods of determining price—may be added in the agreement. In case the price is subject to variations, the agreement must include a guaranteed price to be paid as well as clear references for any additional amounts the farmer may receive, like bonus or premium.
- There is no mention of minimum support price (MSP) that buyers need to offer to farmers.
- Delivery of farmers' produce may be undertaken by either party within the agreed time frame. Sponsors are liable to inspect the quality of products as per the agreement, otherwise they will be deemed to have inspected the produce and have to accept the delivery within the agreed time frame.
- In case of seed production, sponsors are required to pay at least two-thirds of the agreed amount at the time of delivery, and the remaining amount to be paid after due certification within 30 days of date of delivery. Regarding all other cases, the entire amount must be paid at the time of delivery and a receipt slip must be issued with details of the sale.
- Produce generated under farming agreements are exempt from any state acts aimed at regulating the sale and purchase of

farming produce, therefore leaving no room for states to impose MSPs on such produce. Such agreements also exempt the sponsor from any stock-limit obligations applicable under the Essential Commodities Act, 1955. Stock-limits are a method of preventing hoarding of agricultural produce.
- Provides for a three-level dispute settlement mechanism: the conciliation board—comprising representatives of parties to the agreement, the sub-divisional magistrate, and appellate authority.

3. Essential Commodities (Amendment) Act, 2020

An amendment to the Essential Commodities Act, 1955, seeks to restrict the powers of the government with respect to production, supply, and distribution of certain key commodities.
- The Act removes cereals, pulses, oilseeds, edible oils, onions, and potatoes from the list of essential commodities.
- Government can impose stock holding limits and regulate the prices for the above commodities—under the Essential Commodities Act, 1955—only under exceptional circumstances. These include war, famine, extraordinary price rise, and natural calamity of grave nature.
- Stock limits on farming produce to be based on price rise in the market. They may be imposed only if there is: (i) A 100 per cent increase in retail price of horticultural produce, and (ii) A 50 per cent increase in the retail price of non-perishable agricultural food items. The increase is to be calculated over the price prevailing during the preceding twelve months, or the average retail price over the last five years, whichever is lower.
- The Act aims at removing the fears of private investors with regard to regulatory influence in their business operations.
- Gives freedom to produce, hold, move, distribute, and supply produce, leading to harnessing private sector/foreign direct investment in agricultural infrastructure (IDR, 2021).

As per the government, the bills were aimed to liberalise the agricultural sector and allow the farmers to sell their crops to anyone, anywhere in the country. The farmers and activists argued that the bills would hurt the small and marginal farmers, who would not be able to compete with large agri-businesses and lead to the exploitation of farmers by the corporations. Additionally, the farmers were worried that the bills would lead to the dismantling of the Minimum Support Price (MSP) system which ensures that farmers receive a fair price for their crops. Farmers feared that they would be forced to sell their crops at a lower price, which would result in financial losses for them.

The farmers' concerns and reasons for protesting against these laws can be summarised in a few key points such as below:

Potential Impact on Minimum Support Price (MSP): The Minimum Support Price is a government-set price at which the government procures agricultural commodities from farmers to ensure their financial stability. Farmers were apprehensive that the new laws might weaken the MSP system, as they allowed for deregulation of agricultural markets. They feared that private corporations and big agribusinesses could exploit the absence of a regulated market, leading to lower prices for their produce and a loss of income.

Diminished Bargaining Power: The laws proposed the establishment of private agricultural produce markets outside the traditional 'mandis' (regulated markets). Farmers worried that this would reduce their bargaining power, as they would be left to negotiate with private buyers without the protection provided by the mandis. They expressed concerns about being subjected to unfair practices, such as price manipulation and contract farming agreements that could favour buyers.

Lack of Legal Safeguards: Farmers raised concerns about the absence of legal safeguards in the new laws. They argued that the legislation did not provide an effective dispute resolution mechanism or adequate protection against unfair practices. The absence of clear mechanisms for conflict resolution and legal recourse made them apprehensive about the potential exploitation and vulnerability they might face.

Inadequate Consultation and Stakeholder Inclusion: Many farmers believed that the government had not adequately consulted them or taken their concerns into account before passing the laws. They called for wider consultations and meaningful dialogue to address their apprehensions and ensure that their voices were heard in the decision-making process.

Socioeconomic Impact on Farmers: The agricultural sector in India supports a significant portion of the population, and farmers highlighted the potential adverse socioeconomic impacts of the reforms. The agriculture sector contributes nearly 15 per cent of India's $2.9 trillion economy and employs about half of the country's 1.3 billion people (Jazeera, 2020).

The farmers expressed concerns about increased inequality, consolidation of agricultural markets in favour of corporate interests, and the exacerbation of existing challenges faced by small and marginal farmers.

The farmers' protest in India was a widespread movement that garnered significant attention and support, not only within the country but also internationally. The protests represented the collective demands and grievances of farmers who believed that the new agricultural laws could have a detrimental effect on their livelihoods and the agricultural sector as a whole. They called for a repeal of the contentious laws and for the government to engage in meaningful dialogue to address their concerns and ensure a fair and sustainable agricultural system. The initial demands in the month of September 2020 were manifold ranging from agriculture to electricity, oil to disparity of powers between center and state. Later 32 farmers/labour unions came together and many young Punjabi singers including the late Siddhu Moosewala and other artists started to support the agitation. Religious and political organisations from around the world started sending support, while middlemen who would be the first to lose business due to the laws also joined in. Small businessmen, mid-level professionals with agricultural background, and even the industrialists of Ludhiana came forward to support the farmers. By October 2020, national level support was garnered through the umbrella organisation, the All India Kisan Sangharsh Coordination Committee.

Following a massive nationwide one-day strike of farmers together with the trade unionists (Joy, 2020), tens of thousands of farmers from various states, including Punjab, Haryana, Uttar Pradesh, Madhya Pradesh, and Rajasthan, participated in the 'Delhi Chalo' (Let's go to Delhi) march. The police made efforts to stop the march by employing tear gas, batons, and water cannons at the Punjab-Haryana and Haryana-Delhi borders (Slater, 2020). The farmers established protest camps on the outskirts of the city at the Tikri, Singhu, and Ghazipur borders. These turned into protest sites and camps with approximately 300,000 supporters (Sandhu, 2021). The farmers employed many actions to challenge the government and then the conglomerates too. The farmers surrounded the residences of politicians, shut down government buildings, opened toll plazas, disrupted railway lines, boycotted stores and petrol pumps belonging to the conglomerates.

Eyewitness Account of a Journalist about Social Media Usage on Protest Site

Mandeep Punia, a journalist who covered the protests from day one and was even put behind bars, wrote a memoir of his experiences titled, 'Kisan Andolan-Ground Zero'. In the book he has cited several instances of social media usage during the protest period. The social media posts were the talk of the camp site every evening. The virality of social media posts added to the vitality of the protests. The social media began to influence the decision making since November of 2020, when angry posts compelled many unions and associations to join the agitation (Punia 2022). It was used for collective action (Ibid. 43), where V M Singh, a farmer leader informed the cadre of the next protest site through his social media post. Later when farmers from Uttarakhand and UP joined in the protest, many videos went viral (Ibid. 54). As winter set in, pictures of farmers sitting in cold weather prompted social media users to begin donations and contributions (Ibid. 56). Punjabi actor Deep Sidhu, took to Facebook live to make a point about agreeing to the government proposal of revision in the laws. As ministers started a series of speeches trying to talk about the advantages of the laws, the farmers decided to respond only by showing placards with 'yes/no' written on them. Soon the Yes/No movement speeded up and became a popular slogan trending on social media on 5 December 2020. The author says that he saw this slogan on cars, in rallies, on placards. Social media was effectively used for choreography of assembly as meeting venue and time would be sent through messages on WhatsApp. On 23rd January 2021 a map of Outer Ring Road as the proposed route for Kisan parade was uploaded on a social media site and it was viral by next day (Ibid. 60, 71,

100). Social media was used for miscommunication too. As too many members started sending messages on WhatsApp, it led to confusion regarding time and venue of meetings (Ibid. 70). Meanwhile official pages on social media were also set up (Ibid.108). In principle, the farmers had decided to follow the route suggested by Delhi Police. Later however, farmers from UP's Ghazipur border entered Delhi by breaking all barricades and viral video was circulated in all the camp sites (Ibid.110). Another viral video was of a young boy who climbed up a pole on 26 January and hoisted the farmer union flag and Sikh religious flag at Red Fort (Ibid. 119) and later of a boy who died during the agitation, with two versions of the cause of death circulated on social media. This created a rift amongst the farmers (Ibid. 123). Interestingly, despite the soaring popularity of social media the farmers started their own newspaper called *Trolley Times* which was published in Hindi and Gurumukhi (Behl, 2022).

In November 2021, the government finally repealed the three farm laws. The repeal of the laws was a major victory for the farmers. It was also a positive step for democracy in India, and it proved once again the power of the plaza protest and choreography of assembly in such protests.

Given below is the timeline of the Farmers' agitation:

Date	Activity
14 September 2020	Ordinance is brought to Parliament.
17 September 2020	Ordinance is passed in Lok Sabha.
20 September 2020	Ordinance is passed in Rajya Sabha by voice vote.
24 September 2020	Farmers in Punjab announce a three-day rail roko

25 September 2020	Farmers across India take to the streets in response to a call by the All India Kisan Sangharsh Coordination Committee (AIKSCC).
27 September 2020	Farm Bills are **given presidential assent** and notified in the Gazette of India and become Farm Laws.
25 November 2020	After sporadic protests against the new farm laws, including a nationwide road blockade on November 3, farmers' unions in Punjab and Haryana gave the call for a **'Delhi Chalo' movement**. The Delhi Police, however, rejected their request to march to the capital city citing Covid-19 protocols.
26 November 2020	Farmers from Punjab and Haryana start their protest march towards Delhi
27 November 2020	Police used tear gas and water cannons to disperse farmers at border points between Delhi and Haryana/Punjab
28 November 2020	Protesters continue to gather at Delhi's borders
8 December 2020	Farmer unions call for Bharat Bandh, a nationwide strike
14 December 2020	The government holds its first meeting with farmer unions, but fails to reach an agreement on the farm laws
December 30, 2020	Sixth round of talks between the government and farmer unions ends in a stalemate
12 January 2021	Supreme Court suspends implementation of the farm laws and sets up a committee to hold talks with farmer unions
26 January 2021	Farmers' tractor rally in Delhi turns violent, leading to clashes with police and damage to public property
29 January 2021	Eleventh round of talks between the government and farmer unions end without a resolution
26 February 2021	Samyukt Kisan Morcha, a coalition of farmer unions, calls for a nationwide blockade
18 March 2021	Bharat Bandh called by farmer unions to protest against the farm laws
26 May 2021	Farmers' protest completes six months of agitation

9 August 2021	Government introduces three bills in Parliament to repeal the farm laws
10 August 2021	Parliament passes the bills to repeal the farm laws
12 August 2021	Supreme Court disbands the committee set up to hold talks with farmer unions and directs the government to resolve the issue through negotiation
15 August 2021	Farmer unions vow to continue their protests until their demands for a legal guarantee of Minimum Support Price (MSP) and withdrawal of cases against protesters are met
5 September 2021	Bharat Bandh called by farmer unions to protest against rising fuel prices and inflation
9 September 2021	Ninth round of talks between the government and farmer unions end without a resolution
15 September 2021	The Indian Express reports that farmers' protests are likely to continue into the winter months
19 November 2021	PM announces a repeal of farm laws in an address to the nation with the below statement. 'Today, while apologising to the countrymen, I want to say with a sincere and pure heart that perhaps there must have been some deficiency in our efforts, due to which we could not explain the truth like the light of the lamp to some farmers.'
29 November 2021	Both the Houses of Parliament clear Farm Laws Repeal Bill, 2021, via voice votes without any discussion.
8 December 2021	The **government sends a draft proposal** to the farm unions and said that in light of the concessions proposed — including the unconditional withdrawal of all police cases lodged against protesters during the agitation, there was no justification for the agitation to continue and requested the unions to call it off.
9 December 2021	The Samyukt Kisan Morcha (SKM) leaders meet after getting the official proposal from the government and decide to call off its protest at Delhi's borders.

Figure 18: Timeline of Farmer's Protest (Express, 2021)

A Look at the Twitter Data

For the Nirbhaya Case, the analysis was conducted with the help of resources provided by www.topsy.com. This website was suggested to me by the American Library of Congress, Washington DC as a reliable source for tweets. However, now this website is shut down. The website leads the researchers to another website called www.twitterbinder.com. This is the website from where the data related to Farmers' agitation has been acquired. The website www.twitterbinder.com provides tweets related to hashtags requested and also does a sentiment analysis. It provides the economic value of the tweets.

The three hashtags studied were the most popular hashtags during the agitation, ie #Farmersprotest, #tractortotwitter, #Iamwithfarmers. Figure 1 depicts the number of tweets as per hashtags and we find that #Farmersprotest is the most powerful hashtag with more than 90 per cent of tweets and maximum impact.

BINDERS' DETAILS								
	TWEETS	%TOTAL	IMPACTS	CONTRIBUTORS	TWEET/ CONTRIBUTOR	FOLLOWERS/ CONTRIBUTOR	LINKS/ PICS	RETWEETS
#FARMERSPROTEST	151,755	90.18%	6,573,030,994	29,573	513	222,264,60	89,973	0
#TRACTORTOTWITT	9,074	5.39%	14,175,251	3,558	255	3,984,05	5,373	0
#IAMWITHFARMERS	12,154	7.22%	63,524,632	6,622	184	9,592,97	6,534	0

Figure 19: Total tweets in three hashtags, #Farmersprotest, #tractortotwitter, #Iamwithfarmer

Hashtags

For the purpose of this study hashtags have been used as the unit of analysis in order to conduct a sentiment analysis around the subject under discussion. In this case, #farmersprotest turned out to be the most popular hashtag as it clearly outlined the subject of the event without any bias.

The hashtag #farmersprotest provided 90 per cent of the tweets in this sample with maximum impact of 6,573,030,994 and by 29,573 contributors. As compared to the other two hashtags, this one appears to be the most popular.

When one hashtag performs better than others, it typically means that the hashtag is generating higher levels of engagement, visibility, or reach compared to the other hashtags being used. It may be more relevant to the content or topic being discussed and resonates with the target audience and aligns with their interests, resulting in increased engagement and interaction. Some hashtags gain popularity and become trending topics on Twitter. If a hashtag is currently trending, it is more likely to receive higher visibility and engagement as more users are actively searching for and engaging with that specific hashtag. Sometimes hashtags may have a larger audience base, meaning more people are following or actively using those hashtags already. Of course, use of such hashtags gains wider reach, increased impressions, engagements, and potential followers. Specifically, hashtags that are associated with communities, events, or campaigns often generate higher levels of engagement. They create a sense of belonging and encourage community members to participate and interact with the hashtag, leading to increased visibility and engagement.

It's important to note that the success of a hashtag is not solely determined by the number of impressions or engagements. The relevance, context, timing, and quality of the content associated with the hashtag also play a significant role. Amongst the three hashtags #farmersprotest was most neutral and was also the one to clearly define the topic. #iamwithfarmers shows solidarity with the farmers and #tractortotwitter was a trending hashtag that slants towards the use of twitter by the farmers. The three hashtags were trending at the time of selection. Figure 18 clearly shows the three top hashtags during the agitation. Thus, the same has been used for the purpose of this analysis.

Economic Value of a hashtag: The economic value of a hashtag can be difficult to quantify, as it depends on several factors such as the popularity and relevance of the hashtag, the context in which it is used, and the goals of the individuals or organisations using it. In general, hashtags are used to increase the visibility and discoverability of content on social media platforms, particularly Twitter and Instagram. By using a popular or trending hashtag, individuals and organisations increase the reach of their content and potentially attract new followers, customers, or supporters.

TOP HASHTAGS	
HASHTAG	TWEETS
#FARMERSPROTEST	151688
#IAMWITHFARMERS	12141
#TRACTORTOTWITTER	9061
#FARMLAWS	5769
#FARMERS	5009
#FARMLAWSREPEALED	3619
#TRACTOR2TWITTER	3366
#HUMANRIGHTS	3130
#FARMERSPARLIAMENT	2476
#FARMERPROTEST	2435

Figure 20: Top trending hashtags

To someone who followed social media or even the legacy media for news related to farmers' protest, it appeared as though the popular perception about the farm laws protest in India was that it was a legitimate protest by farmers who are concerned about the impact of the new laws on their livelihoods. The protest attracted widespread support from both within India and from the international community.

A number of opinion polls were conducted in India, and they have consistently shown that a majority of the public supports the farmers' protest. For example, Gaon Connection, a trusted rural media platform that conducts surveys, interviews, and carries stories related to the rural hinterland, conducted a survey in November 2020 to understand the perception of farmers in India about the new agriculture laws. The survey was conducted among 10,000 farmers from 22 states.

The survey found that a majority of farmers (52 per cent) were opposed to the new laws. The main reasons for opposition were:
- Fear that the laws would lead to lower prices for their crops.
- Fear that the laws would make it easier for big corporations to exploit them.
- Lack of trust in the government.

The survey also found that a significant number of farmers (35 per cent) were in favour of the new laws. The main reasons for support were:
- The belief that the laws would give them more freedom to sell their crops.
- The belief that the laws would make it easier for them to access markets.
- The belief that the laws would help to reduce corruption in the mandi system.

The survey result showed that large number of farmers (13 per cent) were undecided about the new laws. The survey results suggest that there was a lot of confusion and uncertainty among farmers about the new agriculture laws. The government needs to do more to clarify the provisions of the laws and to address the concerns of farmers (Gupta, 2020). In addition to media reports the plight and sight of the farmers protesting on the roads in the extreme winter of North India obviously created a negative perception in the minds of the media consuming publics. The travellers moving towards Delhi from the North Indian states could actually witness the living conditions of the agitating farmers as seasons changed.

Meanwhile the protests also found support from a number of celebrities and politicians, including Rihanna, Greta Thunberg, Priyanka Chopra Jonas and Meera Harris. These celebrities used their platforms to raise awareness about the protest and to call for the government to repeal the new laws.

The Farmers' agitation was supported by many student bodies, young activists and also media professionals. It was a well-planned agitation although not as spontaneous as the Nirbhaya agitation. Several websites were created by various farmer unions and organisations to provide information, updates, and resources related to the movement. One of the prominent websites associated with the movement is 'www.farmerprotests.com'. The website served as a dedicated platform to highlight the demands, grievances, and objectives of the farmers' agitation. It provided information about the contentious agricultural reforms, including the three farm laws that sparked the protests. The website aimed to raise awareness about the issues faced by farmers and mobilise support for their cause.

In the Nirbhaya case where the agitations had stopped after a month and Twitter activity had slowed down, while the judiciary, legacy media, women's organisations, and legislative action picked up the issue. I, therefore, collected the tweets only for a month. The Farmers' agitation on the other hand, continued for more than a year. The agitation on the road did not end and nor did Twitter activity. Therefore, it was necessary to analyse the Tweets for one whole year specifically from 29 November 2020 to 30 November 2021.

SUMMARY	ACTIVITY	RETWEETS AND LIKES	SENTIMENT	RANKINGS	ECONOMIC STUDY	IMAGES	OTHER STATS	BINDERS
1,479,808 Total Tweets				DATE RANGE 11/26/2020 - 11/30/2021				CHANGE DATES
				TEXT TWEETS 2.86%				42,282
				REPLIES 2.31%				34,116
				RETWEETS 88.63%				1,311,519
1,152,101,082.66 economic value ?		NaN total impressions ?		LINKS AND IMAGES 6.69%				99,028

Figure 21: Total tweets of three hashtags during farmers' agitation

Figure 21 provides the total data breakup into different elements. It shows the exact number of tweets, with the breakup of retweets, text tweets, replies, links, and images.

Date Range: 26 November 2020 to 30 November 2021

Total tweets: Number of tweets for this search in given time period.

Economic Value: Amount of money the hashtag is worth in the market.

Text tweets: Tweets shared with the hashtags that contain nothing but text.

Replies: Replies sent using the hashtags.

Retweets: Amount of tweets and retweets this report has received.

Links and images: Tweets shared with hashtag that contain link or media

Potential Impressions (without RT): These impressions have been calculated with the original tweet ,minus the retweet data.
Potential Reach (without RTs): This reach has been calculated with the data from users who have sent original tweets minus the retweet data.
Original Contributors: Number of users who have shared original tweets with the hashtags.
Original tweets per Contributor: Average number of original tweets per original contributor.
Followers per contributor: Average number of followers per contributor.
Original Tweets: Number of original tweets using the hashtags excluding retweets.
Likes: Number of 'likes' received by the tweets included in this report.
Received retweets: Statistical summary received by this report.

As is visible from the data in the figure, that a total of 1,479,808 tweets were gathered from the three hashtags during the sampling period. Out of the total number of tweets only 168,289 are original tweets which is only 11 per cent. This shows us that most tweeters are actually retweeters. Creating original content for Twitter, whatever the point of view, is not something commonly done. Moreover the original contributors of the tweets are 36,380 which is 21 per cent of all the original tweeters. As per the data, on an average each original content creator has 4.63 tweets to his credit.

Potential Impressions: On Twitter, an impression refers to the number of times a tweet has been viewed by users. Impressions are more important than likes, retweets, or quote tweets because they measure the reach of your content. While likes, retweets, and quote tweets are all forms of engagement, they only measure the interaction of your content with your followers. Impressions, on the other hand, measure the number of times your content has been seen by anyone, including people who are not following you.

A high number of impressions indicates that your content is being seen by a large number of people, which can lead to more engagement and followers. Additionally, impressions can help you to identify which topics resonate with your audience and which types of content are driving the most traffic to your content. Engagements contribute to increased visibility and leads to further amplification of your message. By comparing impressions from different tweets, one can identify the content effectiveness.

It is important to note that while impressions provide useful insights, they do not represent direct engagement or conversions. Tracking other metrics like clicks, retweets, replies, and link visits in conjunction with impressions gives a more comprehensive understanding of the effectiveness of the tweets and overall Twitter strategy. Strategies for improving impressions on Twitter could include tweeting at the right time, using relevant hashtags, creating interesting and engaging content and lastly promotion of content from one social media on other social media platforms.

In the present case we notice a large number of potential impressions, 6,639,924,864. As compared to this, the reach of the Tweets is 311,524,584 which is approximately 5 per cent of the impressions. Reach and impressions are two different metrics that provide insights into the visibility and the potential audience of a tweet. Reach refers to the number of unique Twitter accounts or users who have seen a particular tweet. It measures the potential audience size that the tweet has reached. Reach counts each unique user only once, regardless of how many times they may have seen the tweet, providing an estimate of the unique individuals who have been exposed to your tweet in their timeline. Impressions, on the other hand, represent the total number of times a tweet has been viewed by Twitter users. It includes both multiple views from the same user and views from different users. Impressions can be higher than the reach since a single user can view a tweet multiple times, either by scrolling through their timeline or revisiting the tweet at a later time.

As in our case, having a large number of impressions as compared to reach would mean that users have viewed the tweet several times.

The data also provides economic value and a sentiment score, explained in the following pages.

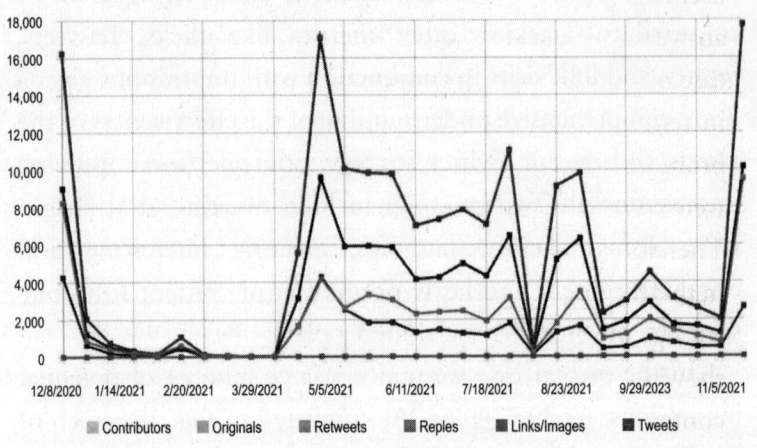

Figure 22: Peaks in Twitter activity

One look at the activity (Figure 22) on the three hashtags proves that original tweets have more reach and impressions.

The highest score can be seen as soon as the agitation started, which is around November-December 2020 and then a dip is registered for a few months, till February 2021 when there was a four-hour Rail Roko (Stop the trains) call, then again in mid-March when there was a call for Bharat Bandh (India Shut down) by farmer unions to protest against the farm laws. In May 2021, on completion of six months of the agitation, much activity is visible, and then in August 2021 when the process of repeal began. The data shoots up in December when PM announced that the government was ready to repeal the laws and apologised in a public address.

Economic Value of Tweets

What is the economic outcome of a tweet? What can be its potential impact on business, marketing, brand reputation, user engagement and financial returns? These are the questions answered by data on the economic value of the tweets. In the case of this study, we are not interested in the economic value in terms of financial returns as the users were not trying to promote a brand to make a financial profit. Yet, the users were trying to promote an idea and increase user engagement. Therefore, it is interesting to see the perceived value of tweets in this data set. Engaging with others through tweets can foster strong connections and build relationships. When tweets showcase positive experiences, testimonials, or user-generated content, they contribute to building social proof and trust. This can enhance credibility and lead to leveraging popular hashtags or participating in relevant conversations.

Economic Value of a User

Metrics such as follower count, engagement rates, influence, and demonstrated impact on business outcomes are often considered when assessing the economic value of a Twitter user. It is the measurable or perceived value that an individual user on the Twitter platform can bring to businesses, brands, or advertisers. In the case of this analysis, the economic value of the user could be the most influential users. Twitter users who are considered influential or establish themselves as thought leaders in specific domains possess higher economic value. Their opinions and recommendations carry weight and impact the decisions and behaviours of their followers towards desired outcomes. Users with a large follower base can potentially reach a broader audience and attract more attention to their tweets or endorsements. The level of engagement a Twitter user generates, such as likes, retweets, replies, and mentions, indicate their influence and the extent to which their content resonates with their audience. Higher engagement rates generally indicate a higher economic value as it suggests a user's ability to drive conversations and capture attention. Besides the quantity, even the quality of content matters. The relevance of a Twitter user's content plays a crucial role in their economic value. Users who consistently share valuable, informative, or entertaining

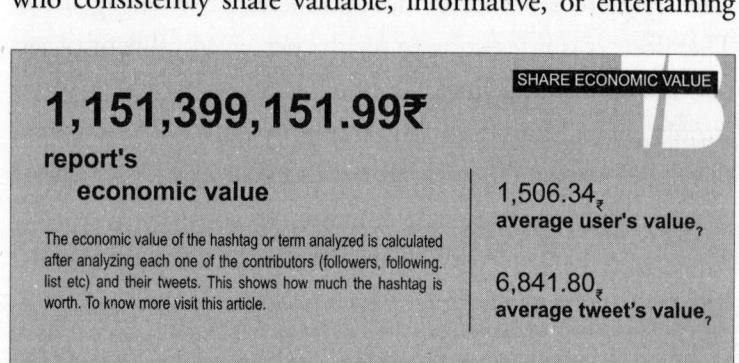

Figure 23: Economic value of the report

content attract and retain a loyal audience, leading to increased engagement and better credibility.

This report (Figure 23) calculated the value of all the tweets combined to provide the economic worth of the hashtag in the market. Rs 1,151,399,151.99/- is the value of the report in case we wanted to use these hashtags and contributors for a business venture. This proves that ideas and opinions have a great scope for promotion through the use of Twitter. As days pass by, the economic value of the report, hashtag and user keeps on changing.

Economic Value of a hashtag: The economic value of a hashtag can be difficult to quantify, as it depends on several factors such as the popularity and relevance of the hashtag, the context in which it is used, and the goals of the individuals or organizations using it. In general, hashtags are used to increase the visibility and discoverability of content on social media platforms, particularly Twitter and Instagram. By using a popular or trending hashtag, individuals and organisations increase the reach of their content and potentially attract new followers, customers, or supporters.

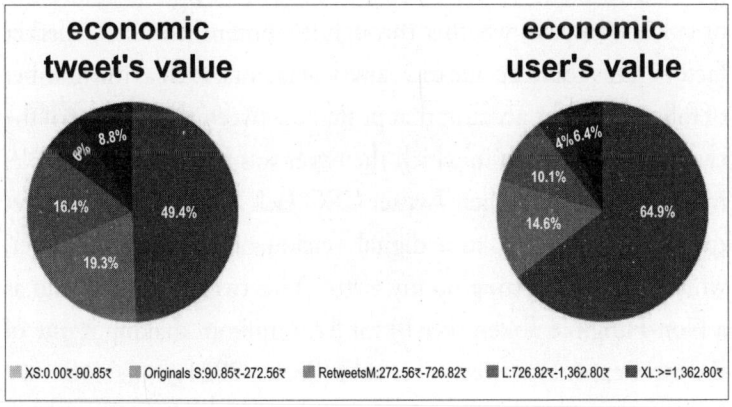

Figure 24: Economic value of tweets and users

Similarly, the average user value is the average amount of money users in this report are worth in the market. A total of all the users values and divided it by the number of contributors gives the average user value which, in the case of this report, is Rs.1506.34.

An average tweet's value is an astounding Rs 6,841.80 which has been calculated by dividing the total of all the tweet values by the total number of tweets. This gives us the average value of each tweet. This analysis proves that each tweet was a powerful source of inspiration, connection, and motivation towards the cause. This also proves the power of the hashtag.

Notice the notation running under the pie chart in Figure 24
XS: 0.00 ₹-90.85 ₹0 **S:** 90.85 ₹ -272.56 ₹7 **M:** 272.56 -726.82 ₹. **L:** 726.82 ₹- 1,362.80 **XL**>1,362.80 ₹

The terms XS, S, M,L,XL denote the economic value exerted by tweets and users. The S users are the ones whose economic value is between Rs 0 to Rs 90.85. However, they form the largest body of tweets and users thereby exerting maximum influence.

Most expensive tweet: The term 'most expensive tweet' generally refers to a tweet that has generated significant financial or cultural impact, whether through its content, context, or other factors. This could be due to a variety of factors, such as the number of followers of the account that posted the tweet, the content of the tweet, or the context in which the tweet was posted. For example, in March 2021, the then Twitter CEO Jack Dorsey posted a tweet that included a link to a digital version of his first-ever tweet, which read 'just setting up my twttr'. This tweet was then sold as a Non-Fungible Token (NFT) for $2.9 million, making it one of the most expensive tweets ever sold (Locke, 2021).

Similarly, tweets from high-profile accounts, such as those of celebrities or politicians, can also be considered 'expensive' if they generate significant impact or engagement. For instance, in 2017, a tweet from former President Barack Obama following the white supremacist rally in Charlottesville, Virginia, became one of the most-liked tweets of all time, with over 4 million likes (Bloom, 2017).

In this case, the news channel NDTV takes credit for the most expensive tweets (Figure 25).

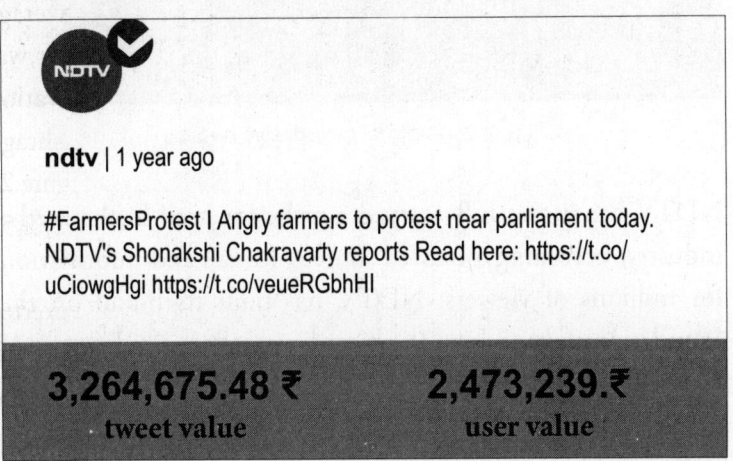

Figure 25: Most expensive tweet

NDTV had reported the proposal of the farmers to organise a Kisan Sansad in groups of 200 during the monsoon session of the parliament. The Delhi government and police allowed farmers to protest till August 9 between 11am and 5pm (Sengar, M.S., Shonakshi Chakravarty, 2021). This tweet is by its correspondent Shonakshi Chakravarty.

The fact that the most expensive tweets come from the same entity speaks volumes about it as a brand (Figures 25, 26, 27). New Delhi Television Network is one of India's premier news networks, renowned for its comprehensive coverage, ethical journalism, and commitment to social impact. As a brand,

ndtv | 1 year ago

"Don't Love Post", Meghalaya Governor Targets BJP Over #FarmersProtest https://t.co/tDEXWhq7Vl https://t.co/NWo5wjP1gV

3,264,674.58 ₹
tweet value

2,473,238.₹
user value

Figure 26: 2nd most expensive tweet

NDTV has successfully carved a niche for itself in the media industry, becoming a trusted source of news and information for millions of viewers. NDTV has built its brand on the foundation of credible and unbiased journalism. With a team of experienced journalists and reporters, the network has upheld high editorial standards and integrity. NDTV's commitment to fact-checking, accuracy, and balanced reporting has earned it the trust and respect of its audience. The network's focus on investigative journalism and in-depth analysis has been instrumental in bringing important stories to light and holding those in power accountable. The channel covers a wide range of topics, including politics, business, sports, entertainment, and social issues. Its comprehensive coverage ensures that viewers have access to diverse perspectives and a well-rounded understanding of current events. NDTV's journalists are known for their expertise and in-depth knowledge, allowing them to provide insightful commentary and analysis. It has consistently pushed the boundaries of traditional journalism by introducing innovative programming formats. Shows like

'The Big Fight', 'We the People', and 'Ravish Ki Report' have become popular for their engaging discussions and thought-provoking content. NDTV's commitment to exploring new formats and embracing digital platforms has helped it stay relevant in an ever-evolving media landscape. The channel has leveraged its brand and platform to drive social impact initiatives such as its coverage of the #farmersprotest. The fact that the most expensive tweets come from NDTV proves its brand value in the market. The network has actively promoted campaigns and initiatives related to education, healthcare, environmental conservation, women's empowerment, and disaster relief. Through its programs such as 'Save Our Tigers' and 'Greenathon', NDTV has raised awareness about critical social issues and mobilised support from viewers, celebrities, and corporate partners. The network's digital platforms provide real-time updates, live streaming, and interactive features, allowing viewers to engage with the content and express their opinions. NDTV's mobile applications and

ndtv | 2 year ago

Famrer Leader Rakesh Tikait. Others Step Up Protest Against Arrests Read more: https://t.co/Cp7sFSwMXD #FarmerProtest https://t.co/Z8WWQnDXPN

3,264,674.58 ₹	2,473,238.₹
tweet value	user value

Figure 27: 3rd most expensive tweet

TOP ACCOUNTS	Value
@ndtv NDTV	2,473,005.59₹
@timesofindia The Times Of India	2,082,039.46₹
@TimesNow TIMES NOW	1,510,896.28₹
@INCIndia Congress	1,389,677.41₹
@htTweets Hindustan Times	1,294,284.43₹
@the_hindu The Hindu	1,199,124.94₹
@ANI ANI	1,149,982.52₹
@AamAadmiparty AAP	989.156.27₹
@YourAnonNews Anonymous	986,723.22₹
@ZeeNews Zee News	973,543.17₹

Figure 28: Top Accounts

social media presence have extended its reach and facilitated greater audience engagement. The network has received prestigious honors, including multiple Ramnath Goenka Excellence in Journalism Awards, Asian Television Awards, and Indian Television Academy Awards. These accolades serve as a testament to NDTV's quality journalism and brand reputation. The network was founded by Radhika Roy and Prannoy Roy as a production house for television news content in the year 1988. From the path-breaking foreign affairs show 'The World This Week' (nominated as one of India's 5 best television programmes since Independence), the first private news on Doordarshan 'The News Tonight', producing India's first 24-hour news channel 'Star News' and the country's first ever 2-in-1 channel Profit-Prime, NDTV has been at the forefront of every single news revolution. It was one of the first private news channels in India and quickly gained popularity for its unbiased and credible journalism. It has since not looked back. Presently it is a subsidiary of AMG Media Networks Limited, an Adani Group Company (About, 2023).

Overall distribution of top accounts in terms of its value is taken away by media organisations rather than any individuals. Only two political parties make it in the top 10, @INCIndia and @AamAadmiParty. The data shows how much a text tweet from any of these accounts is worth. NDTV is right on top, followed by the Times of India Group in second and third positions. Both the newspaper and news channel make their appearance. (Figure 28)

The data looks like this:
- News Channels: 4
- Newspapers: 3
- Political parties: 2
- Anonymous: 1

While all the other handles are well known Indian media organisations and political parties, the name @YourAnonNews may not be well known. This is a verified handle, and its profile says, 'We are Anonymous, we are legion, we do not forgive, we do not forget. Expect us. Prepared to go forward w/it. Here live. Not a cat.' @YourAnonNews has 7.8M followers that include several journalists and media houses. @YourAnonNews is a Twitter account associated with the collective known as Anonymous. Anonymous is a loosely affiliated decentralised

Most Expensive Users		Value
	@ndtv NDTV	368,192,097.83₹
	@IndiaToday IndiaToday	208,496.367.77₹
	@htTweets Hindustan Times	137,972,965.63₹
	@ZeeNewsEnglish Zee News English	60,427,303.82₹
	@TimesNow Times Now	37,772,032.73₹
	@dna DNA	25,406,872.12₹
	@bsindia Business Standard	20,553,060.43₹
	@CNNnews18 News18	16,092,993.15₹
	@the_hindu The Hindu	15,828,114.71₹
	@EconomicTimes Economic Times	15,015,091.63₹

Figure 29: Most expensive users of the analysed hashtags

international activist and hacktivist collective. The Twitter account serves as a platform for sharing news, updates, and statements related to activism, social issues, cybersecurity, and political events from the perspective of Anonymous. The account operates under the pseudonym 'Anonymous', which symbolises the collective rather than an individual. The account is known for its provocative and sometimes controversial tweets, often targeting corporations, governments, and organisations perceived to be engaged in unethical or corrupt practices. The tweets typically highlight issues such as privacy rights, freedom of expression, social justice, and accountability. They do not believe in censorship in any form. They were one of the earliest groups to come forward in support of the Arab Spring movement. They have followed most of the uprisings and protests. The philosophy of Anonymous offers 'insight into a long-standing political question that has gone unanswered with often tragic consequences for social movements: what does a new form of collective politics look like that wishes to go beyond the identity of the individual subject in late capitalism' (Halpin, 2014). It is no surprise that anon finds a place in the top ten most influential websites in this data. While Figure 28 shows the overall expensive tweeters, Figure 29 is a more focussed view of the most expensive tweets by users who used the three hashtags, #farmersprotest, #iamwithfarmers, #tractortotwitter. They are all media organisations and @ndtv takes the lead followed at a distance by @indiatoday, @htTweets and others.

Sentiment Analysis

Sentiment analysis of a corpus of tweets involves the process of determining the overall sentiment or emotional tone expressed in a collection of tweets. It is a text analysis technique that aims to classify each tweet as positive, negative, or neutral based on the sentiment it conveys. www.twitterbinder.com has collected a total of 1,749,808 tweets related to the three hashtags #farmersprotest, #iamwithfarmers, #tractortotwitter. The collected tweets need to be pre-processed to prepare them for sentiment analysis. This typically involves removing noise such as hashtags, URLs, and special characters, as well as tokenising the tweets into individual words. Sentiment analysis often relies on a sentiment lexicon or dictionary, which contains words or phrases associated with positive or negative sentiments. These lexicons assign sentiment scores or labels to words, enabling sentiment analysis algorithms to determine the overall sentiment of a tweet based on the sentiment scores of its constituent words. A sentiment score is a numerical representation of the sentiment (positive, negative, or neutral) expressed in a particular text, such as a review, social media post, or news article. Algorithms use a combination of techniques to analyse text and assign a sentiment score. This score is often represented as a numerical value, with a range of -1 to +1, where -1 represents a highly negative sentiment, +1 represents a highly positive sentiment, and 0 represents a neutral sentiment. As is evident from the sentiment analysis of tweets presented here, the high percentage of neutral sentiment means that the majority of tweets analysed do not express a strong positive or negative sentiment. This indicates that tweets are focussed on a neutral topic or that they express opinions that are relatively balanced. It is important to note that sentiment score can vary according to the context. A high neutral score in a case like this one, where public opinion was the most important yardstick, would actually mean that the issue was not highly polarised on Twitter and that room for discussion and dialogue was present. This score also indicates that there is diversity and differences in perspectives amongst tweeters and that they are not as emotionally invested in the issue as was being generally felt.

The next step is to analyse each tweet in the corpus to determine its sentiment. There are different approaches to sentiment classification, including rule-based methods, machine learning techniques, and deep learning models. Rule-based methods utilise predefined rules or patterns to classify tweets based on sentiment indicators, while machine learning and deep learning models learn patterns and relationships in the data to predict sentiment.

Many a times, the algorithm is unable to gauge the sentiment clearly if sarcasm or irony are present in the Tweets.

However, in this data the neutral sentiment is too high as compared to others, diminishing the chances of such an error.

Once the sentiment analysis is performed, the results can be analysed and visualised to gain insights into the overall sentiment trends within the corpus of tweets. This can involve creating visualisations such as sentiment distribution plots, word clouds, or sentiment timelines to understand how sentiment varies over time or across different topics. Generally, a sentiment analysis of a corpus of tweets provides valuable insights into public opinion and social trends. In this case, the website www.twitterbinder.com has performed the sentiment analysis of the corpus through machine learning tools and created a sentiment timeline. Figure 30 shows the sentiment timeline of the evolution of types of tweets during the time period of 26 November 2020 to 30 November 2021.

When the maximum sentiment in a corpus of tweets is neutral, it means that the majority of tweets in the collection do not exhibit a strong positive or negative sentiment. Neutral

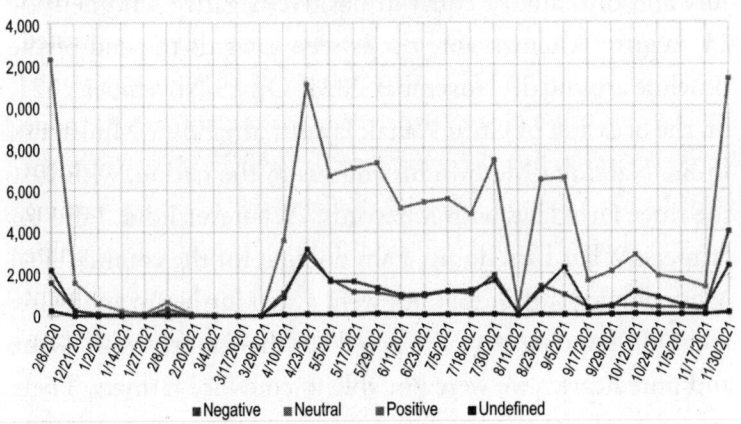

Figure 30: Sentiment timeline

sentiment indicates that the expressed emotions or opinions in the tweets are neither predominantly positive nor negative and that they tend to convey a more objective or balanced viewpoint. As we can observe in Figure 30, while positive and negative tweets are comparably equal, it is the neutral sentiment that stands out. There is the element of topic neutrality in this case. The most popular hashtag #farmersprotest is itself neutral and states the facts as they are without the bias present for sharing general news updates, factual information, or objective observations from different sides of the issue. Many times the subtlety of language nuances are not captured by the machine learning tools and hence the sentiment score may get affected. In Figure 30, we can observe that the neutrality is lost between December 2020 and March 2021 and peaks again in the end of April and early May, during which time farmers celebrated Guru Tegh Bahadur's 400th birthday and later May Day as Majdoor-Kisan Diwas. On 27 May, when the agitation turned six months, the farmers' observed a 'black day'. The neutral sentiment continues to peak till 30 July and dips almost equal to positive/negative sentiment by 11 August. A remarkable rise is seen towards the end of the timeline around 30 November 2021. On 19 November 2021, on the occasion of Guru Nanak Jayanti, the Prime Minister of India, Narendra Modi in his address to the nation, withdrew the three farm laws with the words, 'Whatever I did, I did for farmers. What I am doing, I am doing it for the country.' PM Modi did not stop at that but went a step further to apologise. He said, 'I apologise to the people of the country with a true and pure heart... we were not able to convince farmers. There must have been some deficiency in our efforts that we could not convince some farmers' (Dutta, 2021).

Overall sentiment score looks likes Figure 31:

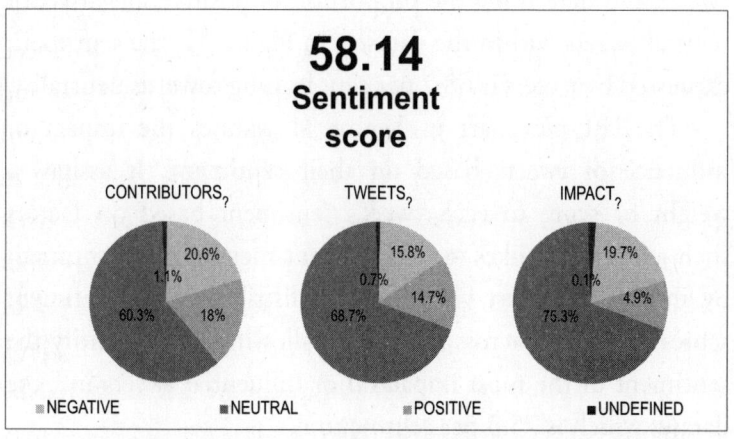

Figure 31: Overall sentiment score

A sentiment score of 58.14/100 indicates that the sentiment expressed in the tweets, associated with the given hashtags, lean towards the positive side. It is not overwhelmingly positive as there may be more neutral elements as seen in the sentiment analysis.

The pie charts in Figure 31 show us 'sentiment' by users, tweets, and impact. All the data shows a slant towards neutrality.

Sentiment by Contributors examines the sentiment expressed by individual users. It aggregates the sentiment of all the tweets posted by each user and categorises them into different sentiment categories (e.g., positive, negative, neutral). The resulting pie chart illustrates the distribution of sentiment across different users, showing predominantly expressed sentiment. In Figure 31, we can observe 60.3 per cent users expressing neutral sentiment towards the issue.

Sentiment by Tweets focuses on the sentiment expressed in each individual tweet. It categorises each tweet into sentiment categories and creates a pie chart showing the distribution of sentiment across all the tweets in the corpus. This chart helps us to understand the overall sentiment composition of the tweets and determine the proportion of positive, negative, or neutral tweets within the dataset. In Figure 31, the sentiment expressed by tweets is 68.7 per cent leaning towards neutrality.

The last pie chart in Figure 31 assesses the impact or influence of tweets based on their sentiment. It assigns a weight or score to each tweet's sentiment based on factors such as retweets, likes, or engagement metrics. The sentiment by impact pie chart visualises the distribution of sentiment scores or weights across the tweets, allowing us to identify the sentiment of the most impactful or influential tweets in the dataset which is 75.3 per cent neutral.

When sentiment stats are observed on a table (Figure 32) one can notice that while neutral sentiment takes the lead, the positive and negative sentiment run neck to neck with negative sentiment being slightly more. The reason for the overall sentiment score being slightly positive is that maximum tweets are neutral. This does show that all sides of the issue were under discussion during the time period. As we can observe, more tweeters, with a better potential impact and economic value of tweets, maintained a neutral stance.

	SENTIMENT STATS				
	TOTAL TWEETS	POTENTIAL IMPACTS	CONTRIBUTORS	ECONOMIC VALUE	LINKS/PICS
NEUTRAL	115,664	4,997,527,958	28,021	9,562,075.62	69.553
POSITIVE	24,697	323,107,696	8,366	644.178.76	13.104
NEGATIVE	26,668	1,310,951,505	9,580	2.448.106.93	15.584

Figure 32: Sentiment data

Observing the sentiment data in Figure 32, one is curious to know something about the contributors who have led to the data being neutral despite the enormous media coverage about violence and destruction from both ends. Figure 33, shows the top accounts in terms of their activity.

MOST ACTIVE	Tweets
@DigitalKisanBot Kisan Bot	2,953
@pacifistrebel The Pacifist Rebel	2,820
@SupreemJohn John	1,640
@VickyGurm143 ਸਰਦਾਰ ਸਾਬ (A Farm...	1,547
@tasversandhu Dnt Lie Loser Mod	1,309

Figure 33: Most active handles

In order to learn more about the contributors, we will have to study their profiles on Twitter. The contributor account that was most active during the agitation is @DigitalKisanBOT

The account is still present on Twitter and as I write this it has 2189 followers and has 37.5K Tweets to its credit. The account mentions its location as Atlanta, Georgia and was started in September 2020. Its bio reads as 'Kisana de samarthan vich pahila Twitter Bot. Eh Bot kisana de haq layi Tweet karda hai. Most Tweets and RTs are automated. #farmersprotest @billingpuneet.' Roughly translated from

Punjabi, it means, 'First Bot designed in support of the farmers. This Bot tweets in the interest of the farmers...' The handle tags @billingpuneet. I am seizing this opportunity to discuss the meaning and relevance of a Twitter bot.

What is a Twitter Bot?

Before going into a deeper analysis of this handle, it is better to understand the meaning of a bot on Twitter. A Twitter bot is an automated software program or script that performs actions on Twitter without direct human intervention. These bots are programmed to execute various tasks on the social media platform, ranging from simple automated actions to more complex interactions. Twitter bots serve different purposes such as automatically posting tweets based on predefined criteria or schedules. They can be programmed for engagement and interaction such as automatically like, retweet, or reply to specific tweets or users based on certain keywords or patterns. Bots can be used to collect and analyse data from Twitter. They can scrape tweets, hashtags, or user profiles to gather information for research, sentiment analysis, or other analytical purposes.

Some bots are created for spamming purposes, spreading misinformation, or engaging in malicious activities such as phishing, hacking, or spreading malware. When they indulge in such negative activity, they violate Twitter's terms of service and can be flagged or suspended.

It is no surprise that the most active handle is a bot. Bots observe every keyword every time it is mentioned and retweet or even create fresh tweets. They of course, turn out to be more efficient than human beings and much faster.

The fact that the bot originated from the USA was intriguing.

I decided to find out more about @billingpuneet. The handle also originates from Atlanta and @DigitalKisanBot follows it. This handle has 116 followers. This is an old handle, started in May 2011. It becomes clear that @billingpuneet started the bot for the purpose of showing solidarity with the farmers.

Other handles on the list are all human beings. The second name on the list is @pacifistrebel. The handle's bio says, 'Human Rights/Civil Rights & A Love for Humanity. Seeking eternal Chardi Kala state of mind. ਨਾਨਕ ਨਾਮ ਚੜ੍ਹਦੀ ਕਲਾ ਤੇਰੇ ਭਾਣੇ ਸਰਬੱਤ ਦਾ ਭਲਾ। Typos are my trademark'. The Punjabi part of the bio is a popular Punjabi prayer which roughly translates to: 'Nanak, with your name comes prosperity and with your blessing, peace for everyone'. The handle was started in January 2021, and it has 1625 followers and 109.8K tweets.

The third most active handle was @SupreemJohn. The handle has only 49 followers and was started in September 2015. So far it has 13.9K tweets. The handle has a picture of the popular film star John Abraham but it is not the film actor's handle.

The fourth handle on the list is @VickyGurm143, it belongs to 'Sardar saab' who qualifies himself as 'A farmer'. It has 275 followers and 9609 tweets.

The fifth position is occupied by @tasveersandhu, whose name on the profile is 'Dnt lie Loser Modi (angry emoji) Ravinder Kaur (Ravinder Kaur in Urdu).' The description on the bio says, 'I WAS I AM and I WILL STAND WITH FARMERS ALWAYS P.S I would like to apologise to anyone I have not offended yet. Please be patient. I will get to you shortly.' The handle was started in August 2009, is operated from Amritsar, and has 993 followers and 45.3K tweets. When the data was checked for most original tweets, we found the same handles occupying the top positions. The list remained unchanged (See Figure 34).

ORIGINAL TWEETS	Tweets
@DigitalKisanBot Kisan Bot	2,953
@pacifistrebel The Pacifist Rebel	2,820
@SupreemJohn John	1,640
@VickyGurm143 ਸਰਦਾਰ ਸਾਬ (A Farm...	1,547
@tasversandhu Dnt Lie Loser Mod	1,309

Figure 34: Most original tweets

MOST POPULAR	Followers
@ndtv NDTV	17,744,948
@timesofindia The Times Of India	14,683,187
@TimesNow TIMES NOW	10,319,094
@INCIndia Congress	9,412,179
@htTweets Hindustan Times	8,704,242

Figure 35: Most popular handles

However, the list changed drastically when the contributor data was fetched for the maximum popularity, i.e. contributors with the highest number of followers in this data set. @NDTV, followed by @TimesofIndia, @TimesNow, and other media organisations occupied the top slots. Only one political party makes an appearance in this list, @AamAadmiParty. @YourAnonNews is present in this list too (See Figure 35).

Handles that have had the most impact i.e. tweets x followers are all media houses with @NDTV taking the lead (See Figure 36).

HIGHEST IMPACT	Impacts
@ndtv NDTV	2,271,187,042
@IndiaToday IndiaToday	1,170,315,151
@htTweets Hindustan Times	792,070,971
@ZeeNewsEnglish Zee News English	372,382,389
@TimesNow Times Now	216,698,598

Figure 36: Highest impact

Top retweet engagers, top likes and most retweets

TOP RTS ENGAGERS	Rts	TOP LIKES ENGAGERS	Likes	MOST RETWEETED	Retweets
@satishacharya Satish Acharya	2,282.33	@Imangadbedi ANGAD BEDI	21,142.00	@NKJammu Navneet us	87,377
@Imangadbedi ANGAD BEDI	1,923.00	@satishacharya Satish Acharya	10,586.33	@indijaswaloye Indi Jaswal	73,263
@srivatsayb Srivatsa	1,676.33	@sherryontopp Navjot Singh Sidhu	9,270.00	@Tractor2twitr Tractor2ट्विटर	39,660
@indijaswaloye Indi Jaswal	1,559.21	@KTRBRS KTR	7,616.00	@karajlahoria97 koraj_Lahoria_	31,879
@sherryontopp Navjot Singh Sidhu	1,360.00	@RoflGandhi_ Rofl Gandhi 2.0	6,530.00	@ikaur_deep ਅਕਾਲਦੀਪ ਸਿੰਘ	24,018

Figure 37: Top average Rts for original tweets with hashtag, top likes and most retweeted

The top retweet engagers are the contributors ranked by average number of retweets they received with their original tweets with hashtags under study. Top likes engagers are the contributors ranked by the average number of likes to their original tweets with hashtags under study. The average number of retweets received are ranked under the column Most retweeted.

As we can see, the first two columns in Figure 37 show some similarities. Contributors who got maximum likes were also the ones who got more retweets to their original tweet. Their ranks shift a bit but overall the top ten has these common handles.

@satishacharya: This handle makes an appearance in the first two positions in the categories of most retweet engagers and most like engagers. Surprisingly, though he got maximum retweets and likes for his original tweets, he does not figure in the most original tweets list (See Figure 37). According to his Twitter handle, Satish Acharya is a cartoonist from Kundapur in Karnataka. He has published several books and has provided the links on his handle. He has 333.9K followers and 42.6K tweets to his credit. His bio reads 'Editorial cartoonist, cricket, films' suggesting his areas of interest. Interestingly, the image of a cartoon drawn and tweeted by him got the top slot in the most liked and most retweeted photograph. However, since it was not technically a photograph it was not included in the analysis.

@Iamangadbedi: Angad Bedi is a film and TV star with 53.6K followers and 13.2K tweets. His bio reads, 'Main PENDU bada URBAN!!' which when translated means, 'I am a very urban villager'.

@srivatsayb: According to his Twitter handle bio, he is a Congress worker. He is followed by 296.2K followers including Priyanka Gandhi Vadra. He has 86.7K tweets. He joined Twitter in June 2009.

@sherryontop: This handle belongs to Navjot Singh Sidhu. The bio reads 'Fr President PPCC, Son of my soil; MLA; Fr Cabinet Minister Punjab; 4term MP; Cricketer; Commentator; Motivational Speaker; TV Personality'. With 1 million followers, he has 1822 tweets to his credit. The cover page of his handle shows a picture of him with Congress leaders Priyanka Gandhi Vadra and Rahul Gandhi.

@Meghupdates: It is an open-source news handle. No identity is revealed in the handle. The bio reads, 'Bringing headlines to you, open source, likes not endorsements, Contact at telegram @-t.me/MEGHUPDATES.' The handle is followed by 221K followers and has 14.8K tweets.

@prakashraaj: The handle belongs to a popular film star. His bio reads, 'let's give back to life', and his cover page shows a mob of people with a caption, 'India is ready for an alternative'. He has 2.7-million followers. He has 4320 tweets to his credit.

@koenamitra: This handle belongs to a film star. Her bio reads, 'Film actor, animal lover, spiritual warrior, gypsy soul.... brat!' She is followed by 268.5K users and has 5522 tweets to her credit.

@KTRBRS: KT Rama Rao is the only politician to figure so prominently through his personal account. His bio reads, 'Personal account of Minister for Municipal Admin & Urban Dev, Industry & Commerce, ITE&C | MLA from Siricilla, Telangana.' He has 4-million followers and 22.1K tweets.

As I was looking at each profile, I realised that there was a judicious mix of pro and anti-farm laws mix in this group of contributors who have been liked and retweeted the most for their original tweets.

Others @indijaswaloye, and @maya206 had the most retweets, while @ROFLGandhi and @MohdZeeshanAyyub had the most likes.

As I studied the list of those handles that have received maximum retweets in this report, I find only one handle is common in any other two lists. @indijaswaloye figures in the list of top handles that have the largest average number of retweets for their original tweet with hashtag (first column in Figure 37) and also the maximum retweets.

@indijaswaloye is a handle from Surrey, UK with 44.4K followers, and 381 tweets. While searching for him I found his parody account too.

Others on the list of most retweeted users are all new handles.

Topping the list is @NKJammu. Her name is Navneet Kaur and her bio does not say anything. However, next to her name is the British flag, although she mentions her location as Global. Her cover page says, 'We don't have to agree on anything to be kind to each other.' She has 6195 followers and 59K tweets. She is followed by @indijaswaloye and @Tractor2twitr. Upon searching for this handle @Tractor2twitr, it was found that the account has been withheld in India in response to a legal demand. I shall discuss the legal aspects in the coming pages.

@karajlahoria97: The account of an activist of the 'Davinder Bambiha group' as he says in the bio. He also adds, 'Fear those people, Those who have a mind in their heart.' His profile picture features the protesting wrestlers, (which is a protest on another issue that is not a part of this sample). He has 2319 followers and 64.7K tweets.

@ikaur_deep belongs to Gagandeep Kaur. Her bio reads, 'And miles to go before I sleep….' And the profile picture is of an avatar. She has 2332 followers and 27K tweets. She mentions her location as Punjab.

@japneet_19: Japneet mentions her location as Punjab and her bio reads, *Dekhi chal mardaniyan rang kartar de, aape mar jande dujiyan nu jo marde*, which roughly translated means, 'Keep watching God's ways, those who kill others themselves die'. She has 3543 followers and 36.5K tweets.

@__Taman: The handle belongs to Tapanpreet Kaur. She has decorated the page with many emojis and her bio reads, *Paix, Amour, Bonheur* which are French words meaning Peace, Love and Happiness. Further the bio reads Punjab, Punjabi and Punjabiyat, which means, Punjab as in the state, Punjabi as in the language spoken in Punjab and Punjabiyat is the culture of Punjab. She has 3546 followers and 9259 tweets.

@_KingRaga_: He claims that he is Rahul Gandhi's fan in his bio. His profile picture is of the Congress leader Rahul Gandhi and cover photo also shows Congress party leadership. The profile picture carries a slogan in Kannada which means, If Congress comes to power, it shall bring prosperity. He is followed by 1221 users and has 78.7K tweets.

@itsBrarBaby: This handle belongs to Jazz, Garam Khayali from Canada. She has 11.3K followers and 241K tweets. Her cover photo shows Bhagat Singh, Rajguru and Sukhdev. Profile picture shows a pretty girl dressed in bridal finery. The picture may or may not be hers.

@Amandeep_45: Amandeep Kaur has a small village girl on her profile picture and a picture of a farmer holding a roti to his forehead on her cover page. Her bio reads *lagi je tere kalje hale chhuri nahin, ih na samajh ki Shahir di halat buri nahin*, which in translation means, 'Till the time you don't have a knife in your heart you are unable to see the worsening condition of the city'. She has 1442 followers and 165.2K tweets.

As the above illustrates, women make a powerful appearance in the most retweeted list while they were in minority in all the other lists so far.

Overall, the group is a combination of men, women of all age groups, pro and antifarm laws, activists, film stars and politicians. Anyone who found a voice and had something to say used the platform and got retweeted and liked by large numbers. A platform where the celebrities and the common people rub shoulders.

As we study the next table at Figure 37, we find that the most liked tweets have already featured in some of the above lists. The same handles, @indijaswaloye, @NKJammu, @Tractor2twtr, @satishacharya, @karajlahoria97 have already been introduced. @NDTV is the only media organisation to have got maximum likes. Others who appear here are @ramanmann1974, and @RaviSinghKA, @rakhitripathi and @saahilmenghani.

@ramanmann1974 is a farmer as it appears from his profile picture and bio. His bio reads, 'Engineer by education; want to make #Farminga profession of hope…again!' He has 33.3K followers and 105K tweets.

The account of @RaviSinghKA is also withheld.

@rakhitripathi: This is the first academician to make it to any list. She says in her bio, 'Against inequality; Associate Professor, Digital technologies and social issues.' She goes on to share a link of the videos of Prof VK Tripathi. She has 57K followers and is located in Delhi. She has 42.9K tweets.

@saahilmenghani is the handle of Sahil Murali Menghani with 104.6K followers and 24.7K tweets. He is an independent journalist and fact checker. His bio says, 'Independent Journalist || Head, Wire's Fact Check Unit || Contributor - UK's Channel 4, & Norway's NRK TV || Over the years- YKA, ToI & News Anchor at CNN.' He shares his Instagram handle in the bio too. So far this is the first journalist who has made an appearance in any of the lists.

MOST FAVORITED	Likes	MOST MENTIONED	Mentions
@indijaswaloye — Indi Jaswal	92,110	@narendramodi — Narendra Modi	4,986
@NKJammu — Navneet us	63,465	@kisanektamorcha — Kisan Ekta Morcha	3,240
@Tractor2twitr — Tractor2ट्विटर	56,781	@pmoindia — PMO India	2,661
@ramanmann1974 — Ramandeep Sing...	49,303	@tractor2twitr — Tractor2ट्विटर	2,297
@RaviSinghKA — ravinder singh	39,655	@rakeshtikaitbku — Rakesh Tikait	1,844

Figure 38: Most favoured and Most mentioned

As far as the most mentioned handles are concerned, as is evident in Figure 38, political leaders, leaders of opposition, political parties, politically active entertainers, and some farmer leaders are mentioned.

@tractor2twitr account, which has been withheld in India,

is also a part of this list. Media and public continue to debate the reasons behind the withholding of certain accounts to the extent that Twitter co-founder Jack Dorsey accused the Government of India of pressuring the platform to block accounts related to farmers' protests and criticism of the government, threatening to shut down the platform and raid employees' homes (Mukhopadhyay, 2023). The government vehemently denied the allegations, with Deputy Minister for Information Technology, Rajeev Chandrasekhar, calling these assertions an 'outright lie'. (Reuters, 2023). There are always two sides to the coin and the discussion here is based on two core values of society. I shall discuss them further in the next chapter.

Moving on, let us look at some other statistics that were collected as part of the sample mostly about the demographics of the sample.

Average tweet per contributor: Most users have tweeted 4.63 tweets during this time frame, using these three hashtags. Figure 39 shows the average number of tweets per contributor. As we can see 66.38 per cent users have only tweeted once and only 7.64 per cent have tweeted more than seven times.

TWEETS/CONTRIBUTORS			4.63 tweets/ contributor
TWEETS	CONTRIBUTORS	%TOTAL	
1	24149	66.38%	
2	4937	13.57%	
3	2090	5.74%	
4	1176	3.23%	
5	712	196%	
6	537	148%	
>=7	2779	7.64%	

Figure 39: Tweets per contributor
Age of Twitter account in years and length of Tweet in characters

The terms XS, S, M, L, XL in the first column (Figure 40) denote the age of the Twitter account counted as the number of years the account has been active. Notice the data, which shows that young accounts were on 7.09 per cent (XS) and 29.24 per cent (S) while the XXL accounts (More than 6 years old) are 42.19 per cent. This proves that although younger accounts were less in number, they commanded more value as compared to older accounts. They used the right hashtags and got better reach and impressions.

Younger Twitter accounts tweeted more frequently and clearly articulated the goals and objectives of the protest, thereby becoming instrumental in attracting support and galvanising participants. Through effective communication, they created a shared sense of purpose, fostered a collective identity, and articulated the demands that resonated with the grievances of the protesters. The younger accounts provided a framework for the movement's aspirations and guided the development of strategic objectives.

It is possible to operate within a broader sociopolitical landscape and navigate the dynamics of power, public opinion, and media coverage. The need is to effectively engage with the

AGE OF THE TWITTER ACCOUNTS				LENGTH OF THE TWEETS			157.35 characters/tweet
YEAR	USERS	%TOTAL		YEAR	USERS	%TOTAL	
XXS (0-1)	24149	0%		XXS (0-40)	3525	2.09%	
XXS (1-2)	4937	7.09%		XXS (40-80)	31067	18.46%	
S (2-5)	2090	29.24%		S (80-120)	31384	18.65%	
M (3-4)	1176	10.42%		M (120-160)	26695	15.86%	
L (4-5)	712	5.4%		L (160-200)	21655	12.87%	
XL (5-5)	537	5.67%		XL (200-240)	18181	10.8%	
XXL (6-∞)	2779	42.19%		XXL (240-∞)	35782	21.26%	

Figure 40: Age of account & Length of tweet

media, disseminate messages to wider audiences, and leverage public support to generate momentum and influence public discourse. All of these were visible during the agitation.

The data about the length of tweet shows that average length of the tweet was 157.35 characters. This is closer to the 140-character limit that Twitter used to have earlier. Yet, 20.26 users, which is the highest figure in this table, have used 240 characters in their tweet. This means that the largest group of people who tweeted about the issue were interested in longer tweets.

Influence as per number of followers: Each tweeter had a minimum of 8-9 followers. Notice data in Figure 41 of contributor influence in terms of followers, which shows the XXS accounts had 15.35 influence as compared to XXL accounts who had 7.14 per cent. Maximum influence was exerted by the accounts that have been categorised as XS, S and M. This proves that a higher number of followers leads to better influence.

CONTRIBUTOR INFLUENCE			4.63 tweets/ contributor
FOLLOWERS	CONTRIBUTORS	%TOTAL	
XXS (0-10)	5584	15.35%	
XXS (10-50)	7895	27.7%	
S (50-200)	7339	20.17%	
M (200-500)	4633	12.74%	
L (500-1000)	3061	8.41%	
XL (1000-5000)	5271	14.49%	
XXL (5000-∞)	2597	7.14%	

Figure 41: As per followers

Most Retweeted and Most Liked Tweet

@satisheharya was the handle that got the most retweets, a total of 3729 times. Next six positions are occupied by @indijaswaloye followed by @RaviSinghKA and @TanDesi. These handles seem familiar because they have appeared in our discussion about most retweeted engagers and most liked engagers. This does prove that a few people dominated the Twitter discourse.

most retweeted tweets

satishacharya | 1 year ago | 3729

3 Farm Bills to be withdrawn! #FarmersProtest #farmbills #elections https://t.co/j8rMPOFTvf

Figure 42: Most retweeted tweet

Similarly, the most liked tweet came from @Iamangadbedi who has closely followed @Satisheharya on the lists of most powerful engagers. This particular tweet (See Figure 24) was liked by 21,142 users. Others who followed are @satisheharya, @AlmeidaJugnu, @SherryOnTopp, @ramanmann1974, @KTRBRS, @GauravPandhi.

Out of all, the new accounts that have appeared in this list are @AlmeidaJugnu and @GauravPandhi.

@AlmeidaJugnu: The full name on the account is Jugnu Grewal Almeida and the bio reads, 'Mum, Realtor, FarmGirl,

Punjab.' The profile picture is of a pleasant woman. The cover picture shows a woman's pout and the statement, 'Well behaved women seldom make history' in bold. She has a total of 6959 tweets and 1223 followers.

most liked tweets

Imangadbedi | 2 year ago | 21142 Likes

Be responsible national media. This is the face of a person who provides food to billions of people... it's the face of a farmer. #IamWithFarmers@diljitdosanjh https://t.co/jV6R1CFW2Q

Figure 43: Most liked tweet

Almeida has pinned a tweet on her profile which incidentally is of the most liked photo as per this data set. Analysis of the two most prominent photos is carried out in the following pages.

@GauravPandhi: Gaurav Pandhi is a Congress party worker. His account is verified, and his bio reads, 'Congressman, AICC Coordinator, Office of Congress President Shri Mallikarjun @Kharge.' He also mentions that Views and Opinions are personal. He has 50.4K tweets and 200.2K followers. He uses his own picture as a profile photo and his cover photo shows the Buddhist Dhamma Chakra and an inscription that says,; Even if you are a minority of one, truth is the truth.' His account provides a link to his website which cannot be reached.

Top Photographer/Top Photo Contributors

The list of top photographers has been drawn up on the basis of the highest number of photos uploaded. These contributors are not photographers in the professional sense, but all Twitter users who uploaded photos on the social media have been put under the umbrella term of top photographer. We have (See Figure 44) already noted some accounts in previous discussion such as @NKJammu and @-KingRaga_ We shall look at the profiles of others mentioned in this list.

The handle which has posted the maximum number of photos is @sidhuparshotam1. The name on the account is Parshotam Singh Sidhu. His is a relatively young account, having started in April 2021. He has 105K tweets and 771 followers. His profile picture is his own photo, and the cover photo is a picture of the Golden Temple. A scroll down his account does show that he has been posting pictures with every tweet. Figure 44 provides the entire list of top photo contributors.

TOP PHOTOGRAPHER	Photos
@sidhuparshotam1 PARSHOTAM SIN...	1,076
@NKJammu Navneet us	672
@_KingRaga_ Rahul Gandhi F...	669
@vashishtvp Er. VP Vashisht	573
@Singhmaan923 SINGHMAAN	468

Figure 44: Top Photo Contributors

Analysis of Top Photo

As explained in Chapter 4 under the section Methodology, the top tweeted photograph is analysed by using a method of visual social semiotics. Since the data has thrown two separate photographs as top tweeted, in the form of most liked, and most retweeted, both photographs are being analysed using the Kress and van Leeuwen framework. This framework recognises that an image simultaneously performs three kinds of meta-semiotic tasks to create meaning. These tasks are called the representational meta-function, interpersonal meta-function, and compositional meta-function. The same framework has been used to analyse the top photograph in the Nirbhaya Case. The framework has been explained in detail in Chapter 4.

Most liked and Most Retweeted Images

Figure 45 : Most liked image from the handle @almeidaJugnu
Retrieved from https://twitter.com/AlmeidaJugnu

Most liked Picture

@AlmeidaJugnu has already been discussed as one of the most liked tweets and it was mentioned that she had pinned a tweet to her profile. This is the pinned tweet and the photograph in the tweet as shown in Figure 45 is the most liked photograph.

Structure and Processes of Representational Meta-Function

As regards structure, in this picture vectors are not present to show the movement of the Representative Personality (RP), therefore, I would not classify the picture as a narrative. The structure is conceptual as RPs tend to be grouped together to present viewers with the 'concept' of who or what they represent. The entire group of women sitting on a tractor is a very powerful image and signifies the power of women in the struggle.

The tweet is from a woman's handle; the main RP is a woman accompanied by at least six other women. There are seven women in the picture. Five are looking at the camera, one is partially hidden, one is far away in the background with her back to the camera.

All women are wearing *salwar kameez* which is a traditional dress of Punjabi women. Significantly all are wearing bright yellow dupatta or stoles. In Punjabi culture, the colour yellow holds significant cultural and traditional symbolism. It is associated with various aspects of Punjabi customs, festivities, and everyday life. For example, during the harvest festival of Baisakhi people traditionally wear yellow-coloured attire as a symbol of abundance, prosperity, and good fortune. Yellow symbolises the golden fields of wheat, mustard, and other crops during the harvest season. It represents the hard work of farmers, the fertility of the land, and the prosperity brought by a successful harvest, the vibrant and warm spirit of the Punjabi people, their zest for life, and their exuberance. It is often associated with the cheerful and hospitable nature of Punjabi culture, with positivity, optimism, and enlightenment. It is believed to uplift the mood, radiate positive energy, and bring about a sense of warmth and cheerfulness.

In the picture the yellow dupatta is eye catching and increases the shareability of the picture. The group of women is sitting on a tractor which itself is symbolic of the farmer, the farm, rural life, rural ethos, or anything to do with farmers, including the farmers' agitation. The farmers had camped at the border of Delhi having arrived in tractors from their villages, they had also held a parallel Kisan Parade in January of 2021 with an entire contingent of tractors. Therefore, the tractor is a symbol of the agitation in this picture. The tractor is also a symbol of power and strength. It represents the women's ability to take control of their own lives and to make their own decisions.

Caption: We did it! #farmerswin, #farmersprotest. Clear, concise, and easily understood, the caption is a winner at many levels. It hits hard with the message. It shows exuberance, a sense of joy in the victory and pride in having won it. It contains an inclusive personal pronoun, 'We', which shows solidarity, and spirit of togetherness. In a very short succinct message the caption speaks to the reader. When accompanied by the picture the caption becomes a powerful statement of farmers unity, women's success in their mission.

The processes are analytical, and symbolic. The RPs are displayed in terms of a 'part-whole' structure. The 'whole' is the agitation and its parts called Attributes are the agitating farmers. It is a symbolic process too because the RPs are important for what they 'mean'. They don't just mean a group of women sitting in a vehicle. The meaning is much beyond that. As attributes of the agitation, they are a smiling, victorious group of women who have shouldered a responsibility and overcome all hurdles and achieved what they set out to do.

The basic structure and processes of representational meta-function make this a very powerful image and the smiles on the women's faces are a symbol of joy and satisfaction. They represent the women's acknowledgement of their accomplishment and their gratitude for the support of their community.

The picture is a reminder of the strength and resilience of women. It is a call to action too.

Thereby, it got 1196 retweets, 81 quotes, 9986 likes, 42 bookmarks.

Structure and Processes of Interpersonal Meta Function are:

Features, Image Act, and Gaze. The image act in this picture involves the eye line of the RP(s) in relation to the viewer. The main RP is looking straight into the camera and therefore appears to be looking into the eyes of the viewer. Social distance and intimacy come into play because social distance is determined by how close RPs in an image appear to the viewer, thereby resulting in feelings of intimacy or distance. In the picture there are seven RPs but five of them figure prominently and they are visible from a far personal distance (from the waist up) and a close social distance because the whole figure of one of the RPs is visible. The angle is frontal and creates stronger involvement on the part of the viewer as it implies that the RP is 'one of us'. The RP also has equal power as the viewer because they are looking at him horizontally. Horizontal frontal angles are the best for introducing involvement and connection in a photograph.

The feature processes are demand and offer. In this picture, the feature of demand is present because the RP looks at the viewer and smiles at him through a horizontal frontal angle of the camera at the far personal and close social distance. The RP demands attention. In this picture it is not one RP but at least five of them demanding action through their gaze.

It is not a surprise that the picture compelled the viewers to get impressed by the message and press the like button catering to the demand.

The basic structure and processes of the compositional meta-function depends on the placement of RPs and allows them to take on different information roles.

In this picture the RPs are placed centrally. They are occupying the entire picture and the main RP is in the center stage. When the RPs are placed in this manner, they provide the nucleus of information to which surrounding elements are subservient. Also, because they are factual, informative, down to earth, practical. The RPs hold the picture together, they are in the foreground and are large. The larger the RP the greater the salience. The picture is sharp with strongly saturated colours having high tonal contrasts that add to the effectiveness of the picture in terms of composition.

Most Retweeted Picture

The most retweeted picture is such a graceful finale to this analysis. I was blown away by the quality of photography both in technical as well as symbolic terms. Kindly look at the picture in Figure 46. The picture is clicked by Ravan Khosa.

Figure 46: Most retweeted photo from the account of @indijaswaloye
Retrieved from https://twitter.com/indijaswaloye

@indijaswaloye has already figured in our previous lists. His tweets have been popular during the agitation. This picture was tweeted on 27 May 2021 with two hashtags, #farmlawsthreattoIndians and #farmersprotest.

In the first glance the picture paints a poignant portrayal of a Sikh farmer, capturing the essence of their resilience, connection to the land, and the laborious nature of their work. It showcases the farmer's sense of purpose, dignity, and commitment, evoking emotions of respect, admiration, and a recognition of the essential role played by farmers in sustaining communities and the agricultural sector. No matter how it is interpreted, the picture is a powerful and moving image of a man who is facing the challenges of life with strength, dignity, and determination. The symbolism in the picture is apparent. The plough is a symbol of hard work and the struggle to provide for one's family. The man's dignified bearing is a symbol of his pride and self-respect.

On a deeper study of the picture one can discern that an elderly Sikh farmer suggests a connection to traditional agricultural practices and a representation of the farming community. The Sikh faith places a strong emphasis on humility, hard work, and selfless service, which are reflected in the character and demeanor of the farmer.

The image of the farmer holding a plough signifies his connection to the land and his role as a cultivator. The plough is a symbol of labour, perseverance, and the farmer's dedication to his agricultural work. It represents the farmer's commitment to sustenance and his integral role in the agricultural landscape.

The choice of off-white clothes worn by the farmer may symbolise simplicity, purity, and a connection to traditional attire. The color choice suggests a sense of authenticity and harmony with nature.

The farmer's straight posture indicates strength, resilience, and a sense of purpose. His calm expression suggests a determination and a deep connection to the land. It may reflect the farmer's ability to endure challenges and maintain composure in the face of adversity. The farmer's gaze towards the horizon symbolises the farmer's vision for a prosperous future, his connection to the cycles of nature, or his contemplation of the tasks at hand. The dignified appearance of the farmer implies a sense of self-respect, honour, and pride in his work. The description of the farmer's soiled hands and tired appearance reflects the physical demands of agricultural labour, highlighting the farmer's hard work, dedication, and connection to the earth.

Although the shadows behind him show the obstacles

faced by him, the stoic expression shows his determination.

Let us now analyse it as per Kress and van Leeuwen framework which analyses the pictures through three kinds of meta-semiotic tasks to create meaning. These tasks are called the representational meta-function, interpersonal meta-function, and compositional meta-function.

The Basic Structure and Processes of Representational Meta-Function are:

Structure could be narrative, which allows viewers to create a story about the Representative Personality/ies (RP) and the images include vectors of motion. They could be conceptual which include images that do not include vectors. I would like to classify this picture as narrative because the elderly Sikh farmer (RP) actually tells a story. Although there is no apparent movement in the picture, the vectors of motion are present. The farmer seems to be moving in the right direction and his eyes are looking beyond the picture and outside of it.

In this picture the processes are actional and reactional because of the way the arms are holding the plough and the narrative is being created by the eye lines that are acting as vectors of motion. We could also include the symbolic process because the man himself is a symbol of farmers' resilience and determination. He is not just a man with a plough but a representative of all the farmers and all their hard work.

Considering the interpersonal meta function, the image act involves the eye line of the RP in relation to the viewer. Our RP is looking towards the horizon and has a worried or sad expression in his eyes. He could be contemplative or apprehensive. His gaze is unwavering and fixed towards the right of the picture. He is not looking at the viewer and not trying to establish any connection. The image is at a far personal distance from the viewer and since he is gazing outwards, he is not demanding any attention but offering a chance to contemplate. The viewer too feels the depth of his gaze. The angle of the picture is horizontal meaning that the RP has the same power as the viewer. They are both equals.

With regard to the compositional meta function, in this picture the RP is on the left side of the image and has the value of being 'given' knowledge which could mean that there is an easy familiarity between the viewer and the RP.

As already explained in the methodology, this value is based on the fact that we read from left to right in English. This does not necessarily apply to languages in which reading occurs from right to left or in columns.

The RP in this picture is in the centre providing the nucleus of information to which surrounding elements are subservient. The salience of the RP in this picture is immense.

The ability of an RP to capture the viewer's attention depends on the size of the picture, its sharpness of focus, tonal contrast and colour contrast. All the elements are in perfect order making the picture instantly attractive and memorable.

The RP is very much in the foreground, very aptly representing the agitation. No wonder the picture attracted the users, and it was retweeted 3448 times, quoted 176 times, and liked 3291 times.

Synthesis and Insights
Unpacking Findings, Unveiling Perspectives

> *Research is what I'm doing when I don't know what I'm doing.*
> - **Wernher von Braun (1912-1977)**, German American Physicist and Rocket Engineer whose team launched the first US satellite into space.

THIS QUOTE RESONATES in my mind as I embark on the process of discussing the findings. It encapsulates the essence of a researcher's journey, evoking a sense of anticipation and trepidation. With each step, fresh research questions emerge, prompting the evolution of innovative methodologies to unravel their mysteries. As intriguing findings unfold, they beckon to be shared with those eager to participate in the journey. The process itself becomes an enlightening expedition, fostering personal growth and discovery. As we come together, you and I, we are poised to unveil the culmination of our initial quest and the beginning of a new one.

In this ever-evolving landscape of technology, media, and communication systems, momentous changes are destined to unfold. Let us pause and reflect on this moment in time which is a profound convergence of human intellect and artificial intelligence. By the time you read this, the methods employed and the medium used may have metamorphosed into new forms. This study is not just about media and methods, it is about humans coming together online and offline in the form of protests. Rest assured, as long as human existence endures, revolutions will continue to shape our collective destiny. Some revolutions shall manifest at the technological level, while others shall resound within the depths of our humanity. Humans shall always find causes to gather in city squares, to organise and raise their voices. Remarkably, it is in the fusion of technological and human revolutions that true marvels arise. And so, this study shall stand as a testament to this pivotal decade, preserved in time—a profound encapsulation of our age.

I shall commence this discussion by drawing inspiration from Christianson's classification of the four stages of revolution—emergence, coalescence, bureaucratisation, and decline. The preceding pages have unfurled the narratives of two distinct cases, each traversing the aforementioned stages. While the Nirbhaya rape case swiftly surged to its zenith and waned, the farmers' agitation unfolded over an extended period, spanning more than a year. These cases, though disparate, warrant no direct comparison. In the Nirbhaya case, a unanimous sentiment prevailed, leaving no room for dissent or contention. The protests epitomised an outpouring of anguish, despair, shock, and collective grief. Conversely, the farmers' agitation manifested as a revolt, a defiance against the prevailing order—a resolute rebellion resonating within a collective voice.

The two share certain similarities despite their distinct contexts. Both movements witnessed widespread public outcry and garnered significant attention across the nation. They exemplified collective mobilisation and highlighted the public's demand for justice and societal change. Both movements represented a form of resistance against perceived injustices and sought to challenge the existing systems and policies. They ignited a sense of solidarity and unity among the participants, fostering a shared sentiment of outrage and empathy. The Nirbhaya case addressed issues of gender-based violence and women's safety, while the farmers' agitation revolved around concerns related to agricultural reforms and livelihoods, both serving as reminders of the power of collective action and both being successful in bringing about the desired change.

To keep the discussion focused, a systematic navigation of data is being undertaken to substantiate each objective delineated in Chapter IV.

Two extensive tweet corpora were collected and subjected to an overarching analysis in accordance with the first objective. The tweets, obtained from the online archive service www.topsy.com, encompassed three hashtags (#Nirbhaya, #delhigangrape, #Delhirape) to capture the public discourse on Twitter. The archivist site provided insights into 'all time influencers', 'exposure', 'sentiment', and 'top links'. Acceleration, peak, and momentum analyses unveiled the most frequently used terms in the tweets. An examination of volume, content patterns, topics, and prominent users during the specified timeframe (16 December 2012 to 16 January 2013) was done. Out of the total 335,528 tweets, 168,518 originated from India. Twitter appeared to democratise the pursuit of justice by facilitating the inclusion of the common man in the discussion, removing barriers of social status. However, public attention waned over time as other events took precedence, though the impact of the movement transcended the online realm. The issue gradually diminished in significance by 9 January 2013.

The analysis for the Nirbhaya Case utilised resources provided by www.topsy.com, a recommended source from the American Library of Congress, Washington DC. However, it is important to note that the website has since been discontinued. Consequently, I redirected my efforts to www.twitterbinder.com, which served as the data source for the farmers' agitation. This website provided tweets associated with the requested hashtags, as well as sentiment analysis and economic value metrics. The three hashtags examined, namely #Farmersprotest, #tractortotwitter, and #Iamwithfarmers, represented the most prevalent hashtags during the agitation. The total number of tweets collected for the period spanning 26 November 2020 to 30 November 2021 was 1,479,808. It is crucial to acknowledge that a direct comparison between the number of tweets in the two cases is not feasible, as the data for one case spans a month while the other covers a year. Additionally, it is noteworthy that the analysis of sentiment and economic value was exclusive to the farmers' agitation and was not conducted during the Nirbhaya Case, reflecting the evolving nature of Twitter analytics over time.

The second objective entailed the identification of influential individuals who garnered significant attention through mentions, retweets, and overall engagements regarding the subject under investigation. In both the Nirbhaya case and the farmers' agitation, diverse stakeholders such as the organised media sector, celebrities, and the general public participated in the discourse. However, in the farmers' agitation, media involvement was more prominent, with a few specific channels taking the lead, while celebrity engagement was comparatively limited. Interestingly, a particular Twitter account, @DigitalKisanBot, emerged as the most active contributor during the farmers' agitation. When a bot tweets, it means that an automated program or script has been designed to generate and post content on the social media platform Twitter. Bots can be programmed to perform a variety of tasks such as sharing news updates, providing customer support, posting automated responses, or spreading information based on predefined criteria. Bots can interact with other users, reply to mentions or messages, and even retweet or like other tweets. The purpose of bot-generated tweets can vary depending on the intentions of the creator. Some bots aim to provide helpful and relevant information, while others may be designed to manipulate public opinion or engage in spam-like behaviour. The presence of bots in online discourse raises concerns about discerning machine-generated content from human-generated content, as individuals can employ machines to serve their specific purposes. Heightened vigilance is necessary to critically evaluate and comprehend information and interactions in the face of evolving technological landscapes.

Since a bot is the highest tweeter, it appears as though the job of opinion building will be handed over to artificial intelligence in the future. In that case, Web 3.0 is likely to change the dynamics of social activism and future opinion leaders will create what we can imagine as 'Botopinion' which will be a highly calculated, ever-changing take on events as they continue to happen. Botopinion indices will be used for the purpose of target-oriented dissemination of content including advertising.

The third objective was to find the influence of media organisations on the number and impact of tweets. In both the Nirbhaya case and the farmers' agitation, media organisations played a prominent role as influencers. Among the top influencers, the majority consisted of renowned news channels, and one newspaper, the Hindustan Times, being represented. The substantial presence of news channels on Twitter indicates their influential role in shaping affective news. Affective news streams are conceptualised by Papacharissi and Oliveira (2012) in their study of #Egypt, highlight the collaborative construction of news based on subjective experiences, opinions, and emotions within an ambient news environment. Affective news signifies the convergence of medium, masses, and messages into an interconnected entity. Yet, to better understand the transfer of agendas from social media to news channels, further investigation is necessary. Among the influential channels, @NDTV stands out with its breaking news alerts from India, boasting a significant number of tweets and followers. During both the Nirbhaya case and the farmers' agitation, @NDTV, @httweets, @zeenews, and @timesnow emerged as the most prominent channels. Media organisations, notably @NDTV and @TimesofIndia, dominated the top slots in terms of followers and impact, also media organisations held the highest distribution of top accounts based on value, with only @INCIndia and @AamAadmiParty, representing political parties, making it into the top 10. This data sheds light on the significance of text tweets from these accounts, with NDTV occupying the foremost position, followed by the Times Group. Both newspapers and news channels wielded considerable influence within this landscape.

The economic impact of hashtags during the farmers' agitation has been examined. Among the analysed data sets, specific hashtags like #Delhigangrape and #farmersprotest had gained considerable prominence, being utilised by roughly 90 per cent of Twitter users, indicating their significant economic value. The economic value of a hashtag is influenced by factors such as its popularity, relevance, contextual usage, and the goals of individuals or organisations employing it. By capitalising on a popular or trending hashtag, individuals and organisations can expand the reach of their content, potentially attracting new followers, customers, or supporters. Thus, the economic value of a hashtag represents a conceptual framework for assessing its market worth. However, it is important to note that in this context, the economic value represents a theoretical value of the tweet and hashtag, as the tweets were not directly selling products but establishing brand value for the users.

In the analysed report, @NDTV has emerged as the most valuable tweeter, with a cumulative value of all the tweets being Rs 1,121,219,060.80/-. This valuation provides an economic estimation of the hashtags and contributors if they were to be utilised for a business venture. It substantiates the notion that ideas and opinions can be effectively promoted through Twitter. Moreover, the report indicates an average user value of Rs 1466.86/-, and the average value of a tweet is remarkably high at Rs 662.46. This analysis underscores the influential nature of each user and each tweet, serving as a potent source of inspiration, connection, and motivation toward the cause. It further emphasises the power of hashtags in driving engagement and impact. Although users with very few followers called S users, possess an economic value ranging from Rs 0 to Rs 88.47, they constitute the largest segment of tweets, exerting significant influence. The term 'most expensive tweet' generally pertains to a tweet that has generated substantial financial or cultural impact, driven by factors such as the account's follower count, the tweet's content, or the contextual circumstances surrounding its posting. In the ranking of most expensive tweets, @NDTV scores the top three slots establishing its position as the most influential media market leader in both these cases. It is significant knowledge because the cases are nine years apart and the channel has maintained its lead.

The presence of TV channels and newspapers in the highest tweeting, economically viable and most influential tweets suggest a collaboration between new and legacy media. By establishing their presence online, the legacy media organisations benefit from direct interaction with users, using hashtags to categorise content, and sharing multimedia for enhanced storytelling. They are prone to certain challenges such as oversimplification of news, misinformation, and adapting to Twitter's unique characteristics. However, the combination is powerful and influential.

One would have imagined celebrity tweets to throng the Twittersphere with their opinions and their many followers lapping up every word. The study has proved otherwise. We will look at the two aspects of prominence as we discuss celebrity involvement on social media. Prominence in news comprises two interconnected aspects, the status quo and status conferral. The status quo aspect reflects the prevailing power structures and societal norms that influence individuals, events, or topics that receive media attention. Established figures, such as political leaders and celebrities, often garner extensive coverage due to their existing influence. This perpetuates power imbalances and can marginalise alternative voices.

On the other hand, status conferral pertains to the media's ability to confer visibility, credibility, and influence on subjects through coverage and repetition. News organisations shape public perceptions by selecting and highlighting stories they deem significant, which can amplify voices and issues that might otherwise remain on the periphery. While the media plays a central role in status conferral, public interest and social media also influence prominence. Since both are present in the findings, it is reasonable to assume that media professionals, organisations, and celebrities collectively contribute to a space infused with diverse viewpoints. This collaborative construction primarily involves the most privileged individuals, representing the elitist segment. However, as the data has shown the most popular tweet did not really need a celebrity.

In the case of celebrities, politicians, and other influencers, their presence and engagement on Twitter signify the first tier of elitism, while their established status and influence in the offline world contribute to the second tier. This amalgamation of real-world and virtual status grants them the ability to surpass other Twitter users and ascend to the list of influencers. The notable figures, including @adityarajkaul, @kanchangupta, @rahulkanwal, @raheelk, @vikramchandra, @asher_wolf, @kamaalrkhan, @ayeshatakia, and @gulpanag, from the Nirbhaya case represent a combination of film stars, politicians, and other influential individuals. Although top politicians were not extensively active on Twitter, it is commonly assumed that influencers utilise social media to maintain their brand image. By leveraging their extensive reach and engaged audience, influencers effectively set agendas by drawing attention to specific topics, issues, or events. Their strategic content creation and dissemination prioritise certain subjects, thereby influencing public discourse and garnering attention. The compelling storytelling techniques employed by influencers enhance their agenda-setting potential. In the present data set, the minimal involvement of celebrities highlights the status conferral role of tweeters as becomes apparent when ordinary individuals interact with celebrity influencers. Notably, the common individuals in the Nirbhaya case were not famous personalities but were certainly not ordinary as they held positions in elite circles such as directors of organisations or members of political parties. Additionally, the economic value analysis of users, hashtags, and tweets in the farmers' protest reveals that the average tweet holds a remarkable value of Rs 662.46, underscoring their influential role as a source of inspiration, connection, and motivation. Users with lower economic values, ranging from Rs 0 to Rs 88.47, constitute the largest group of contributors, exerting significant influence. The most active non-bot handles, such as @pacifistrebel, @SupreemJohn, @VickyGurm143, and @tasveersandhu, consistently occupied top positions in terms of overall activity and original tweets, demonstrating the significance of consistency and regularity in tweeting for both maintaining existing prominence and establishing new identities.

The sentiment analysis of tweets focused solely on the farmers' agitation due to its contentious nature and clear existence of two opposing sides. In contrast, the sentiment in the Nirbhaya case was evident without any significant debate. The overall data demonstrates a leaning towards a neutral sentiment, which forms the core finding of the sentiment analysis. Despite the presence of physical evidence, such as ongoing protests, loss of lives disruptions in transportation, separate tractor marches on Indian Independence Day, and persistent demonstrations by supporters in cities like Chandigarh, the tweets predominantly expressed neutral sentiment. It is noteworthy that the online protest seemed to involve individuals residing in the United States, Canada, and various parts of India, while the plaza protests were primarily conducted by farmers in North India.

Upon further examination of the most active tweeters during the Farmers' agitation, the most prominent being the handle, @DigitalKisanBot, appeared to be a Twitter bot created in support of the farmers' cause. Its creator, @billingpuneet, is located in Atlanta, USA. Other notable handles that garnered maximum retweets and engagements include @satishacharya, a cartoonist from Karnataka, @prakashraaj, a popular South Indian film star, and @KTRBRS, a politician from Telangana among others. The diversity of these tweeters in terms of geographic location and potentially differing opinions contributes to the overall neutral sentiment observed in the final sentiment analysis. While it is challenging to ascertain whether the sentiment in the real world was truly neutral, the data reinforces the notion that the sentiment expressed in the Twittersphere leaned towards neutrality.

The last objective was to analyse the top tweeted photograph. The prominent photographs occupying the top positions on Twitter reflect the sensibilities of its users. All three images exhibit a social relevance that transcends political motivations and biases, instead emphasising values such as humanity, fair play, justice, and peace. These photographs serve to reaffirm our belief in the inherent goodness of ordinary individuals.

The comprehensive analysis holds significant meaning as it demonstrates that the Twitter community has not developed a mere mob mentality. A considerable number of users continue to strive for a balanced approach, expressing positive intentions. This observation bodes well for the collective progress of the human race as a whole, highlighting the capacity of individuals to uphold noble principles even within the realm of social media.

By showcasing socially relevant photographs at the forefront and elucidating the prevalent sentiments and aspirations of Twitter users, this analysis provokes contemplation on the potential of digital platforms to inspire positive change, foster compassion, and promote a shared sense of justice and peace.

Having fulfilled the objectives I will shift gears and move the discussion towards the theoretical implications of this report.

The convergence of the offline and online worlds occurs at the intersection where media influences shape public discourse. When examining the Agenda Setting theory, it is widely accepted that the media plays a significant role in guiding what topics the public should focus on. Consequently, the media outlet that reports news first, typically sets the agenda. In the present context, online media takes precedence by breaking news stories and occupying a prominent position. It follows logically that the flow of agenda should move from online to offline media. However, our data reveals that traditional media platforms such as television and newspapers dominated the Twitter domain in terms of tweet volume about the protests. This suggests that offline media transitions to the online realm and actively establishes the agenda, as Twitter serves as a platform rather than a content creator. Media organisations garnered the highest engagement among all those who tweeted, including influencers and celebrities. Therefore, it is inadequate to assume a unidirectional agenda flow, as the agenda-setting process is primarily driven by organised media institutions leveraging this rapid and dynamic platform.

Twitter's influence is evident through its rapid information dissemination and its ability to prioritise content based on user engagement. The viral nature of the platform's hashtags further enhances its role in agenda-setting and shaping public discourse. The data analysis reveals the presence of various cue systems on Twitter, enabling users to provide feedback through different forms of interaction, such as quote retweets, retweets, comments, and likes. Additionally, the effective utilisation of the platform's 280-character limit, along with the use of hashtags and nonverbal cues, enriches communication among users. While Twitter offers both synchronous and asynchronous communication, this study primarily focuses on asynchronous conversations, and the comparative richness of these modes of communication has not been extensively examined. It is worth noting that conversations predominantly occur through retweets, as original tweets are comparatively fewer in number.

As I move on to discuss the concept of public sphere as given by Habermas, one look at the digital divide in India is imperative. It is fashionable to say that social media is the new public sphere, and it may be true too but in a very limited way. The population of India is not just vast in numbers but also vast in terms of diversity. For one, India faces a problem of digital divide although it may not be in the sense that is mistakenly understood. The concept of the digital divide, as defined by the Organisation for Economic Development and Cooperation (OECD) pertains to the disparity among individuals, households, businesses, and geographic areas of varying socio-economic levels, with regard to access to

Information and Communication Technologies (ICTs) and in their utilisation of the internet for diverse activities (Mahendru, A., et al., 2022).

The digital divide encompasses not only the accessibility and availability of digital hardware and software but also the aspect of media literacy. Within the spectrum of media literacy, content prosumers represent the privileged 'haves' of the digital divide, while those who passively consume content without critical engagement are the most disadvantaged. It is no longer solely about possessing a medium; rather, it is about effectively harnessing its potential. In India, socio-economic inequalities, cutting across gender, class and urban/non-urban categories, further contribute to various dimensions of this divide.

When Twitter and other social media platforms are compared to the Habermasian public sphere, the digital divide becomes evident. India, with its 1.4 billion population, has approximately 15 million active Twitter users, ranking fifth globally after the United States, Japan, Brazil, and the United Kingdom (Twitter users, stats, data and trends, 2023). The stark disparity lies within these numbers. The 15 million users constitute only about 1 per cent of the population, and among this 1 per cent, the fraction actively creating content is even smaller.

Despite these disparate figures, the power of Twitter derives from the influential circle within which it operates. This 1 per cent population encompasses individuals who occupy positions of power, whether as decision makers, policy influencers, or intellectual and financial elites. Consequently, their opinions trickle down through the mechanism of diffusion, as posited by the theory of Diffusion of Innovations, wherein new ideas or practices are communicated over time among members of a social system. In today's context, social media channels serve as these communication channels. Therefore, this elite circle represents the contemporary public sphere, exerting significant influence. In this data set, the public sphere aspect stood out, as the news value of 'prominence' was present in both its forms, i.e. maintenance of status quo and status conferral.

The public sphere notion of Habermas defines Twitter as a platform where views are exchanged, and public opinion is being formed. Habermas has stressed on the role of media and democracy, and the contribution of the public sphere towards revitalising both. The open network of Twitter elite forges 'weak ties' amongst the users. The weak ties are visible in the form of the largest number of retweets in these data sets. Users are happier connecting with other users while retweeting their tweets. Significantly, the top engagers in this case have been common people with persuasive tweets. Contributors who got maximum likes were also the ones who got more retweets to their original tweet. One look at the handles makes one realise the democratisation of the platform where film stars, politicians, and common people rub shoulders. In the Nirbhaya Case they were, @amishra77, @Vidyut, @gsurya, @yearning4d_sky, @against_pseudos, @nkumar, @historyneedsyou, @youranonnews, @shellylakhani and @wajahatali and in the farmers' agitation @satishacharya, @Iamangadbedi, @srivatsayb, @sherryontop, @Meghupdates @prakashraaj, @koenamitra, @KTRBRS, @indijaswaloye, @maya206, @ROFLGandhi, @MohdZeeshanAyyub, @NKJammu, @karajlahoria97, @ikaur_deep, @japneet_19, @__Taman, @_KingRaga_, @itsBrarBaby and @Amandeep_45 are all found in this list. One user who finds mention in both the data sets is @youranonnews.

The data has shown that the oldest handles were perceived as more trustworthy as the older accounts had better engagement and more retweets. This is despite the fact that many new accounts were started for the protests and created a large body of data. The age of the account could signify credibility, trustworthiness, commitment, and consistency but it could also signify expertise in content creation through regular practice. Sometimes old handles point at a historical archive of previous such movements. They also show the involvement of the user in the issue. These are my observations of older handles as compared to the new ones in the context of the data from this corpus.

Unlike the Nirbhaya protests, which were more or less leaderless and thrived on public angst, the farmers' agitation was more organised with identifiable leaders on the ground. Leaders on online platforms were from different parts of the country and their participation on ground was not visible. The ground level leaders assume the responsibility of organising and coordinating various aspects of the movement. They play a crucial role in strategising, planning, and executing protest activities, including determining protest locations, scheduling events, and mobilising participants. They have the ability to foster unity among diverse groups, and a keen understanding of the logistical requirements for sustaining long-term protests. Such coordination was not visible in the corpora.

Granovetter's seminal work, *The Strength of Weak Ties* highlights the potential of weak ties formed through retweeting and quote tweeting in facilitating diffusion, social mobility, political organisation, and social cohesion across diverse networks (Granovetter, 1973). In both the datasets examined, users who had never met in person were able to connect on virtual platforms and share news and views by tagging others. The use of hashtags further facilitated the formation of interest-based communities, encompassing both individuals and celebrities. This phenomenon can be understood through the lens of collective action theory also, as users recognised the importance of voicing their opinions and formed a collective represented by the hashtag.

The Nirbhaya case exemplified a spontaneous collective that united for a cause, while the farmers' movement was driven by a rational evaluation of the potential benefits of achieving their goal compared to the costs associated with participating in collective action, such as time, effort, and resources. Their decision to participate was ultimately vindicated.

Hashtags help to build communities around the topic under discussion. By participating in conversations and using relevant hashtags, users have engaged with others and built relationships and networks to encourage engagement and interaction with content. It was observed that some hashtags were more popular than others. It is the universal appeal of the hashtag that makes it popular. The rampant usage of hashtags not only attracts the attention of users to a specific topic and makes it easy to search for a particular content but also acts as a beacon for the media persons to follow. Journalists have always covered topics that are considered 'trending', but the emergence of Twitter and hashtag activism has introduced a new dynamic to this process. The trends are now algorithmically ranked, making it easier for journalists to determine the significance of a topic currently popular amongst the public. The journalists do face the challenge of deciding when a Twitter trend deserves news coverage and whether the hashtag itself is newsworthy. Many a times, news stories that are propelled by hashtag activists have successfully drawn the attention of the public and reporters to previously overlooked angles. However, it is important to note that while hashtag activism can introduce a story or perspective into the mainstream news cycle, it often does not lead to sustained coverage of that particular story. The prevalence of hashtag activism is closely tied to the nature of social medium which is a continuous stream of content. The news media relied on editor-curated headlines, but now the ball is in the hands of the prosumers as they create and promote hashtags. This real-time news gathering and dissemination process prioritises the news value of 'timeliness' with the most recent content taking precedence. Hashtags serve as a way for readers to express their preferences within this fast-paced environment, as traditional indicators like an outlet's 'most read' lists may not capture the full spectrum of what people are consuming online. Hashtag activism has clearly introduced a new dimension to journalism, allowing readers to influence the news cycle by emphasising certain topics through social media trends. While it can be effective in bringing attention to specific issues, the transient nature of trends within the continuous stream of information makes sustained coverage a challenge. Journalists need to navigate these dynamics to ensure they capture the breadth of readers' interests in an era where the digital landscape is rapidly evolving.

The data sets have thrown up several pictures that were popularly tweeted or retweeted. The analysis of the photographs have shown how powerful this medium is, for sharing experiences, eliciting emotions, and engaging audiences. They were successful at capturing attention, conveying messages, evoking empathy, and amplifying the impact of the tweets.

High-quality and compelling photographs connect with the users at a subliminal level amidst the abundance of textual and multimedia content. McLuhan's medium being the message, it was evident in the form of Twitter being a powerful platform for online activists to share their views, and it also provided reach and access to the messages by reducing the barriers to entry and participation. The level of interactivity and engagement increased amongst the non-related publics too fostering a sense of community and collaboration. Online participants used the medium to frame narratives through visual imagery evoking strong reactions from the online as well as offline community as is evident from the popularity of the photographs. This medium provides speed and vitality and changes the course of events by its mere presence. Hashtags, trending topics, and viral videos propel a movement into the mainstream consciousness, attracting widespread attention and support. Marshall McLuhan's relevance remains undisputed.

Originally, it was the concept of Choreography of Assembly that motivated me to undertake this significant task. The relationship between choreography and protest has already been established. However, the factors influencing people's participation, the mechanisms through which collectives are formed, both online and offline, and the inclusion or exclusion of physical and online spaces for protests, remain important questions. Gerbaudo discusses this choreography in terms of power dynamics played out during protests rather than physical movements (Gerbaudo, 2012). Online protests often begin as leaderless revolutions, as observed in the Nirbhaya case and to some extent in the farmers' agitation. New leaders emerged daily, including leaders who created 'bots' such as @DigitalKisanBot, leaders whose accounts were withheld, celebrities showing solidarity, and passionate individuals who retweeted extensively. Gerbaudo categorises these leaders as 'soft leaders', 'reluctant leaders', and 'anti-leaders', all of whom were evident in our data. The choreography of these movements is not directed by a single leader, but rather by multiple leaders who influenced and motivated at different points in time. Nevertheless, the hashtags #delhigangrape and #farmersprotest continued to command significant attention in our corpus, solidifying the space occupied by these movements. The role of physical space has always been crucial in analysing choreography. Kitchin and Lupton (2018) investigated the role of place in shaping Twitter publics using the Women's March in 2017 as a case study within the context of the Black Lives Matter movement. The authors argued that Twitter engagement during the Women's March was influenced by the physical locations of users, with discourse varying among users in different places (Kitchin, A. T., & Lupton, D., 2018). Similar arguments can be made regarding the farmers' agitation, as the farmers strategically occupied several borders of New Delhi, the capital of India. By doing so, they disrupted transportation between the capital and neighbouring states such as Punjab, Haryana, and Uttar Pradesh. This unintentionally compelled a large number of daily commuters to alter their routes and search for alternatives. Consequently, this choreography on a grand scale involved unwitting participants who deviated from their usual paths and inadvertently became part of the protest's choreography. Even those who disagreed with the protest were compelled to participate through these unique detours.

Planned choreography was also evident in various instances, such as in the Nirbhaya case, where the girl's statement ignited a movement that defied prohibitory orders. Additionally, during the farmers' protest, different leaders orchestrated planned choreography on various occasions, as documented by journalist Mandeep Punia's account (on pages 162 and 163). Judith Butler offers an intriguing perspective on choreography through her discussion of the 'right to appear', which extends beyond the content displayed on placards. This decision, made collectively by individuals who constitute the mass, embodies the essence of choreography (Butler, 2015). Body movements and actions, such as raising fists, waving flags, marching together in parades, utilising symbols like tractors, shedding tears, vocalising chants and slogans, and engaging in acts of property damage and midnight vigils, were all evident in both protests. Protesters may not fully comprehend the impact of their actions on the protest's outcome, but the fervour with which these actions are performed holds immense power. The strength of weak ties is also demonstrated here, as the emotional investment in the protest often exceeds the awareness that this unity is temporary and will eventually decline with the revolution's inevitable ebb. Individual gestures unify collective movements (Gerecke, A. and Laura Levin, 2018), as evidenced in our analysis of tweets.

Gerbaudo's analysis of the risks associated with online protests aligns with the findings observed in the datasets, where the individuals actively participating online differed from those present on the physical plaza. As previously discussed, the Twitter users represented a global prosumer, and the celebrities tweeting in support of the protests were not physically present to demonstrate solidarity with the on-ground protestors. Twitter's platform effectively obscured the underlying power dynamics within these social movements. Although the online movements appeared leaderless and exhibited a discourse characterised by 'horizontalism', the actual power structures were well-defined and closely monitored.

Public squares turned into centers of networks of mobilisation in a way which substantiates Manuel Castells' vision of a centre-less network. Castell has carved out common patterns of networked social movements that provide a useful set of analytical categories:

1. Multimodal networking of emerging social movements. They connect online and offline networks, the society with the movements, etc. They can work without a centre or hierarchical leadership as evidenced in both the cases.
2. This de-centered structure maximises chances of participation in the movement and reduces the possibility of repression.
3. Incidents that trigger online outrage usually happen in the physical environment, not in virtual spaces. Hence the role of the internet is mainly instrumental and cyber-activism translates only into an influential movement by occupying urban space. This is absolutely true in both the cases. The social media is still a medium used for offline causes.
4. 'A third space' between communication networks and physical action is a space of autonomy.
5. On account of taking inspiration from other movements around the world he states that 'movements are local as well as global at the same time'.
6. Incidents that turn into media events and consequentially in the causation of networked social movements are 'spontaneous in their origin, usually triggered by a spark of indignation'.
7. One of the most striking characteristics is the accelerated pace with which messages, news and images are spread. According to Castells, movements become viral when they generate hope.
8. Multimodal networks create a feeling of 'togetherness' not in

the classic sense of community because there is no shared set of values but a common purpose.
9. On account of integrating multiple demands and generally lacking a unifying ideology, Castells categorises networked social movements as 'programmatic movements' (Castells, 2012).

The success of online movements relied heavily on evoking high levels of emotional engagement, as demonstrated by the soul stirring content present in the tweets analysed. Both cases under examination were deeply felt, and this evocative aspect translated into the horizontal discourse observed on Twitter. The data unequivocally showcased the prevalence of emotion within these movements. Recognising the nuanced interplay between online and offline participation contributes to a deeper understanding of the choreography of social movements.

With regard to the theory of Collective Action, the gap between online and offline action was created by the fact that those who were online were different from those who were offline. The protestors at the site were not the ones coordinating the narrative online. Farmers on the site had limited resources and faced collective action problems that made it difficult to coordinate and achieve their goals. The phenomenon of 'free rider' was evident in both Nirbhaya and the Farmers' agitation cases because tweeters online participated from afar and engaged in collective action as the perceived benefits outweighed the costs. Many others engaged in collective action because they perceived that their actions would make a difference in achieving the goal. The theory provides a framework for understanding how participants worked together to achieve common goals, despite the obstacles and challenges they may face.

A worrying observation in the data was that some accounts were found to be withheld due to legal issues. There are many opinions about the reasons behind certain accounts getting withheld. This requires a studied opinion. As far as I can understand, it is a debate involving the basic core values of the society which are Freedom vis-à-vis Order. In the following paragraph I am discussing these two aspects in detail:

We need to realise that the emergence of social media platforms has transformed the way people communicate and express their opinions. However, this increased connectivity has also given rise to challenges for governments, including the need to regulate content and maintain law and order. Freedom and order are two core values that underpin society. They represent fundamental principles that societies strive to balance in order to create a harmonious and functioning community. While these values may seem inherently contradictory, they are interdependent and necessary for the stability and progress of any society. The concept of core values in society has been proposed and discussed by various philosophers, sociologists, and thinkers throughout history. While it is challenging to attribute core values to a single individual, several influential figures have contributed in shaping our understanding of these values. We can, in this context, mention John Locke, an English philosopher from the seventeenth century, who advocated for natural rights and the social contract theory. He emphasised the importance of individual freedom, property rights, and limited government. Similarly, a prominent philosopher and political economist of the nineteenth century, Mill argued for the importance of individual liberties, including freedom of thought, expression, and association. He emphasised the idea of liberty as a core value necessary for humans flourishing. Immanuel Kant, a noted German philosopher of the eighteenth century, proposed the concept of categorical imperative, which emphasises the moral duty and respect for the autonomy of individuals. He considered human dignity and freedom as fundamental values. Jean-Jacques Rousseau, a French philosopher from the eighteenth century, explored the social contract theory and the idea of the general will. He emphasised the need for a balance between individual freedom and the common good. John Rawls, an influential American political philosopher of the twentieth century, developed the theory of justice as fairness. He argued for the importance of individual rights and liberties, coupled with the principle of distributive justice to ensure a just society.

It is important to note that the understanding and interpretation of core values in society are subject to ongoing philosophical debates and cultural variations. Different societies emphasise different values based on their historical, cultural, and political contexts. The identification and prioritisation of core values often emerge through collective dialogue, social consensus, and the evolving needs and aspirations of communities. In fact famous Indian philosopher and economist, Chanakya has mentioned the power of punishment as protection of this world and next. I quote, 'It is the power of punishment alone, when exercised impartially in proportion to the guilt, and irrespective of whether the person punished is the King's son or an enemy, that protects this world and the next' (Rangarajan, 1992).

Freedom is a cherished value that encompasses various dimensions, including individual liberty, autonomy, and the ability to express oneself without undue interference. It is the foundation of democracy and human rights, recognising that individuals should be able to make choices, pursue their goals, and express their thoughts and beliefs freely, as long as they do not infringe upon the rights and freedoms of others.

Key aspects of freedom include freedom of speech, freedom of the press, freedom of assembly, freedom of religion, and freedom of thought. These freedoms empower individuals to participate in civic life, engage in public discourse, hold diverse opinions, and contribute to the democratic process. They provide space for creativity, innovation, personal development, and protection of minority rights. In fact, right to freedom of speech and expression, assembly, association or union, movement, residence, and right to practice any profession or occupation are enshrined in the Indian Constitution under Articles 12 to 35 contained in Part III of the Constitution. Some of these rights are subject to security of the State, friendly relations with foreign countries, public order, decency, or morality (Publications, 2000).

Having understood that, one also realises that freedom does not imply absolute license or disregard for societal well-being. It is subject to reasonable limitations to prevent harm, protect public interests, and ensure the rights and freedoms of others. Balancing freedom with responsibility is crucial to maintain social cohesion and prevent the abuse of rights. That's where the other core value of 'order' comes into place. Order refers to the maintenance of a structured and predictable society where laws, rules, and regulations are established and enforced. It encompasses the notion of social stability, adherence to legal frameworks, and the resolution of conflicts through peaceful means. Order provides the necessary framework for individuals to coexist, pursue their goals, and live without fear of violence or chaos. A well-functioning society requires order to ensure public safety, protect property rights, guarantee equal opportunities, and facilitate economic development. It establishes a sense of predictability and trust among individuals, allowing for cooperation, social interaction, and the smooth functioning of institutions. Order is essential for the proper functioning of justice systems, the enforcement of laws, and the protection of human rights. Order should be based on the rule of law, impartiality, and accountability, ensuring that laws are fair, just, and applied equitably to all members of society. Striking a balance between order and freedom requires thoughtful governance, public participation, and mechanisms for redress and justice.

A mature society is capable of achieving this balance. A harmonious balance between freedom and order is a continuous challenge. While too much order can stifle individuality and restrict progress, an excessive focus on freedom without any regard for order can lead to anarchy and erosion of the social fabric. Striking the right balance requires an ongoing dialogue, democratic processes, and the recognition that both values are essential for a functioning and just society. As societies evolve, the balance between freedom and order may shift in response to changing circumstances and societal needs. It is the responsibility of individuals, institutions, and governments to engage in constructive discussions, respect diverse perspectives, and work towards an equilibrium that upholds fundamental rights while maintaining social stability and public welfare.

With this background I am casting a look at the legal framework of the Indian system in the context of regulation of content in cyberspace specifically the farmers' agitation.

India has enacted several laws to regulate cyberspace, notably the Information Technology Act, 2000, and its subsequent amendments. These laws empower the government to act against individuals or platforms involved in activities deemed to be against national security, public order, or the sovereignty and integrity of the nation. The relevant provisions include Section 69A, which enables the blocking or banning of online content, and Section 79, which deals with intermediary liability.

Section 69A in The Information Technology Act, 2000

Section 69A empowers the government to issue directions for blocking public access to any information through any computer resource.

1. Where the Central Government or any of its officers specially authorised by it in this behalf is satisfied that it is necessary or expedient to do so, in the interest of sovereignty and integrity of India, defense of India, security of the State, friendly relations with foreign States or public order or for preventing incitement to the commission of any cognisable offence relating to above, it may subject to the provisions of sub-section (2) for reasons to be recorded in writing, by order, direct any agency of the Government or intermediary to block for access by the public or cause to be blocked for access by the public any information generated, transmitted, received, stored or hosted in any computer resource.
2. The procedure and safeguards subject to which such blocking of access by the public may be carried out, shall be such as may be prescribed.
3. The intermediary who fails to comply with the direction issued under sub-section (1) shall be punished with imprisonment for a term which may extend to seven years and shall also be liable to fine.

Section 79 in The Information Technology Act, 2000

Section 79 Exemption from liability of intermediary in certain cases.

1. Notwithstanding anything contained in any law for the time being in force but subject to the provisions of sub-sections (2) and (3), an intermediary shall not be liable for any third-party information, data, or communication link made available or hosted by him.
2. The provisions of sub-section (1) shall apply if-
    a) the function of the intermediary is limited to providing access to a communication system over which information made available by third parties is transmitted or temporarily stored or hosted; or
    b) the intermediary does not-
    i. initiate the transmission,
    ii. select the receiver of the transmission, and
    iii. select or modify the information contained in the transmission;
    iv. the intermediary observes due diligence while discharging his duties under this Act and also observes such other guidelines as the Central Government may prescribe in this behalf.
3. The provisions of sub-section (1) shall not apply if-
    a. the intermediary has conspired or abetted or aided or induced, whether by threats or promise or otherwise in the commission of the unlawful act;
    b. upon receiving actual knowledge, or on being notified by the appropriate Government or its agency that any information, data, or communication link residing in or connected to a computer resource, controlled by the intermediary is being used to commit the unlawful act, the intermediary fails to expeditiously remove or disable access to that material on that resource without vitiating the evidence in any manner.

For the purpose of this section, the expression 'third party information' means any information dealt with by an intermediary in his capacity as an intermediary. (Kanoon, 2023)

The law must be followed in toto, and punishment can only be levied as per the law. During the farmers' agitation, Twitter became a crucial platform for the exchange of information and the mobilisation of protesters. However, certain tweets and accounts were flagged for potential incitement of violence or spreading misinformation. The Indian government, acting under the IT laws, issued orders to withhold specific Twitter accounts to ensure public safety and prevent the escalation of tensions. The government's decision to withhold Twitter accounts was based on concerns regarding the misuse of social media to spread fake news, incite violence, and disrupt law and order. It viewed these measures as necessary to safeguard the larger public interest and maintain peace and stability in the country. The actions were within the ambit of the legal provisions provided by the IT laws. While critics of the government's actions argue that the withholding of Twitter accounts infringes upon freedom of speech and expression it needs to be understood that resolving the tension between freedom of speech & expression and the need to regulate online content is a complex task. While individuals have the right to express their opinions, this right is not absolute and must be balanced with responsibilities towards national security and public order. Striking an appropriate balance requires robust legal mechanisms, transparent processes, and effective measures to ensure that legitimate concerns are addressed without unduly infringing upon fundamental rights. The case of Twitter accounts being withheld during the farmers' agitation in India serves as a significant example of the challenges faced by governments in regulating online content. It underscores the need for continuous dialogue between the government, social media platforms, civil society organisations, and legal experts to develop comprehensive frameworks that strike an equitable balance between freedom of expression and societal interests. Enhancing transparency, promoting user education, and fostering collaboration among stakeholders can contribute to a more inclusive and effective governance of cyberspace.

The Ripple Effect
Implications and Recommendations

> At this moment in history when bodies gather primarily at shopping malls and when protest is frequently conducted through the ongoing circulation of petitions, I want to argue that this physical interference makes a crucial difference.
> -**Susan Leigh Foster**, Choreographies of Protest

AS WE DELVE deeper into the findings and deliberations presented throughout this study, a multitude of reflections come to the forefront. It is evident that further research is necessary to fully understand the nuances of Twitter usage in India, particularly in the context of social activism. The study has opened up many areas of further research and the data has provided incredible insights and opened our eyes to many new trends. This book provides insights into how social media has been leveraged for effective collective action specifically with verifiable data about two prominent social movements in India. More studies can be conducted using other examples of social movements, using different styles of data collection, and focusing a range of research methods, including qualitative interviews, ethnographic field work, and participatory research, to gain a more comprehensive understanding of the complex social and political dynamics that influence the use of Twitter in India. By doing so, researchers can contribute to a more nuanced understanding of the transformative potential of social media in India and shed light on the complex relationship between technology and social change. The study provides practical implications for activists and policymakers alike and informs the development of policies and strategies for future users of the digital domain.

One key realisation is that social media has become an indelible presence in our lives, demanding our attention and necessitating the judicious and optimal utilisation of its potential. However, the future of platforms like Twitter, which currently serve as conduits for news dissemination, appears uncertain. The looming possibility of increased regulation or demands for payment from intermediaries raises concerns about the potential dwindling of news-related content on Twitter. The intricate issue of the intermediary's freedom becomes a contentious matter, and the remarkable transformation of McLuhan's medium into a message becomes an intriguing phenomenon to observe. Within the realm of these complex dynamics, two overarching concerns stand out, deserving detailed discussion as the culmination of this research. These concerns lie at the heart of this chapter, guiding us towards a deeper understanding of the evolving landscape of social media and its implications for the dissemination of news and the freedom of intermediaries.

These two concerns, if addressed with genuine commitment, possess the potential to alleviate a majority of the challenges arising from technological advancements and the susceptibility of the public to manipulation. These concerns revolve around crucial areas of digital literacy and media education.

The significance of digital literacy and media education in fostering critical engagement within the context of the digital age cannot be overstated. The multifaceted nature of these subjects encompasses not only technological proficiency but also the ability to critically evaluate information and engage in ethical digital practices. The transformative power of these subjects empowers individuals with the essential skills and competencies to navigate the intricate and ever-changing digital landscape, augmenting their ability to promote informed citizenship, combat misinformation, and nurture responsible digital participation. By equipping individuals with the necessary tools to discern truth from falsehood, these educational endeavours play a pivotal role in creating a society that is better equipped to foster a sense of responsibility among individuals, encouraging them to actively participate in shaping the digital landscape in a conscientious manner. To maximise the impact of digital literacy and media education, it is imperative to integrate these subjects into school and college education systems, adult education systems and lifelong learning initiatives. Such integration will not only empower individuals but also contribute to the collective well-being of society, as digitally literate citizens become active contributors in the dissemination and consumption of information, ensuring the preservation of democratic values and critical thinking.

Looking back at 2017, Buckingham (Buckingham, 2017), underscored the convergence of digital literacy and media education in his article titled 'Digital media literacies: Rethinking media education in the age of the internet'. Buckingham expanded the definition of literacy beyond mere competence-based learning, recognising the value and limitations of this notion in the context of the digital age.

This research has also revealed the profound impact of technology, as observed in instances such as the utilisation of bots during the farmers' agitation, where even the judicious use of technology can manipulate narratives. In this study, we discovered that a bot, surpassing human-created content, emerged as the most active handle. This prominence allowed for rapid dissemination of one person's (the bot creator) opinion, thereby creating misleading perceptions.

It is crucial to question whether the creators of such bots possess the necessary awareness of the social diversity within our country and are attuned to issues of reliability and bias. Even if we assume their intentions are well-meaning, their expertise lies solely in technical competency. It is akin to the influence wielded by artificial intelligence experts, where those who shape the functionality of machines inadvertently dictate how human beings ought to operate. In light of these considerations, it becomes evident that addressing the concerns of digital literacy and media education holds immense promise for mitigating the negative effects of technological advancements and fostering an informed, critically engaged citizenry.

In his 2018 article titled *An Approach to Digital Literacy through the Integration of Media and Information Literacy*, Learning explores two practices of information and media literacy and through an examination of their histories and practices proposes a future direction for digital literacy concluding that media literacy lacks a 'full engagement' with digital literacy (Learning, 2018). The present study sheds light on significant findings that warrant careful consideration and attention. The outlined results underscore the importance of addressing these persistent issues.

The following key findings have directed my attention towards these concerns:

1. @DigitalKisanBot emerged as the most active tweeter, indicating the influential role played by this account in the studied phenomena.
2. Notably, in both cases, ordinary individuals actively engaged with media houses, vying for prominence on the Twitter platform.
3. Both common citizens and celebrities have served as influential voices, further highlighting the democratising nature of Twitter as a medium of expression.
4. During the Nirbhaya case, emotionally charged tweets played a significant role in driving conversations. A careful examination of the top keywords, such as 'Asarambapu', 'Northandrew', 'bhawalpur', 'campaign', and 'impassioned', reveals the emotive nature of these tweets. The prolonged trend of 'Asarambapu' can be attributed to his regressive and scandalous remarks concerning Nirbhaya's ordeal, inciting strong responses from users and prolonging the limelight on him.
5. Analysis of the dominant sentiments expressed during the Nirbhaya case reveals keywords like 'violence', 'democracy', 'fearless', 'women', 'shame', 'rape', 'identified', and 'protestors'. Twitter's rapid nature allows sentiments to gain popularity swiftly, providing a metric to gauge public sentiment and its velocity.
6. The most retweeted photograph gained traction as concerned citizens added their opinions and perspectives, contributing to the discourse surrounding the issue.
7. Interestingly, the core issues faced by farmers, as mentioned earlier, did not prominently feature in the top tweets, suggesting a potential gap between the on-ground concerns and the online discourse.
8. Slogans like *Dilli Chalo* did not gain significant traction on Twitter, indicating a potential disconnect between the offline slogans and their resonance in the digital realm.

9. The economic value associated with tweets, amounting to crores of rupees, highlights the substantial impact each tweet has in fostering connections and building relationships.
10. Likewise, the level of engagement generated by Twitter users, including likes, retweets, replies, and mentions, serves as an indicator of their influence and the extent to which their content resonates with the audience.
11. Higher engagement rates generally correlate with greater economic value, signifying a user's ability to drive conversations and capture attention effectively.
12. The enduring popularity of established media firms on Twitter, such as @NDTV as the most popular media handle, further exemplifies the intermedia relationship between traditional media outlets and the Twitter platform.
13. A concerning observation was the account withholding of several users due to legal reasons, indicating a potential lack of digital literacy among users.

These findings highlight the pressing need to address issues such as digital literacy and media education.

It is essential for social media users to develop skills to assess the credibility, accuracy, and bias of information sources, cultivating a discerning and sceptical approach to media consumption and content creation. Media literacy also enables individuals to protect their privacy, advocate for their digital rights, and participate in informed civil discourse.

Moreover, the presence of bots as influential entities on social media platforms indicates the increasing influence of artificial intelligence in content creation and regulation. It is crucial to train AI developers on ethical programming, cognitive biases, and robust privacy safeguards to prevent potential misuse. The ethical use of AI in all fields of learning should be integrated into school curricula. Additionally, legal measures need to be adopted to ensure the transparent and secure use of AI technologies, such as combining AI with blockchain technology to enhance trust, safety, and the integrity of shared information.

Integration of digital literacy into formal education systems, will contribute to a thriving democracy and promote the ethical and responsible use of technology.

The following specific recommendations emerge from the aforementioned discussion:

1. Introduce media education at the middle school level to cultivate future media-literate citizens who possess the necessary skills to the digital landscape.
2. Incorporate media and digital literacy into existing adult and continuing education programs, recognising the importance of lifelong learning in adapting to evolving technologies and media landscapes.
3. Promote media and digital literacy through popular media channels, by utilising engaging and accessible formats to reach a wide audience and raise awareness about responsible digital practices.
4. Include media and digital literacy as a core subject in school curricula, ensuring that students from diverse backgrounds are equipped with the necessary knowledge and skills to critically engage with media content.
5. Provide comprehensive training for AI professionals that incorporates socio-political and ethical considerations, enabling them to develop AI systems that align with societal values and protect against potential misuse.
6. Establish legal safeguards and measures to prevent the misuse of intermediaries by individuals with technological expertise,

ensuring the protection of user rights and maintaining the integrity of digital platforms.
7. Promote widespread knowledge about identifying bots, fake information, and rumours, empowering users to discern reliable sources and combat the spread of misinformation.
8. Empower users to recognise and address issues such as cyberbullying, trolling, and offensive content, while also raising awareness about their rights and responsibilities in the digital sphere. Implementation of these recommendations will help in creating digitally literate citizens who will be able to take educated decisions towards the formation of a healthy digital culture.

Pathways Forward
Lessons from the Activism Landscape

> *So, this movement or stillness, this parking of my body in the middle of another's action, is neither my act nor yours, but something that happens by virtue of the relation between us.*
>
> -Judith Butler (Butler, 2015)

THREE YEARS AFTER the tragic incident that shook the nation, the story of Nirbhaya was once again retold. The echoes of public outrage reverberated through the streets, as protestors took to their feet. The month of December in 2015 bore witness to a familiar tale of collective outcry, as people demanded justice for Nirbhaya. The Twittersphere buzzed with conversations, while newspaper columns recounted the harrowing narrative of denied justice and the pent-up fury of the public. However, amidst these recurring events, a notable difference emerged. The newspapers now boldly spoke her name, Jyoti Singh.

Asha Devi and Badri Singh, the courageous parents of Jyoti, made a conscious decision to reveal their daughter's name, believing that there was no reason to bear the burden of shame. It was a profound shift in perspective. The public gathering held on 16 December 2015, became a poignant occasion known as *Nirbhaya Chetna Diwas*, marking the moment when Nirbhaya repossessed her true identity as Jyoti Singh. The very logic that had compelled the public and the media to conceal her name was now challenged, as Jyoti's mother fervently appealed for her daughter to be addressed by her rightful first name. Henceforth, this chapter honours her as Jyoti.

In reflecting upon this transformative chapter of Jyoti's story, one cannot help but feel a sense of wistful nostalgia. It serves as a reminder of the collective journey embarked upon by the nation—a journey that sought to reclaim her identity and honour her memory. The significance of this moment extends beyond a mere change in name; it represents a profound shift in societal attitudes and perceptions. It symbolises the courage to confront the shadows of shame and stand tall in the face of adversity. As we delve deeper into the intricacies of this chapter, it is essential to appreciate the historical context and the lasting impact of this pivotal moment. It is through thoughtful examination and reflection that we can truly comprehend the significance of Jyoti's resurgence, not only in terms of her name but also in terms of the broader social and cultural implications that accompany it.

The Twittersphere buzzed with activity, while newspaper columns once again recounted the narrative of justice denied and public anger. Tweets filled the digital space, discussing three years of perceived inaction, the release of the juvenile offender, the urgent need for new legislation, the tragic plight of Jyoti's parents, the call to abandon the name 'Nirbhaya,' and invitations to join the protests at Jantar Mantar. It is worth noting that during the period of 2013-14, the tweets primarily focused on raising awareness, with limited discussions about tangible action on the streets. However, after three years of significant advancements and wider reach of social media, one observed an intensified connection between the virtual realm and the real world.

This notable evolution in the digital discourse reflects the growing interplay between online activism and offline mobilisation. The tweets, serving as digital expressions of public sentiment, demonstrated an increased awareness of the need for collective action in the physical realm. The virtual platform became a catalyst for organising and mobilising individuals, amplifying their voices, and fostering a sense of unity in demanding justice and societal change. This is where the aspect of 'Choreography of Assembly' started to influence me.

I believed in the expanded role of social media in facilitating activism amongst the online communities. It also signified a shift from solely raising awareness to actively engaging in discussions on tangible steps and encouraging participation in street demonstrations. This enhanced connection between the virtual and real worlds underscored the transformative potential of digital platforms in shaping public discourse, influencing public opinion, and mobilising collective action.

Media persons were visible attending events and tweeting about them. The give and take from tweets to newspapers and also television was apparent and emotional undertones clearly visible in the news.

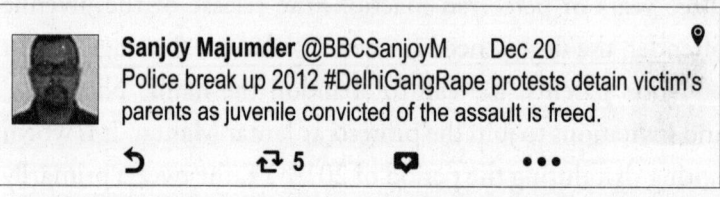

Figure 47: Sanjoy Mujumdar's tweet about the police action on protestors.

During these protests, Jyoti's parents, who were quiet entities in the background, took centre-stage in not just

Lessons from the Activism Landscape 259

Figure 48: An example of a tweet inviting people to participate in the memorial meet.

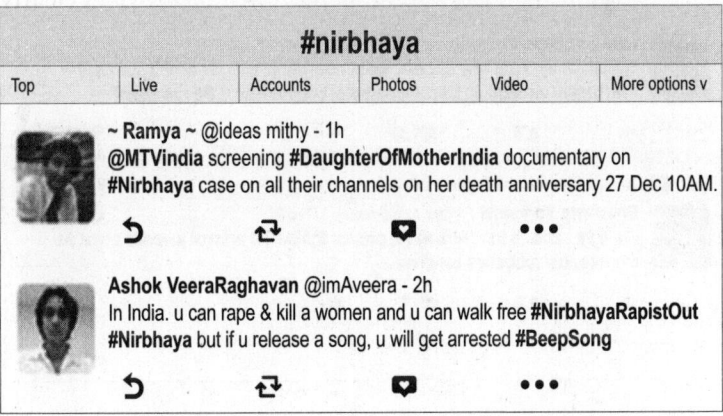

Figure 49: Tweets informing about programmes on TV related to Nirbhaya case

protesting on the streets but also interacting with the media. They appeared for television bytes and newspaper interviews to voice their anger and also employed the tools of social media to provoke action from the community in the real world. The tweets that invited people to attend the protest rallies were sent out on behalf of the parents. This trend also shows the use of the social media for empowering those who were considered voiceless. While three years ago, it was the media that used these tools as the common man gathered and jostled on the streets, this time the tools were being used more democratically.

Figure 50: New hashtags that were trending in the period. #nirbhayaneedjustice, #nirbhayarapistout

Newspapers and television news extensively covered every action undertaken by Jyoti's parents, granting significant attention to their endeavours. The primary catalyst for the revived protests stemmed from the imminent release of the juvenile offender. Having undergone three years of rehabilitation, his scheduled release was set for 20 December 2015. Jyoti's parents consistently asserted that the juvenile was the most heinous among all the perpetrators. They emphasised that individuals of such nature posed a substantial threat to the life and freedom of the general populace. Accordingly, they advocated for the establishment of stringent mechanisms to effectively monitor such offenders, thus safeguarding the community from potential harm. Moreover, they advocated for the fortification of laws pertaining to the protection of women and children, recognising the need for enhanced legal provisions in addressing these pressing societal concerns.

The complainants had also stated that the rate of recidivism (committing crimes again) is fairly high (The Times of India, 2015). The parents protested on the streets of Delhi and received support from civil society, prominent personalities from art, media, theatre, public service, and non-governmental organisations.

With the participation of Jyoti's parents, the case gained an emotional angle, thus making the news even more 'affective'. Political statements began to be made and the buck was passed from one party to the other. The activism on the streets and in the media created a climate for action. Finally, The Juvenile Justice (Care and Protection of Children) Amendment Bill 2015 was passed on 22 December 2015. The Juvenile Justice Act 2015 (Care and Protection of Children), as amended by Presidential acceptance, took effect in 2021. According to this anyone who is between the ages of 16-18 years and has committed a heinous offence (such as rape and murder) may be tried as an adult, irrespective of date of apprehension. As per the law, Juvenile Justice Boards and Child Welfare Committees will be constituted in each district. The board will conduct preliminary enquiry to determine whether the juvenile offender is to be sent for rehabilitation or to be tried as an adult. (www.newsindianexpress.com/nation/juvenile-justice-act).

The Nirbhaya case remains an indelible and poignant chapter in our shared consciousness. Its impact reverberated throughout India, compelling the nation to confront the harsh realities of gender-based violence and catalysing a call for change. This watershed moment sparked an agitation that not only sought justice for the victim but also shook the foundations of complacency and apathy. It compelled us to reassess the delicate equilibrium between personal freedoms and societal order, prompting the establishment of a robust mechanism for punishment. As we reflect upon this transformative journey, we are reminded of the enduring power of collective action and the profound significance of striving for a society that upholds the principles of justice, compassion, and equality for all.

The prolonged farmers' agitation, spanning over a year and resonating across the Twittersphere with resolute protest, had culminated in a triumphant outcome with the repeal of the contentious agricultural laws. This momentous event marked a significant shift in the discourse, as a new wave of Twitter users emerged, employing the popular hashtag, #FarmersProtest to amplify their voices on diverse subjects. These encompassed a range of topics, including the advocacy for the prohibition of genetically modified food, the promotion of organic farming practices, the recognition and elevation of farmer leaders, and even engagment in discussions concerning international issues. This evolution in the discourse showcased the dynamic nature of social media platforms as catalysts for raising awareness and fostering dialogue on multifaceted issues beyond the original cause. It highlights the potential of online activism to transcend its initial boundaries and ignite conversations on broader concerns that resonate with a diverse range of individuals.

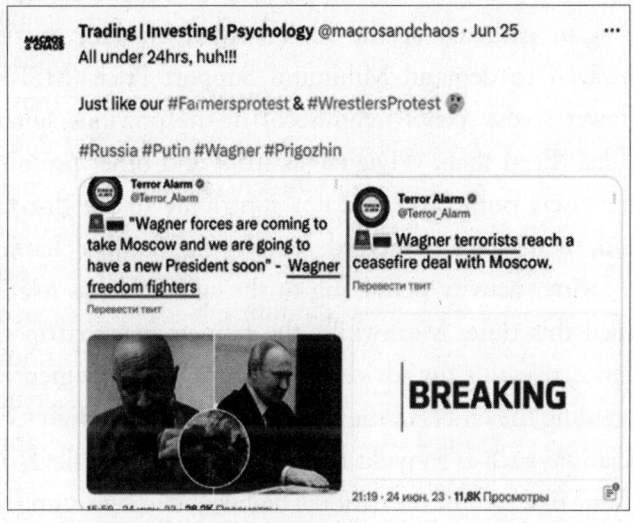

Figure 51: The hashtag being used for unrelated topics

Over the course of one year, the hashtag associated with the farmers' agitation gained substantial popularity, becoming a prominent tool for garnering attention and support. However, the widespread adoption of the hashtag also resulted in a dilution of its exclusivity as a distinct and easily searchable entity, partly due to limited digital literacy among users. In June 2023, the farmers initially expressed solidarity with wrestlers in their ongoing protest, but this alliance was short-lived and garnered lukewarm engagement on Twitter. The wrestlers' agitation was by Olympic medal winning wrestlers following an FIR registered by them against the chief of the Wrestling Federation of India. The discussion is beyond the scope of this study but is being mentioned here because the farmers had briefly shown interest in joining hands with them in their protest.

Notably, @DigitalKisanBot, that had been highly active during the protests in 2020-2021, remained silent. As farmers once again gathered at the Pipli border, blocking National Highway 4 to demand Minimum Support Price (MSP) for Sunflower seeds, scenes reminiscent of the previous agitation unfolded. Even then, @DigitalKisanBot and other prominent Twitter users from 2021 did not contribute to the discourse. Instead, new voices emerged, employing familiar hashtags. Also, Twitter activity pertaining to the agitation was relatively subdued this time. Meanwhile, the farmers persisted in their resistance, rejecting the advice of the Haryana Government, and disregarding the orders of the Punjab and Haryana High Court. Associations such as Sanyukt Kisan Morcha (SKM) called for an indefinite blockade of the national highway, demonstrating their unwavering commitment to the cause despite legal constraints.

The protestors also demanded the release of farmer leaders arrested on June 6 from Shahabad when they tried to block the national highway (online, 2023). After 33 hours of agitation at the borders, they decided to end the protest. The fervour that once filled the digital sphere gradually subsided, leaving behind a sense of quiet introspection. While the hashtags were being employed elsewhere and online discussions seemed to have come to a halt, the real-life struggle persisted, unaffected by the ebb and flow of virtual engagement. It is in this juncture of reflection that we recognise the inherent limitations of online activism, which can surge and recede like a passing wave. The true essence of the movement lies not in the tweets or retweets, but in the unwavering dedication of the farmers who continued to press for their demands, disregarding the shifting tides of social media trends. As we contemplate the significance of this moment, we are reminded that true change often transcends the confines of digital platforms, finding its roots in the tangible actions and resilience of those on the ground.

In the intricate web of online and offline dynamics, the direct connection between virtual activism and real-world actions may elude statistical validation. Yet, the presence of a connection becomes apparent through the interplay of various elements. Journalists, embrace the digital realm by weaving their narratives through tweets and retweets, use hashtags to shape public opinion and the discourse changes gears with each click of the 'share' button. The common person, too, approaches this virtual space, utilising the platform to propagate ideologies, voice perspectives, and disseminate factual information. Furthermore, legacy media institutions, once confined to traditional channels, have now established their significant presence within these online domains, extending their reach and influence. As we engage in contemplation, we recognise that the convergence of online and offline realms forms a complex interplay of human expression and collective action, blurring the boundaries between the two. While the direct correlation may remain elusive, the symbiotic relationship between virtual platforms and tangible realities sparks an ongoing dialogue, shaping the course of our shared narrative.

As the relentless flow of tweets persists, demanding,

condemning, praising, encouraging, informing, lamenting, and embodying every conceivable mood, it becomes evident that public participation has surged, and a diverse array of viewpoints has emerged. Meanwhile, within the intellectual elite of our society, academic discussions on the merits of these protests persist, unravelling the complex debate between retribution and reformation. Arguments against succumbing to over-sentimentalism while formulating or repealing laws, deliberations concerning the government's efforts to pacify, and diverging viewpoints remain unresolved. In the case of the farmers' agitation, the initial tweeters may have faded away as days passed, but the farmers endure, steadfastly protesting for the same issues that came to the fore in the turbulent year long protest of 2020-21 and resurfacing in the month of June 2023. Discussions persist, echoing with the voices of those grappling with this unresolved matter.

The life of a tweet remains ephemeral, fleeting, although it finds its place of immortality within the archives, whether tangible or digital. With each twist and turn of events, the narrative resurfaces, infused with renewed perspectives and newfound dimensions. The cycle of discourse, perpetual and unfathomable, reminds us of the unresolved nature of this issue and the enduring quest for understanding and resolution.

In this integration of emotions and data, the culmination of this endeavour underscores the intricate complexity of societal dilemmas, urging us to continue the pursuit of knowledge, empathy, and thoughtful dialogue. The story unfolds and new chapters are written, we observe the transformative power of critical engagement, holding steadfast to the belief that within the matrix of unresolved issues lies the potential for growth, change, and the realisation of a more just and equitable society.

Endnote

Throughout history, the deliberate destruction of books and texts has occurred for various reasons, encompassing cultural and religious motivations. Notably, early Christian texts suffered extensive erasure comparable to public burnings, reflecting the Church and clergy's attempts to control access to disapproved literature (Knuth, 2006). In England of 1641, the abolition of the Star Chamber briefly allowed unhindered publication before the enforcement of pre-censorship through licensing orders. John Milton's influential work, *Areopagitica* (1644), eloquently articulated the concepts of freedom of speech and press, challenging censorship practices (Milton, 1644). These instances exemplify the efforts of the Crown to regulate books, writing, reading, and independent thought. The concept of 'public sphere', initially represented by authoritative figures, predates the formation of bourgeois public spheres as explained by Habermas (1991).

The control of thought and the exchange of ideas has transcended eras and involved various entities, including the Church, Clergy, and the Crown throughout the history of nations.

In contemporary times, we thought that the consumer is finally the king with citizen driven content, but the influence of corporates has become prominent. They employ AI-driven algorithms to categorise consumers into echo chambers, determine the information we consume, and impose restrictions on accessing archival data. Third-party data scraping for marketing or academic research purposes, such as sentiment analysis or trend analysis using big data research tools, faces challenges due to evolving policies, exemplified by Twitter's recent changes in policy (Times of India, 2023). Although primarily a corporate conflict surrounding generative AI tools and data gathering, its impact directly affects researchers. This development serves as a cautionary signal for scholars engaged in scraping-based research, highlighting potential obstacles and considerations in their methodologies.

In the intellectual pursuits, a subtle yet noticeable shift signals a potential encroachment upon the cherished freedom to explore the depths of archival data. This apprehension stirs a profound concern, for it is through research that we have witnessed the blossoming of innovative methodologies and the dawning of new possibilities. -

As I contemplate, I find comfort in the unwavering belief that every day brings the promise of a new beginning. The resilience of human ingenuity and the boundless nature of knowledge cannot be confined. The spirit of research is ever persistent and will find its way through uncharted territories, discovering new methodologies to traverse the undiscovered.

Steering through the delicate balance between freedom and control, let us firmly uphold the spirit of research that transcends the mere constraints of time and place. In this noble pursuit, we shall boldly navigate through the seas of change with our sails unfurled, guided by our dedication to the boundless realm of knowledge that awaits us all.

References

Abraham, T. (2012). 'Sathin Bhanwari Revisited.' *Indian Journal of Gender Studies*, 19(1), pp. 149-157.

Alejandro, J. (2010). '*Journalism in the age of social media.*' University of Oxford: Reuters Institute Fellowship Paper.

Al Maskati, N. A. (2012). 'Newspaper coverage of the 2011 protests in Egypt.' *Journal of International Communication Gazette.*

Alison, L. E. (2006). 'Examining group rape: A descriptive analysis of offender and victim behaviour.' *European Journal of Criminology*, 3(3), pp. 357–381.

Anderson, L. (2011). 'Demystifying the Arab Spring: Parsing the differences between Tunisia, Egypt, and Libya'. *Foreign Affairs*, pp. 2-7.

Barnes, J. (1954). 'Class and committees in a Norwegian Island Parish.' *Human Relations*, 7, pp. 39-58.

Barron, P. (2011). 'News bites can satisfy all appetites.' Retrieved October 26, 2013, *British Journalism Review*: http://bjr.sagepub.com/content/22/2/23

Backstrom, L. (2011). 'Supervised random walks: predicting and recommending links in social networks.' *Proceedings of Fourth International Conference on Web Search and Data Mining.* pp. 635-644. WSDM. pdf?3l.73PGQrpQfYrnwWeoXV3BFjhETfA_p

Bassiouney, R. (2012). 'Politicizing identity: Code choice and stance-taking during the Egyptian revolution.' *Discourse Society,* 23(2), pp.107-126.

Bart, Cammaerts, Alice Mattoni, Patrick McCurdy. (2013). *Mediation and protest movements.* Intellect books.

Barthes, R. (1970). *Mythologies.* Paris: Seuil, Pocket edition 1.

Basu, I. (2015, 03 02). Nirbhaya's rapist blames her for December 16 brutality. Retrieved from *The Huffington Post*: http://www.huffingtonpost.in/2015/03/02/nirbhaya-rapist-december-_n_6782062.html

Basuroy, T. (2022). www.statista.com. Retrieved from https://www.statista.com/statistics/255146/number-of-internet-users-in-india/:

Bechmann, A. (2012). Mapping actor roles in social media: Different perspectives on value creation in theories of user participation. Retrieved October 29, 2013, from *New Media & Society*: http://nms.sagepub.com/content/early/2012/11/22/1461444812462853

Behl, N. (2022). India's farmers' protest: An inclusive vision of Indian democracy. *American Political Science Review*, 116(3), pp. 1141-1146. Retrieved from https://www.cambridge.org/core/journals/american-political-science-review/article/indias-farmers-protest-an-inclusive-vision-of-indian-democracy/78B4021417116DCC65F05177645AA34F

Belair-Gagnon, V. Mishra, S. and Agur. (2014). 'Reconstructing the Indian public sphere: Newswork and social media during the Delhi gang rape case.' *Journalism: Theory, Practice and Criticism*. Online First. Retrieved 21 January 2015, from http://hal.univ-lille3.fr/hal-00839288

Bhargava, Y. (2015). Ban on porn sites doesn't go down well. Retrieved from *The Hindu:* http://www.thehindu.com/news/national/govt-orders-ban-on-over-850-porn-sites/article7495179.ece

Bhattacharyya, R., & Banerjee, S. (2021). 'Farmers' agitation in India: An analysis of Twitter discourse.' *Journal of Social and Political Sciences,* 4(3), pp. 788-794.

Black Lives Matter Topic Overview. (2014). Retrieved from https://www.gale.com/open-access/black-lives-matter:

Bloom, E. (2017). Obama's response to Charlottesville is now the most 'liked' tweet of all time. Retrieved June 5, 2023, from www.cnbc.com: https://www.cnbc.com/2017/08/15/obamas-charlottesville-response-could-be-the-most-popular-tweet-ever.html

Bimber, B., Flanagin, A. J., & Stohl, C. (2012). *Collective action in organizations: Interaction and engagement in an era of technological change.* Cambridge: Cambridge University Press.

Blog. (2023). Media and information literacy: Need, importance, example. Retrieved from www.knowledgehut.com: https://www.knowledgehut.com/blog/learning/media-and-information-literacy

Boyd, A. M. (2011). 'To see and be seen: Celebrity practice on Twitter.' Convergence: *The International Journal of Research into New Media Technologies,* 17(2), pp. 139–158.

Boyd, D. S. (2010). 'Tweet, tweet, retweet: Conversational aspects of retweeting on Twitter.' HICSS-43, IEEE, Kauai, HI.

Bruns, A. (2005). *Gatewatching, not gatekeeping: Collaborative online news*. New York: Peter Lang.

Brownmiller, S. (1993). *Against our will: Men, women, and rape*. Ballantine Books: Reprint edition.

Buckingham, D. (2017). 'Digital media literacies: Rethinking media education in the age of the internet.' Research in Comparative and International Education, DOI:10.2304/rcie.2007.2.1.43.

Bruns, A., & Burgess, J. (2012). 'Researching news discussion on Twitter: New methodologies.' *Journalism Studies,* 13(5-6), 801-814.

Bute, S. (2014). 'The role of social media in mobilizing people for riots and revolutions: Four case studies in India.' In B. Eds., Social Media in Politics, Public Administration and Information Technology (pp. 355-366). Springer Switzerland International.

Butler, J. (2015). Notes toward a performative theory of assembly. Retrieved from https://www.degruyter.com/document/doi/10.4159/9780674495548/html: doi.org/10.4159/9780674495548

Byrne, J. L. (2002). 'Click her': A content analysis of internet rape. *Gender & Society,* 16 pp. 689, http://gas.sagepub.com/content/16/5/689.

C. Willis, S. Bowman. (2003). *We media: How audiences are shaping the future of news and information*. California: The Media Centre at the American Press Institute.

Castells, M. (2012). *Network of outrage and hope: Social movements in the internet age*. Cambridge: Polity Press.

Cha. (2010). 'Measuring user influence in Twitter: The million follower fallacy.' Association for advancement of artificial intelligence (www.aaai.org). Retrieved May 5, 2013, from http://snap.stanford.edu/class/cs224w-readings/cha10influence.pdf

Chadwick, A. (2011). 'The political information cycle in a hybrid news system: The British prime minister and the 'bullygate affair'. *The International Journal of Press/Politics,* 16(1), pp. 3-29.

Chan, C. K.-1. (2020). 'Public opinion during the Hong Kong protests: A big data analysis of Twitter data.' *International Journal of Communication,* 14, pp. 1234-1254.

Chandler, D. (2001). Semiotics for beginners. Retrieved from http://www.aber.ac.uk: http://www.aber.ac.uk/media/Documents/S4B/semiotic.html

Chaudhuri, M. (2000). 'Feminism' in print media. Retrieved October 29, 2013, from http://ijg.sagepub.com/content/7/2/263: http://ijg.sagepub.com/content/7/2/263

Cheong, F. A. (2011). 'Social media data mining: A social network analysis of tweets during the 2010-2011 Australian floods'. *PACIS Proceedings* (p. 46). http://aisel.aisnet.org/pacis2011/46.

Chopra, S. (2014). *The big connect: Politics in the age of social media.* Random House Publishers India Private Limited.

Christiansen, J. (2009). 'Four stages of social movements.' EBSCO Research Starters.

'Click here'A content analysis of internet rape sites. (10/2002, 16(5):). *Gender & Society.* 689-709. Retrieved from Gender & Society. 16(5), pp. 689-709. DOI: 10.1177/089124302236992.

Cockbain, E. (2013). Grooming and the 'Asian sex gang predator': the construction of a racial crime threat. Retrieved October 29, 2013, from *Race & Class*: http://discovery.ucl.ac.uk/1420144/1/Race_Class-2013-Cockbain-22-32.pdf

Comor, E. (2011). 'Critiquing the fantastic prosumer: Power, alienation and hegemony.' *Contextualizing and Critical Sociology,* 37(3), pp. 309-327.

Cunningham, S. (2012). 'Emergent innovation through the coevolution of informal and formal media economies.' *Television New Media,* 13(5), pp. 415-430.

Daft, R. L. & Lengel, R. H. (1984). 'Information richness: a new approach to managerial behavior and organizational design.' In L. &. Cummings (eds), *Research in organizational behavior.* pp. 191-233. Hollywood: IL: JAI Press.

Daniels, J. (2012). 'Race and racism in internet studies: A review and critique.' *New Media Society,* pp. 1 –25.

Dasgupta, M., & Sharma, A. (2021). 'Farmers protest 2020: A content analysis of Twitter discourse.' *International Journal of Humanities and Social Science Research,* 9(1), pp. 40-49.

Dataportal. (2021). Global overview report. Retrieved from https://datareportal.com/reports/digital-2021-global-overview-report.

Dave, S. (2013). Planning Commission India goes social. Retrieved from www.yourstory.com: https://yourstory.com/2013/03/planning-commission-india-goes-digital-hosts-first-ever-google-hangout

David C. Pyrooz, Scott E. Wolfe, Cassia Spohn. (2011). 'Gang-related homicide charging decisions: The implementation of a specialized prosecution unit in Los Angeles.' *Criminal Justice Policy Review,* 22(1), pp. 3-26.

Davis, J. L. (2018). 'Tweeting for social justice: How Black Lives Matter activists use Twitter to shape discourse and affect change.' *Journal of Race, Ethnicity and Politics*, 3(1), pp. 1-25.

De Choudhury, M., Sharma, S., Logar, T., & Eekhout, W. (2018). 'Gender and power dynamics in hashtag campaigns: implications for social media advocacy.' *In Proceedings of the 2018 CHI Conference on Human Factors in Computing Systems*, 31. Montreal, Canada.

Dean G. Kilpatrick & Ron Acierno. (2003). 'Mental health needs of crime victims: Epidemiology.' *Journal of Traumatic Stress*, 16(2), pp. 119–132.

Debolina Dutta and Oishik Sircar. (2013). 'India's winter of discontent: Some feminist dilemmas in the wake of a rape.' *Feminist Studies*, 39(1), 293-306. Retrieved from ww19318w.jstor.org/stable/237.

Derrick de Kerckhove, *Eric McLuhan*. (2011).

Deshmukh-Ranadive, J. (2005). 'Are democracy and human rights valid within domestic units? Some theoretical explorations.' *Indian Journal of Gender Studies*, pp. 99-113.

Desouza, S. (2012). 'The strength of collective processes: An outcome analysis of women's collectives in India.' *Indian Journal of Gender Studies*, 19, pp. 373-392.

Diken, B. (2005). 'Becoming abject: Rape as a weapon of war.' *Body Society*, 11(1), pp. 111-128.

Dixon, M., & Levine, A. (2012). 'Beyond the streets: The choreography of protest.' *Social Movement Studies*, 11(3&4), pp. 367-383.

Dixon, M., & Riseman. (2013). *The choreography of protest: The dance of collective action in public space*. Routledge.

Dixon, S. (2022). Twitter: Number of worldwide users 2019-2024. Retrieved from https://www.statista.com/statistics/303681/twitter-users-worldwide/.

Donath, J. (2004). Sociable Media. *Encyclopedia of human computer interaction*, pp. 627-633.

Dutta, P. K. (2021). PM Modi withdraws farm laws that were not in force. Why now? Retrieved June 07, 2023, from www.indiatoday.com: https://www.indiatoday.in/news-analysis/story/pm-modi-withdraws-farm-laws-why-now-1878593-2021-11-19.

'Rumors-Editorials.' (E. P. Matteo Ciastellardi, Ed.) *International Journal of McLuhan Studies*, 1(1).

E. McLuhan, & F. Zingrone, eds. (1995). *Essential McLuhan by Marshall McLuhan*. New York: Basic Books.

E. Rogers. (1986). *Communication technology: The new media in society*. New York: Free Press.

Edelman, M. (2001). 'Social movements: Changing paradigms and forms of politics.' *Annual Review of Anthropology*, 30, 285-317. Retrieved June 19, 2023, from http://www.jstor.org/stable/3069218.

Elias Said-Hung, A. S.-T.-D.-T.-C.-B. (2013). Ibero-American online news managers' goals and handicaps in managing social media. Retrieved october 29, 2013, from *Television New Media*: http://tvn.sagepub.com/content/early/2013/02/19/1527476412474352

Elmer, G. (2013). 'Live research: Twittering an election debate.' *New Media & Society*, 15(1), pp. 18-30.

Emma Tonkin, Heather D. Pfeiffer, Greg Tourte. (2013). 'Twitter, information sharing and the London riots?' *Bulletin of the American Society for Information Science and Technology*, 38(2), pp. 49–57.

Eun-Ju Lee and Soo Yun Shin. (2012). 'When the medium is the message : How transportability moderates the effects of politicians' Twitter communication.' *Communication Research*, pp. 1–12.

Evelyn Nakano Glenn, Grace Chang, Linda Rennie Forcey. (1994). *Mothering: Ideology, experience, and agency*. Psychology Press.

Express, I. (2021). *The Indian Express*. Retrieved from https://indianexpress.com/article/india/one-year-of-farm-laws-timeline-7511961/

Faust, S. W. (1994). *Social network analysis*. Cambridge: Cambridge University Press.

Felmlee, D. (2020). The geography of sentiment towards the Women's March of 2017. PLOS ONE, 15. doi:10.1371/journal.pone.0233994

FICCI. (2022). Tuning into consumer- Indian M&E rebounds with a customer-centric approach. Retrieved from https://assets.ey.com/content/dam/ey-sites/ey-com/en_in/topics/media-and-entertainment/2022/ey-ficci-m-and-e-report-tuning-into-consumer_v3.pdf

Foster, S. L. (2003). 'Choreographies of protest.' *Theatre Journal*, 55(3), pp. 395–412. doi:10.1353/tj.2003.0111.

Foulger, D. (2004). Models of the communication process. Retrieved June 15, 2015, from http://davis.foulger.info/research/unifiedModelOfCommunication.htm

Fu, K. W., Chan, C. K., & Chau, M. (2020). 'Assessing the credibility of social media sources for Hong Kong protest news.' *Journalism & Mass Communication Quarterly*, 97(2), pp. 563-583.

Fulk, J. S. (1990). A social influence model of technology use. organizations and communication technology. Newbury Park, CA: Sage.

G. Ku. (2002). Intermedia agenda setting in the 2000 presidential Campaign: Influence of the candidate's website on traditional news media. Ph.D thesis. Norman, Oklahoma: University of Oklahoma : ProQuest Information and Learning Company.

Gans, H. (1979). Deciding what's news. New York: Pantheon.

Gerbaudo, P. (2012). Tweets and the streets: Social media and contemporary activism. Pluto Press.

Gerecke, A., & Levin, L. (2018). 'Moving together in an era of assembly.' *Canadian Theatre Review*, 176, pp. 5-10. doi:10.3138/ctr.176.001

Ghose, R. (2022). What social activism will look like in Web 3.0. Retrieved from www.rabble.io: https://www.rabble.io/blog/what-social-activism-will-look-like-in-web3

Gladwell, M. (2010). Why the revolution will not be tweeted. Retrieved from *The New Yorker*: http://www.newyorker.com/reporting/2010/10/04/101004fa_fact_gladwel

Goh, D., & McLaughlin, E. (2020). 'The role of Twitter in the Hong Kong protests.' *Communication Research and Practice*, 6(1), pp. 1-15.

Gordon, W. (2003). *McLuhan for beginners*. New York: Orient Blackswan, ISBN 8125024735.

Govindu, V. M. (2019). A novel form of political protest. Retrieved June 19, 2023, from www.hindustantimes.com: https://www.hindustantimes.com/india-news/a-novel-form-of-political-protest/story-3IASzDI7pwcMPJjDFHoodN.html

Granovetter, M. (1973). 'The strength of weak ties.' *American Journal of Sociology*, 78(6), pp. 1360–80.

Gunther Kress and Theo van Leeuwen. (1996). *Reading images: The grammar of visual design*. London: Routledge, UK.

Gupta, S. (2020). The Gaon connection. Retrieved May 30, 2023, from https://en.gaonconnection.com/every-second-respondent-farmer-in-the-west-zone-supports-the-new-agri-laws-gaon-connection-survey/: https://en.gaonconnection.com/category/gaon-connection-survey/

Gupta-Cassale, N. (2000). 'Bearing witness: Rape, female resistance, male authority and the problems of gender representation in popular Indian cinema.' *Indian Journal of Gender Studies*, 7(2), pp. 231-248.

Gustavo S. Mesch, Ilan Talmud, and Anabel Quan-Haase. (2012, September). 'Instant messaging social networks: Individual, relational, and cultural characteristics.' *Journal of Social and Personal Relationships*, 29(6), pp. 736-759.

Habermas, J. (1989). *The structural transformation of the public sphere: An inquiry into a category of bourgeois society*. USA: MIT Paperback edition.

Habermas, J. (1991). The public sphere. In Mukerji, & M. Schudson, Rethinking popular culture. *Contemporary Perspectives in Cultural Studies*. pp. 398-404. Berkeley/Los Angeles: University of California Press.

Habermas, J. (2014). *Stanford Encyclopedia of Philosophy*. Retrieved from http://plato.stanford.edu/entries/habermas/#TheComAct

Halpin, H. (2014). The philosophy of Anonymous. Retrieved June 5, 2023, from https://archive.org/details/ThePhilosophyOfAnonymous_201708/page/n9/mode/2up

Hariman, R., & Lucaites, J. L. (2016). *Choreography & Protests. In No Caption Needed: Iconic Photographs, Public Culture, and Liberal Democracy*, 2nd ed. University of Chicago Press.

Harrison, C. (2003). 'Visual social semiotics: Understanding how still images make meaning.' *Technical Communication*, 50(1), pp. 46-60.

Herman, M. (2014). Twitter breaks news, but will it break journalism. Retrieved from www.memeburn.com: http://memeburn.com/2010/07/twitter-breaks-news-but-will-it-break-journalism/

Hermida, A. (2013). 'Journalism: Reconfiguring journalism research about Twitter, one tweet at a time.' *Digital Journalism*, 1(3), pp. 295-313.

Hewlette, S. (2010). British Journalism Review. Retrieved October 26, 2013, from http:/bjr.sagepub.com/content/21/1/10.citation

Hilly, J. (2011). I've seen tomorrow and its female. Retrieved October 26, 2013, from *British Journalism Review*: http://bjr.sagepub.com/content/22/2/39

Howard, P. N., Duffy, A., Freelon, D., Husain M. M., Mari, W., & Mazaid, M. (2011). *Opening closed regimes: what was the role of social media during the Arab Spring?* Seattle, USA: University of Washington.

Ib T Gulbrandsen and Sine N Just. (2011). The collaborative paradigm: towards an invitational and participatory concept of online communication. *Media, Culture & Society*, 33, pp. 1095-1108.

Idle, A., Nunns, A., & Nadia. (2011). *Tweets from Tahrir: Egypt's revolution as it unfolded, in the words of people who made it*. New York: OR Books.

IDR. (2021). *Indian Development Review*. Retrieved from https://idronline.org/the-farm-bills-all-you-need-to-know/?gclid=CjwKCAjw_YShBhAiEiwAMomsEIouTXJnWYj5wL57KFupzfG6NpNX-gPMiHBVO_IJ_BK6PJ9vumnvohoCPVAQAvD_BwE:

Ifukor, P. (2010). 'Elections' or 'selections'? Blogging and twittering the Nigerian 2007 general elections.' *Bulletin of Science, Technology & Society*, 30(6), pp. 398-414.

Indi Jaswal (2021), Today Hashtag Retweet, #FarmLaws_#ThreattoIndians, #FarmersProtest, (Twitter Post) Retrieved from https://twitter.com/indijaswaloye

Ingram, M. (2001). Was what happened in Tunisia a Twitter revolution? Retrieved from www.Gigaom.com: http://gigaom.com/2011/01/14/was-what-happened-in-tunisia-a-twitter-revolution/

International federation of journalists Asia Pacific. (2013). Building resistance, organising change: Press freedom in South Asia 2012-13. Unesco Digital Library.

Jazeera, A. (2020). Why Indian farmers are protesting against new farm laws. Retrieved May 30, 2023, from www.aljazeera.com: https://www.aljazeera.com/news/2020/9/23/why-are-indian-farmers-protesting-against-new-farm-bills

Jessica Woodhams, Claire Cooke, Leigh Harkins and Teresa da Silva. (2011). Leadership in multiple perpetrator stranger rape. Retrieved October 29, 2013, from *Journal*

Jewitt, R. (2009). 'Commentaries: The trouble with twittering: Integrating social media into mainstream news.' *International Journal of Media and Cultural Politics*, vol. 5 no. (3), pp. 233-246.

Jiang, M., Luo, X., & Zhu, H. (2020). 'How Weibo and Twitter were used in the Hong Kong protests: A comparative analysis of the networked public sphere.' *Telematics and Informatics*, 52. doi:101410

Jodi Lane and James W. Meeker. (2003). 'Fear of gang crime: A look at three theoretical models.' *Law & Society Review*, Volume 37, Number 2, pp. 425-456.

Johnson, J. (2012). 'The power of Twitter.' *British Journalism Review*, vol. 23 no. (4), pp. 15-17.

Joy, S. (2020). At least 25 crore workers participated in general strike. Retrieved from *Deccan Herald*: https://www.deccanherald.com/national/at-least-25-crore-workers-participated-in-general-strike-some-states-saw-complete-shutdown-trade-unions-920200

Jugnu Grewal Almeida (2019) We did it!#farmerswin, #Farmersprotest (Twitter post) Retrieved from https://twitter.com/AlmeidaJugnu

Juris, J. S. (2012). 'Reflections on #occupy everywhere: Social media, public space, and emerging logics of aggregation.' *The Scholar & Feminist Online*, 10(1).

Juris, J. S. (2015). Reflections on #Occupy Everywhere: Social media, public space, and emerging logics of aggregation. In P. Joyce (Ed.), *The social in the slobal: Social theory, governmentality and global politics*. pp. 196-223. Routledge.

Just, I. T. (2011). 'The collaborative paradigm: towards an invitational and participatory concept of online communication'. *Media, Culture & Society*, 33, pp. 1095-1108.

Jütersonke, O., Muggah, R., & Rodgers, D. (2009). 'Gangs, urban violence, and security interventions in Central America'. *Security Dialogue*, 40(4-5), pp. 373-397.

K. Ryan. (2009). Twitter study reveals interesting results about usage. Retrieved from Pear analytics: http:/www. pearanalytics.com/blog/wp-content/uploads/2010/05/TwitterStudy

Kadushin, C. (1976). 'Networks and Circles in the Production of Culture.' *American Behavioral Scientist*, pp. 69-84.

Kadushin, C. (2012). *Introduction to social network theory.* USA: Oxford University Press.

Kahn, A. S. (2003). Rape is not a natural act. Retrieved October 29, 2013, from *Psychology of Women Quarterly*: http://pwq.sagepub.com/content/27/3/273

Kanoon, I. (2023). Retrieved from www.indiakanoon.com: https://indiankanoon.org/doc/10190353/

Katrin Weller, Axel Bruns, VoJean Burgess, Merja Mahrt, Cornelius Puschmann, Steve Jones. (2014). Twitter and society. NY: Peter Lang Publishing, 9781433121708.

Kaur, S. K. (2013). Impact of social media on politics. *Gian Jyoti Journal*, 3(4), 23-29. Retrieved 20 January, 2015, from www.gjimt.ac.in/GianJyotiE-Journal.htm

Keith V. Bletzer and Mary P. Koss. (2006). 'After-rape among three populations in the Southwest: A time of mourning, a time for recovery.' *Violence Against Women*, Volume 12 Number 1, 5-29.

Kemp, S. (2023). DIGITAL 2023: INDIA. Retrieved from https://datareportal.com/reports/digital-2023-india#:~:text=India%20was%20home%20to%20467.0,per cent%20of%20the%20total%20population.: https://datareportal.com/reports/digital-2023-india#:~:text=India%20was%20home%20to%20467.0,percent%20of%20the%20total%20population.

Kevin L. Nunes, Chantal A. Hermann and Katie Ratcliffe. (2013). Implicit and explicit attitudes toward rape are associated with sexual aggression. Retrieved October 26, 2013, from *Journal of Interpersonal Violence*: http://jiv.sagepub.com/content/early/2013/06/04/0886260513487995

Khalil, J. F. (2012). Youth-generated media: A case of blogging and Arab youth cultural politics. Retrieved October 29, 2013, from *Television New Media*: http://tvn.sagepub.com/content/14/4/338

Kitchin, A. T., & Lupton, D. (2018). 'Know your place!' The role of place in the formation of Twitter publics.' *Information, Communication & Society*, 2(7), pp. 940-956.

Korn, A., & Efrat, S. (2004). 'The coverage of rape in the Israeli popular press.' Violence Against Women, 10(9), 1056-1074.

Knuth, R. (2006). *Burning books and leveling libraries: Extremist violence and cultural destruction*. Connecticut: Praeger, ISBN 9780275990077.

Krishnan, A. (2023). *Reuters Institute Digital News Report, 2022*. Retrieved from https://reutersinstitute.politics.ox.ac.uk/digital-news-report/2022/india: https://reutersinstitute.politics.ox.ac.uk/digital-news-report/2022/india

Ku, G. (2002). Intermedia agenda setting in the 2000 presidential Campaign: Influence of the candidate's website on traditional news media. Ph.D thesis . Norman, Oklahoma, University of Oklahoma: ProQuest Information and Learning Company.

Kumar, A., & Vaidya, A. (2021). 'Tweeting protests in India: network study of farmers' protest on Twitter.' *Information, Communication & Society*, vol. 24 no. (11), pp. 1669-1686.

Kumar, P. (2010). 'Sanma told Me: Narratives of gendered violence'. *Indian Journal of Gender Studies*, vol. 17 no. (3) pp. 403–427.

Kwak, H. L. (2010). 'What is Twitter: A social network or a news media.' *Proceedings of the 19th International Conference on the World Wide Web*. New York: ACM. pp. 591-600.

Labi Siffre (2012). RT @WajahatAli: Don't stop your daughter from going out, teach your son how to behave!! #DelhiGangRape #WarAgainstWomen (Twitter post) Retrieved from https://twitter.com/search?q=wajahat%20ali%20%23Delhigangrape&src=recent_search_click

Lardinois, F. (2010). The short lifespan of a tweet: Retweets only happen within the first hour. Retrieved from Readwrite: http://readwrite.com/2010/09/29/the_short_lifespan_of_a_tweet_retweets_only_happen

Laura Rapp, Deeanna M Button, Benjamin Fleury-Steiner and Ruth Fleury-Steiner. (2010). 'The internet as a tool for black feminist activism: Lessons from an online antirape protest.' *Feminist Criminology*, vol. 5 no. (3) pp. 244–262.

Learning, M. (2018). 'An approach to digital literacy through the integration of media and information literacy.' *Media and Communication*, vol. 7 no. (8), pp. 4–13.

Leibling, A. J. (1960). 'The wayword press: Do you belong in Journalism?' *New Yorker*, pp. 105-109.

Leeuwen, G. K. (1996). *Reading images: The grammar of visual design*. London, UK: Routledge.

Leirvik, T., & Karlsson, M. (2020). 'Climate activism and social media: A case study of Fridays for Future.' *Environmental Communication*, vol. 14 no. (7), pp. 906-919.

Lia-Paschalia Spyridou, Maria Matsiola, Andreas Veglis, George Kalliris and Charalambos Dimoulas. (2013). 'Journalism in a state of flux: Journalists as agents of technology innovation and emerging new practices.' *International Communication Gazette*, pp. 76-98.

Lisa A. Paul, Heidi M. Zinzow, Jenna L. McCauley, Dean G. Kilpatrick and Heidi S. Resnick. (2013). Does Encouragement by Others Increase Rape Reporting? Findings From a National Sample of Women. Retrieved October 29, 2013, from *Psychology of Women Quarterly*: http://pwq.sagepub.com/content/early/2013/09/11/0361684313501999

Liu, Y., & Zhou, R. (2020). 'Analysis of the use of Twitter during the Hong Kong protests from the perspective of communication ecology.' *Mobile Networks and Applications*, 252990-3000.

Locke, T. (2021, 3 22). Jack Dorsey sells his first tweet ever as an NFT for over $2.9 million. Retrieved 6 5, 2023, from www. cnbc. com: https://www.cnbc.com/2021/03/22/jack-dorsey-sells-his-first-tweet-ever-as-an-nft-for-over-2point9-million.html#:~:text=The%20 tweet%2C%20which%20says%2C%20%E2%80%9C,sold%2C%20 just%20like%20physical%20assets.

Lotan, G. E. (2011). 'The revolutions were tweeted: Information flows during the 2011 Tunisian and Egyptian revolutions.' *International Journal of Communication*.

Ifukor, P. (2010). 'Elections' or 'selections'? Blogging and twittering the Nigerian 2007 general elections. Bulletin of Science, *Technology & Society*, 30(6), pp. 398-414.

Jewitt, R. (2009). 'Commentaries: The trouble with twittering: Integrating social media into mainstream news.' *International Journal of Media and Cultural Politics*, 5(3), pp. 233-246.

Johnson, J. (2012). 'The power of Twitter.' *British Journalism Review*, 23(4), pp. 15-17.

Juris, J. S. (2012). 'Reflections on #occupy everywhere: Social media, public space, and emerging logics of aggregation.' *The Scholar & Feminist Online*, 10(1).

Juris, J. S. (2015). Reflections on #Occupy everywhere: Social media, public space, and emerging logics of aggregation. In P. Joyce (Ed.), The social in the global: Social theory, governmentality and global politics. Routledge. pp. 196-223.

Kanoon, I. (2023, June 14. Retrieved from www.indiakanoon.com

Kadushin, C. (1976). 'Networks and circles in the production of culture.' *American Behavioral Scientist*, pp. 69-84.

Kadushin, C. (2012). *Introduction to social network theory*. USA: Oxford University Press.

Kahn, A. S. (2003). Rape is not a natural act. Retrieved October 29, 2013, from *Psychology of Women Quarterly*: http://pwq.sagepub.com/content/27/3/273

Kahn, A. S. (2014). *Stanford Encyclopedia of Philosophy*. Retrieved from http://plato.stanford.edu/entries/habermas/#TheComAct

Kadushin, C. (2014). *The philosophy of anonymous*. Retrieved June 5, 2023, from https://archive.org/details/The Philosophy of Anonymous_201708/page/n9/mode/2up

Kamal, A. (2021). *What social activism will look like in Web 3.0*. Retrieved from www.rabble.io

Kanoon, I. (2023). Retrieved from www.indiakanoon.com

Katrin Weller, Axel Bruns, VoJean Burgess, Merja Mahrt, Cornelius Puschmann, Steve Jones. (2014). *Twitter and society*. NY: Peter Lang Publishing, 9781433121708.

Kemp, S. (2023). *DIGITAL 2023: INDIA*. Retrieved from https://datareportal.com/reports/digital-2023-india#:~:text=India%20was%20home%20to%20467.0,percent%20of%20the%20total%20population.

Khalil, J. F. (2012). Youth-generated media: A case of blogging and Arab youth cultural politics. Retrieved 29 October 2013, from *Television New Media*: http://tvn.sagepub.com/content/14/4/338

Louise E. Porter and Laurence J. Alison. (2001). 'A partially ordered scale of influence in violent group behavior, An example from gang rape.' *Small Group Research*, 32(4), pp. 475-497.

Louise E. Porter and Laurence J. Alison. (2005). 'The primacy of decision-action as an influence strategy of violent gang leaders.' *Small Group Research*, 36(2), pp. 188-207.

Louise E. Porter and Laurence J. Alison. (2006). 'Examining group rape: A descriptive analysis of offender and victim behaviour.' *European Journal of Criminology*, 3, pp. 357-381.

Lotan, G., Graeff, E., Ananny, M., Gaffney, D., Pearce, I., & Boyd, D. (2011). 'The revolutions were tweeted: information flows during the 2011 Tunisian and Egyptian revolutions.' *International journal of Communications*, 5, pp. 1375-1405.

Lysenko, V. V. (2012). 'Moldova's internet revolution: Analyzing the role of technologies in various phases of confrontation.'

Mahendru, A., Dutta, M., & Mishra, P. R. (2022). *'Digital divide Indian inequality report.'* Retrieved from Oxfam India: https://d1ns4ht6ytuzzo.cloudfront.net/oxfamdata/oxfamdatapublic/2022-12/Digital%20Divide_India%20Inequality%20Report%202022_PRINT%20with%20cropmarks.

Marshall McLuhan, Q. F. (2001). *The medium is the massage*. Gingko Press; 9th edition.

Maeyer, J. D. (2012). Towards a hyperlinked society: A critical review of link studies. Retrieved from *New Media & Society*: http://nms.sagepub.com/content/early/2012/12/04/1461444812462851.abstract

Mark Phillips, F. M. (2015). Media coverage of violence against women in India: a systematic study of a high profile rape case. *BMC Women's Health*, 15(3), pp. 3-15.

Marwick, A., & Boyd, D. (2011). 'To see and be seen: Celebrity practice on Twitter.' *Convergence: The International Journal of Research into New Media Technologies*, 17(2), pp. 139–158.

M. P. Koss, J. A. Bailey, N. P. Yuan, V. M. Herrera. (2003). Depression and PTSD in survivors of male violence: Research and training initiatives to facilitate recovery. *Psychology of Women Quarterly*, 27, pp. 130-142.

M. Newman. (2003). The structure and function of complex networks. *SIAM Review*, 45(2), pp. 167-256.

McCombs, M. (1972). The agenda-setting function of mass media. *Public Opinion Quarterly*, 36, pp. 176-187.

Mehta, D., & Sharma, R. (2021). Social media as a tool of political communication: A study of the #FarmersProtest in India. *International Journal of Communication*, 15, pp. 2514-2534.

Melde, C. M. (2009). Exploring the use of victim surveys to study gang crime: Prospects and possibilities. *Criminal Justice Review*, 34(4), pp. 489-514.

M. P. Koss, J. A. Bailey, N. P. Yuan, V. M. Herrera. (1994). 'The Global Health Burden of Rape.' *Psychology of Women Quarterly*, 18(4), pp. 509-537.

Mary P. Koss, Lori Heise, Nancy Felipe Russo. (1994). 'The global health burden of rape' *Psychology of Women Quarterly.*, 18(4), pp. 509-537.

Meraz, S. (2011). The many faced 'you' of social media. http:/ijoc.org.

Middaugh, E., & Kim, Y. (2020). 'Social media and global climate activism: The effectiveness of Twitter and Instagram as tools for mobilizing the masses.' *Environmental Communication*, 14(3), pp. 293-307.

Milillo, D. (2006). 'Rape as a tactic of war: Social and psychological perspectives.' *Affilia*, 21(2), pp. 196-205.

Milton, J. (1644). Areopagitica. London: Clarendon Press service.

Mishra, P., Rajnish, R., & Kumar, P. (2016). Sentiment analysis of Twitter data: Case study on digital India. In *International Conference on Information Technology (InCITe) - The Next Generation IT Summit on the Theme - Internet of Things: Connect your Worlds.* Noida, India. pp. 148-153. doi: 10.1109/INCITE.2016.7857607.

Mohsin, A. (2004). Gendered nation, gendered peace. Retrieved from http://ijg.sagepub.com/content/11/1/43.

Moody-Ramirez, M. (2020). 'News media framing of Black Lives Matter and the protest paradigm: An analysis of news coverage and social media content.' *Journal of Black Studies,* 51(7), pp. 640-657. Retrieved April 7, 2023.

Moon, Haewoon Kwak Changhyun Lee Hosung Park Sue. (2010). What is Twitter, a social network or a news media? *Proceedings of the 19th international conference on World wide web,* pp. 591-600. New York.

Morozov, E. (2009). 'Iran: Downside to the "Twitter revolution'. *Dissent,* pp. 10-14.

Mukesh Singh Sengar, Shonakshi Chakravarty. (2021). Angry farmers protest near parliament: 10 points. Retrieved from www.ndtv.com.

Mukhopadhyay, S. (2023). Jack Dorsey on farmers protest. Retrieved from www.livemeint.com.

Murthy, D. (2011). 'Twitter: Microphone for the masses?'. *Media, Culture & Society,* 33(5), pp. 779–89.

Napoli, P. M. (2008). Revisiting 'mass communication' and the 'work' of the audience in the new media environment. Donald McGannon Communication Research Centre, New York, USA.

Nasir, S. (2014). Finding voice through social media: A critical analysis of women's participation in the online public sphere in India. University of Canterbury.

NDTV. (2023). About. Retrieved from ndtv.com: https://www.ndtv.com/convergence/ndtv/corporatepage/index.aspx

Nigam, S. (2014). 'Violence, protest and change: A socio-legal analysis of extraordinary mobilization after the 2012 Delhi gang rape'. *International Journal of Gender and Women's Studies,* 2(2), pp. 197-221.

Neogi, A. S., & Mahendru, K. A. (2021). 'Sentiment analysis and classification of Indian farmers' protest using Twitter data.' *International Journal of Information Management Data Insights,* 1(2). doi: https://doi.org/10.1016/j.jjimei.2021.100019

Newman, M. (2003). 'The structure and function of complex networks.' *SIAM Review*, 45(2), pp. 167-256.

Negroponte, N. (1995). *Being digital*. New York: Alfred A. Knopf, Inc.

Nwammuo, A. N. (2015). 'The views of women of press coverage of rape cases in Nigeria: A misrepresentation or an under-representation?'. *An International Journal of Language, Literature and Gender Studies* (LALIGENS), Ethiopia, 4(1), pp. 163-182.

Oberlo. (2023). www.Oberlo.com. Retrieved from https://www.oberlo.com/statistics/number-of-twitter-users-by-country#:~:text=India%20ranks%20next%2C%20in%20third,1.9%25%20of%20the%20total%20population.

O'Hara, S. (2012). 'Monsters, playboys, virgins, and whores: Rape myths in the news media's coverage of sexual violence.' *Language and Literature*, 21(3), pp. 247–259.

Oosterhoff, B., & Palmer, L. N. (2018). '#MeToo and the women's march: How Twitter use reflects the changing landscape of feminism.' *Journal of Feminist Scholarship*, 13.

OurWorldInData.org. (2019). The rise of social media. Retrieved from OurWorldInData.org.

Owen, S. (2013). 'Little mermaids and pro-sumers: The dilemma of authenticity and surveillance in hybrid public spaces.' *International Communication Gazette*, 75(5-6), pp. 470-483.

Oyama, C. J. (2001). Visual meaning: A social semiotic approach. In J. T. V, Handbook of visual analysis. London: Sage Publications. pp. 134-156.

Palmer, L. (2012). 'iReporting' an uprising: CNN and citizen *Journalism in Network Culture*. Retrieved October 29, 2013, from Television New Media: http://tvn.sagepub.com/content/14/5/367.

Pang, N., & Kim, Y. M. (2018). 'All lives matter' vs. 'Black lives matter': A comparison of how Twitter users respond to police brutality.' *Communication Research Reports*, 35(5), pp. 413-423.

Gupta, P., Kumar, S., Suman, R., & Kumar, V. (2021). 'Sentiment analysis of lockdown in India during COVID-19: A case study on Twitter.' *IEEE Transactions on Computational Social Systems*.

Papacharissi, Z. (2012). 'Without you, I'm nothing: Performances of self on Twitter.' *International Journal of Communication*, 6, pp. 1998-2006.

Papacharissi, Z., & de Fatima Oliveira, M. (2012). 'Affective news and networked publics.' *Journal of Communication*, 1-17.

Papacharissi, Z. (2015). *Affective publics: Sentiment, technology, and politics.* Oxford UP.

Parmalee, J. H. (2013). 'The agenda-building function of political tweets.' *New media and Society*, 1-17.

Potts. (2009). 'Peering into disaster: Social software use from the Indian Ocean earthquake to the Mumbai bombings.' *Proceedings for the 2009 International Professional Communication Conference. Waikiki, HI. Hawaii: Professional Communication Society.*

Prasoon, G., Kumar, S., Suman, R., & Kumar, V. (2021). 'Sentiment analysis of lockdown in India during COVID-19: A case study on Twitter.' *IEEE Transactions on Computational Social Systems.*

Publications, D. (2000). *India Book 2020 - A Reference Annual.* New Delhi: Publications Division, I&B Ministry. Retrieved from https://knowindia.india.gov.in/profile/fundamental-rights.php#:~:text=Right%20to%20freedom%20of%20speech,order%2C%20decency%20or%20morality.

Punia, M. (2022). *Kisan andolan ground zero 2020-21* (2 ed.). New Delhi: Rajkamal Publications.

Rozee, P. D., & Koss, M. P. (2001). 'Rape: A century of resistance.' *Psychology of Women Quarterly*, pp. 295-311.

Perline, R. (2005). 'Strong, weak and inverse power laws.' *Statistical Science*, 20(1), pp. 68-88.

Cottle, S. (2010). Participant observation: Researching news production. In A. Hansen, *Mass communication research methods.* pp. 25-65. New York: New York University Press.

FICCI. (2023). FICCI report on E&M sector. Retrieved from https://ficci.in/publication.asp?spid=23783.

Reich, Z. (2011). 'Comparing reporters' work across print, radio, and online: Converged origination, diverged packaging.' *Journalism & Mass Communication Quarterly*, vol. 88 no. 2, pp. 285-300.

Report, F. (2023). FICCI report on E&M sector. Retrieved from https://ficci.in/publication.asp?spid=23783.

Reuters. (2023). Retrieved from www.nbcnews.com.

Rich, F. (2011). 'Wallflowers at the revolution.' *The New York Times*, p. http://www.nytimes.com/2011/02/06/opinion/06rich.html?_r=1.

Rangarajan, L. (1992). *The Kautilya Arthashastra*. Calcutta: Penguin.

Rani, N. (2013). 'Internet, 'political communication and media inclusion in India - A conceptual perspective.' *Journal of Media and Development*, vol. 1 no. (2), pp. 156-176.

Ray, A. R. (17 (3) 2010). 'Understanding gender justice and perception of lawyers in India.' *Indian Journal of Gender Studies*, Special Issue: Violence, Law and Feminist Politics.

Report, F. (2023). *FICCI report on E&M sector*. Retrieved from https://ficci.in/publication.asp?spid=23783.

Reuters. (2023). Retrieved from www.nbcnews.com.

Rich, F. (2011). 'Wallflowers at the revolution.' *The New York Times*, p. http://www.nytimes.com/2011/02/06/opinion/06rich.html?_r=1.

Robin, G. D. (1977). 'Forcible rape_ institutionalized sexism in the criminal justice system.' *Crime and Delinquency*, Volume: 23 Issue: 2, pp. 136-153.

Rodman, G. (2003). The Net Effect: The public's fear and the public sphere. Virtual publics: Policy and communication in an electronic age, pp. 11-48.

Ruby, D. (2023). Social Media Users In The World — (2023 Demographics). Retrieved from https://www.demandsage.com/social-media-users/.

Ruby, D. (2023). Social media users in the world — (2023 Demographics). Retrieved from https://www.demandsage.com/social-media-users/.

S. Cottle. (2010). Participant observation: Researching news production. In A. Hansen, *Mass communication research methods*. New York: New York University Press. pp. 25-65.

Ahmed, S., Jaidka, K., & Cho, J. (2017). 'Tweeting India's Nirbhaya protest: a study of emotional dynamics in an online social movement.' *Technology, Media and Social Movements*.

Lundrigan, S., & Mueller-Johnson, K. (July, 2013). 'Male stranger rape: A behavioral model of victim-offender' interaction. *Criminal Justice and Behavior*, vol. 40 no. 7, pp. 763-783.

Salter, M. (2013). Justice and revenge in online counter-publics: Emerging responses to sexual violence in the age of social media. Retrieved October 29, 2013, from *Crime Media Culture*: http://cmc.sagepub.com/content/early/2013/07/10/1741659013493918.

Sandhu, A. (2021). Dispatches from India's Farmers Protest. Retrieved from *Zoccolo Public Square*: https://www.zocalopublicsquare.org/2021/04/19/dispatch-from-indias-farmers-protest/ideas/dispatches/.

Said-Hung, E. (2013). Ibero-American online news managers' goals and handicaps in managing social media. *Television New Media*. Retrieved October 23, 2013, from http://tvn.sagepub.com/content/early/2013/02/19/152747641.

Sam, P. (2013). Democratisation of information. in (R. K. Jha, Ed.) Yojana, 57, 5-6.

Sambrook, R. (2009). Citizen journalism and the BBC. Retrieved 2012, from *Nieman Harvard Foundation For Journalism*. http://www.nieman.harvard.edu/reports/article/100542/Citizen-Journalism-and-the-BBC.aspx.

Sanyal, S., & Saha, S. (2021). '"Tractors vs Tweets": Framing the farmers' protests in India on Twitter.' *Communication & Society*, vol. 34 no. (2), pp. 61-76.

Shankland, S. (2009). The Twitter effect: Possibilities and limits. Retrieved from www.news.cnet.com.

Saifuddin Ahmed, Kokil Jaidka, Jaeho Cho. (2017). 'Tweeting India's Nirbhaya protest: A study of emotional dynamics in an online social movement.' *Technology, Media and Social Movements*.

Said-Hung, E. (2013). Ibero-American online news managers' goals and handicaps in managing social media. *Television New Media*. Retrieved October 23, 2013, from http://tvn.sagepub.com/content/early/2013/02/19/152747641.

Sam, P. (2013). Democratisation of information. in (R. K. Jha, Ed.) Yojana, 57, 5-6.

Sanyal, S., & Saha, S. (2021). '"Tractors vs Tweets": Framing the farmers' protests in India on Twitter.' *Communication & Society*, vol. 34 no. (2), pp. 61-76.

Shankland, S. (2009). The Twitter effect: Possibilities and limits. Retrieved from www.news.cnet.com.

Sarkar, L. (1994). Rape: 'A human rights versus a patriarchal interpretation.' *Indian Journal of Gender Studies*, 1, 69.

Sarwar, M. S., & Saleem, H. (2021). 'Farmers' protests in India: analysis of Twitter discourse.' *International Journal of Business and Society*, 22(S4), pp. 107-124.

Schectman, J. (2009). 'Iran's Twitter revolution? Maybe not yet. *Business Week.*

Schonfeld, E. (2010). Costolo: Twitter now has 190 million users tweeting 65 million times a day. USA: Tech Crunch. Retrieved from *Tech Crunch*.

Schneider, N.-C., & Titzmann, F.-M. (2014). "The voice of the youth" Locating a new public sphere between street protest and digital discussion. Berlin: Frank & Timme, Reihe: Kommunikationswissenschaft, Band 6.

Sebastian Valenzuela, Arturo Arriagada, Andres Scherman. (2014). 'Facebook, Twitter, and Youth Engagement: A Quasi-experimental study of social media use and protest behavior Using propensity score matching.' *International Journal of Communication*, 8, pp. 2046-2070. Retrieved January 2015.

Sharma Sanur, Gupta Preeti, Bhatnagar Vishar. (2012). Anonymisation in social network: a literary survey and classification. *Intl Journal of Social Network Mining*, Vol.1 No.1, pp. 51-63.

Sharma, R. K., & Narayan, R. (2021). 'Farmers' protests in India: A Twitter-based analysis of public opinion.' *Journal of Social Sciences Research*, 7(1), pp. 1-10.

Shekhar, R. (2013). Delhi rape case: Main accused Ram Singh commits suicide in Tihar Jail. Retrieved from *The Times of India*: http://timesofindia.indiatimes.com/city/delhi/Delhi-rape-case-Main-accused-Ram-Singh-commits-suicide-in-Tihar-Jail/articleshow/18902304.cms.

Shepherd, J. (2023). The Social Shepherd.

Shin, E. J. L. (2012). 'When the Medium Is the Message: How transportability moderates the effects of politicians' Twitter communication.' *Communication Research*, 1-12.

Shirky, C. (2011). 'The political power of social media.' *Foreign Affairs*, vol. 90 no. (1), pp. 28-41.

Simmel, G. (1950). *The Sociology of Georg Simmel.* NY: Free Press.

Simon Kemp, b. (2023). Digital 2023: India. Retrieved from https://datareportal.com/reports/digital-2023-india#:~:text=Numbers%20published%20in%20Twitter's%20 advertising,total%20population%20at%20the%20time.:

Singh, A. K. (2021). 'Social media and farmers' protest in India: A study of Twitter.' *International Journal of Business and Administration Research Review*, vol. 4 no. (2), pp. 27-31.

Singh, A. R. (2015). 'Semiotic analysis of tweets: A study of #Nirbhaya, #Delhigangrape.' *JMComm*15.35.

Singh, M. P. (2013). Asaram: Rape victim should've pleaded for mercy. Retrieved from *The Hindu*: http://www.thehindu.com/news/national/asaram-rape-victim-shouldve-pleaded-for-mercy/article4283466.ece

Sinnappan, S., Farrell, C., & Stewart, E. (2010). 'Priceless tweets! A study on Twitter messages posted during crisis: Black Saturday.' *ACIS Proceedings* (p. Paper 39). http://aisel.aisnet.org/acis2010/39.

Sircar, D. D. (2013). 'India's winter of discontent: Some feminist dilemmas in the wake of a rape.' *Feminist Studies*, 39(1), pp. 293-306. Retrieved from www.19318w.jstor.org/stable/237

Slater, J. (2020, December 4). "Why India's farmers are in revolt in the middle of a pandemic. Retrieved from T*he Washington Post:* https://www.washingtonpost.com/world/asia_pacific/india-farmers-protest-delhi-reforms/2020/12/04/98db8634-3414-11eb-9699-00d311f13d2d_s

Smelser, N. J. (1962). *Theory of collective behaviour*. NY: New York Free Press.

Snyder-Yuly, T. O. (2007). Any four black men will do: Rape, race, and the ultimate scapegoat. Retrieved October 13, 2013, from *Journal of Black Studies*: http://jbs.sagepub.com/content/37/6/859

Sonesson, G. (1989). *Pictorial concepts: Inquiries into the semiotic heritage*. Lund: Lund University Press.

Sperber, D., & Wilson, D. (1995). *Relevance*, 2nd edition. Oxford, UK: Blackwell.

Sruthijith, K. (2013). Individuals with a big base of followers on social media turn unofficial spokespersons for political parties. Retrieved from *The Economic Times:* http://articles.economictimes.indiatimes.com/2013-07-22/news/40728029_1_youth-cong

Stahl, J. (2013). Thou Shalt Not Stoop to Political Point-Scoring: A journalist's guide to tweeting during a crisis. Retrieved from www.slate.com: https://slate.com/technology/2013/04/boston-marathon-bombing-all-the-mistakes-journalists-make-during-a-crisis-like-the-boston-attacks.html

St-Louis, H. (2014). Comic Book Bin. Retrieved April 20, 2015, from www.comicbookbin.com: www.comicbookbin.com

Strate, L. (2012). The medium and Mcluhan's message. (R. Y. PALABRA, Editor) Retrieved May 21, 2015, from http://www.razonypalabra.org.mx/: http://www.razonypalabra.org.mx/

Surjit Kaur and Manpreet Kaur. (2013, Oct-Dec). 'Impact of Social media on politics.' *Gian Jyoti E-Journal*, Volume 3(Issue 4), 23-29. Retrieved January 20, 2015, from www.gjimt.ac.in/GianJyotiE-Journal.htm

T. O'Reilly. (2004). The architecture of participation. Retrieved from http:/oreilly.com/pub/a/oreilly/tim/articles/architecture of participation: http:/oreilly.com/pub/a/oreilly/tim/articles/architecture of participation.html.

Tang, L., & Yang, P. . (2011). 'Symbolic power and the internet: The power of a 'horse'. *Media, Culture & Society*, vol. 33 no. (5), pp. 675-691.

Techcrunch. (2021). India new rules. *TechCrunch*. Retrieved from www.scribd.com: www.scribd.com

Terranova, T. (2000). 'Free Labor: producing culture for the digital economy.' *Social Text*, Vol. 18, No. 2, pp. 33-58.

Thunberg, G. (2019). Twitter post. https://twitter.com/GretaThunberg/status/1167138038193058817 .

Tian, Q. (2011). 'Social anxiety, motivation, self-disclosure, and computer-mediated friendship: A path analysis of the social interaction in the blogosphere.' *Communication Research*, vol. 40 no. (2), pp. 237–260.

Times of India. (2023). Explained: What is data scraping and why Elon Musk is changing Twitter rules over it' . Retrieved from www.timesofindia.com: www.timesofindia.com

Titzmann, F. (2014). The voice of the youth: Locating a new public sphere between street protest and digital discussion. In N. C. S. M. Titzmann, in Studying youth, media and gender in the post liberalized India: Focus on and beyond the Delhi Gang Rape. Berlin: Frank & Timme, Reihe: Kommunikationswissenschaft, Band 6.

Titzmann, F. (2014b). Studying youth, media and gender in the post liberalized India: Focus on and beyond the Delhi gang rape. In N. C. S. M. Titzmann, "The voice of the youth" Locating a new public sphere between street protest and digital discussion. Berlin: Frank & Timme, Reihe: Kommunikationswissenschaft, Band 6.

TNN. (2013). Delhi gang-rape incident: Asaram blames Nirbhaya, sparks furore. Retrieved from *The Times of India*: http://timesofindia.indiatimes.com/india/Delhi-gang-rape-incident-Asaram-blames-Nirbhaya-sparks-furore/articleshow/17933863.cms

Tom P. Bakker and Claes H. de Vreese. (2011). 'Good news for the future? Young people, internet use and political participation.' *Communication Research*, 38(4), pp. 451–470. Retrieved October 26, 2013, from http://crx.sagepub.com/content/38/4/451:

Tracey Owens Patton and Julie Snyder-Yuly. (2007). 'Any four Black men will do-rape, race, and the ultimate scapegoat.' *Journal of Black Studies*, vol. 37 no. 6, pp. 859-895.

Tripathi, N. (2023). India can lead the Web3 revolution, but lack of regulations can be a business-killer. www.Forbesindia.com. Retrieved June 19, 2023, from https://www.forbesindia.com/article/take-one-big-story-of-the-day/india-can-lead-the-web3-revolution-but-lack-of-regulations-can-be-a-businesskiller/84997/1

Tufekci, Z. (2017). *Twitter and tear gas: The power and fragility of networked protest*. Yale University Press.

Twitter users, stats, data and trends. (2023,). Retrieved from Dataportal: https://datareportal.com/essential-twitter-stats

Ullah, M. S. (2013). 'ICTs changing youths' political attitudes and behaviors in Bangladesh.' *International Communication Gazette*, vol. 75 no. 3, pp. 271-283.

Valente, T. W., Rogers, E. M. (1995). 'The Origins and development of the diffusion of innovations paradigm as an example of scientific growth.' *Science Communication*, vol. 16 no. (3), pp. 242-273.

Vallinyagam, R. (2013). Fast-track-court-awards-death-sentences-to-convicts-of-Delhi-Rape-case_a1252.htm. Retrieved May 21, 2014, from http://www.lejournalinternational.fr

Vergeer, M. (2012). Politics, elections and online campaigning: past, present . . . and a peek into the future. Retrieved October 29, 2013, from *New Media & Society*: http://nms.sagepub.com/content/early/2012/09/24/1461444812457327

Viswanath, S., & Banerjee, B. (2019). '#Rape: Exploring Twitter as a platform for public deliberation on sexual violence in India.' *Feminist Media Studies*, 19(2), pp. 242-257.

W. T. Gordon, C. M. (2003). *Understanding media: The extensions of man* by Marshall McLuhan originally published in 1964. CA: Gningko Press.

Warner, K. (2004). 'Gang rape in Sydney: Crime, the media, politics, race and sentencing.' *Australian & New Zealand Journal of Criminology*, 37, 344.

Wasco, S. M. (2003). 'Conceptualizing the harm done by tape: Applications of trauma theory to experiences of sexual assault.' *Trauma Violence Abuse*, vol. 4 no. 4, pp. 309-322.

Waugh, P. (2011, 6). Content must always be king. Retrieved October 26, 2013, from *British Journalism Review*: http://bjr.sagepub.com/content/22/2/45

Westkott, M. (2012). 'Feminist criticism of the social sciences'. *Harvard Educational Review*, pp. 422-430.

White, A. M. (1999). Talking feminist, talking Black: Micromobilization processes in a collective protest against rape. *Gender and Society*, p. http:/gas.sagepub.com/content/13/1/77.

Williams, B. (2000). 'Unchained Reaction: The collapse of media gatekeeping and the Clinton-Lewinsky scandal.' *Journalism*, vol. 1 no. (1), pp. 61-85.

Willis, C. (2003). *We Media: How the audience are shaping the future of news and information*. The Media Centre, American Press Institute.

Wilson, C. (2020). 'The moment when four students sat down to take a stand.' Smithsonian Magazine. Retrieved July 9, 2023, from https://www.smithsonianmag.com/smithsonian-institution/lessons-worth-learning-moment-greensboro-four-sat-down-lunch-counter-180974087/

www.communicationtheory.org. (2023). Gatekeeping theory. Retrieved from www.communicationtheory.org

www.ischool.berkeley.edu. (n.d.). The grass-mud horse, Online censorship, and China's national identity. Retrieved June 20, 2023, from www.ischool.berkeley.edu

Yang, J., Liang, H., Li, Y., & Huang, C. (2017). 'Analyzing sentiments in tweets about the women's march.' *In Proceedings of the 2nd International Conference on Big Data and Internet of Things* (pp. 190-197). Beijing, China from December 20-22, 2017. BDIOT 2017.

Yar, M. (2012). 'Crime, media and the will-to-representation: Reconsidering relationships in the new media age.' *Crime Media Culture*, vol. 8 no. 3, pp. 245-260.

Yardi, S. (2010). 'Tweeting from the town square: Measuring geographic local networks.' *Proceedings of the International AAAI Conference on Weblogs and Social Media*. I (pp. 194-201). New York: AAAI. ICWSM '10.

Yedekci, E. (2018). 'New social movements and video activism in the context of "Choreography of Assembly".' Turkiye Iletisim Arastirmalari Dergisi-*Turkish Review of Communication Studies*, 30. doi: 10.17829/turcom.468322

Zee, M. (2014). http://zeenews.india.com/news/delhi/december-16-delhi-gang-rape-case-chronology-of-events_917760.html. Retrieved May 21, 2014, from www.zeenews.com

Zeidan, A. (2023). History of Twitter. Retrieved from *Encyclopedia Britannica*: https://www.britannica.com/topic/Twitter#ref286818

Zhang Shixin, Ivy, E. D. (2013). 'The future of journalism and journalism education.' *Convergence Newsletter*.

Zhang, W. (April 2013). 'Redefining youth activism through digital technology in Singapore.' *International Communication Gazette*, vol. 75 no. 3, 253-270.